CHAPTER 15

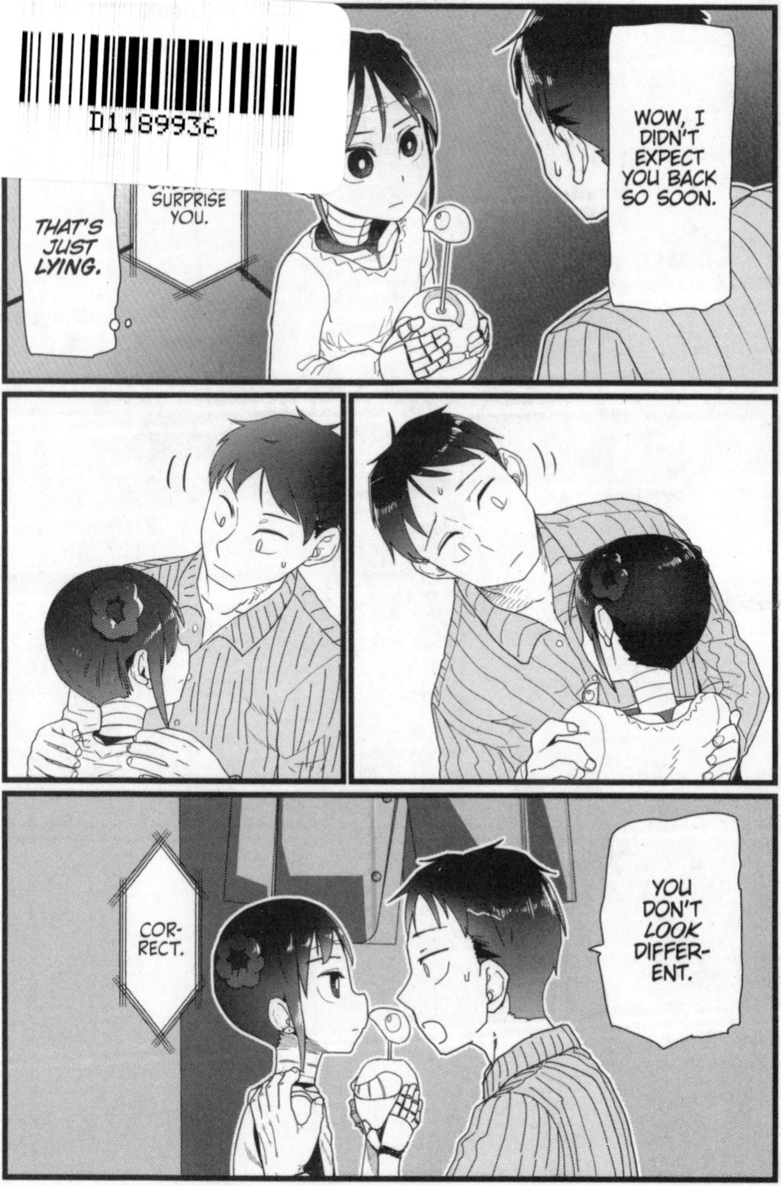
WOW, I DIDN'T EXPECT YOU BACK SO SOON.
SURPRISE YOU.
THAT'S JUST LYING.
YOU DON'T LOOK DIFFER-ENT.
COR-RECT.

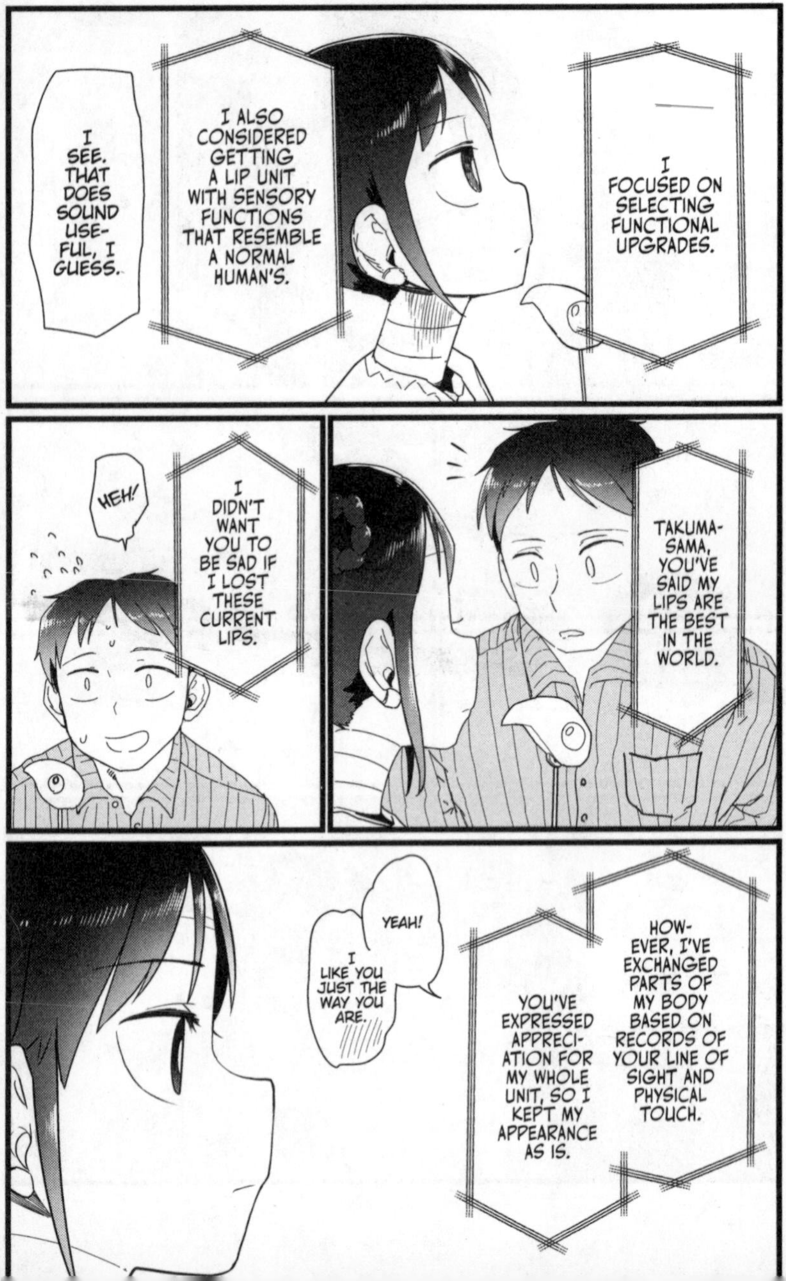
—
I FOCUSED ON SELECTING FUNCTIONAL UPGRADES.
I ALSO CONSIDERED GETTING A LIP UNIT WITH SENSORY FUNCTIONS THAT RESEMBLE A NORMAL HUMAN'S.
I SEE. THAT DOES SOUND USE-FUL, I GUESS.
TAKUMA-SAMA, YOU'VE SAID MY LIPS ARE THE BEST IN THE WORLD.
I DIDN'T WANT YOU TO BE SAD IF I LOST THESE CURRENT LIPS.
HEH!
HOW-EVER, I'VE EXCHANGED PARTS OF MY BODY BASED ON RECORDS OF YOUR LINE OF SIGHT AND PHYSICAL TOUCH.
YOU'VE EXPRESSED APPRECI-ATION FOR MY WHOLE UNIT, SO I KEPT MY APPEARANCE AS IS.
YEAH!
I LIKE YOU JUST THE WAY YOU ARE.

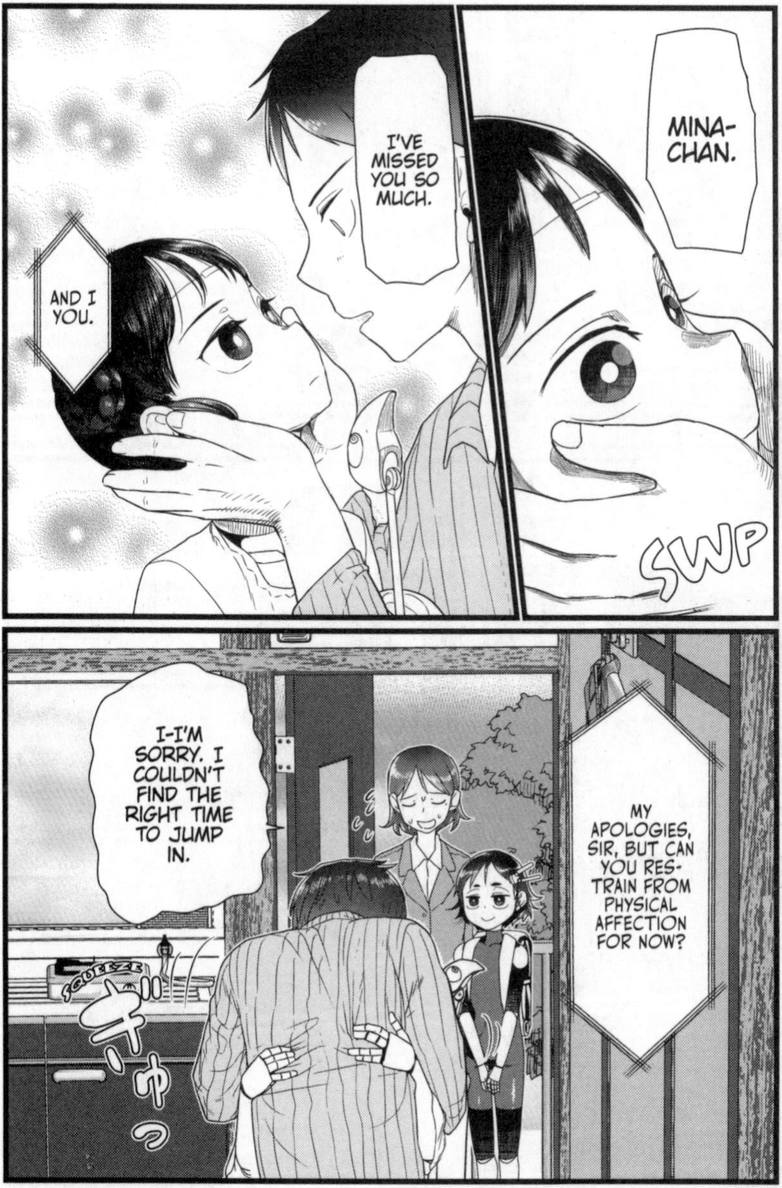
MINA-CHAN.
SWP
I'VE MISSED YOU SO MUCH.
AND I YOU.
MY APOLOGIES, SIR, BUT CAN YOU RES-TRAIN FROM PHYSICAL AFFECTION FOR NOW?
I-I'M SORRY. I COULDN'T FIND THE RIGHT TIME TO JUMP IN.
SQUEEZE

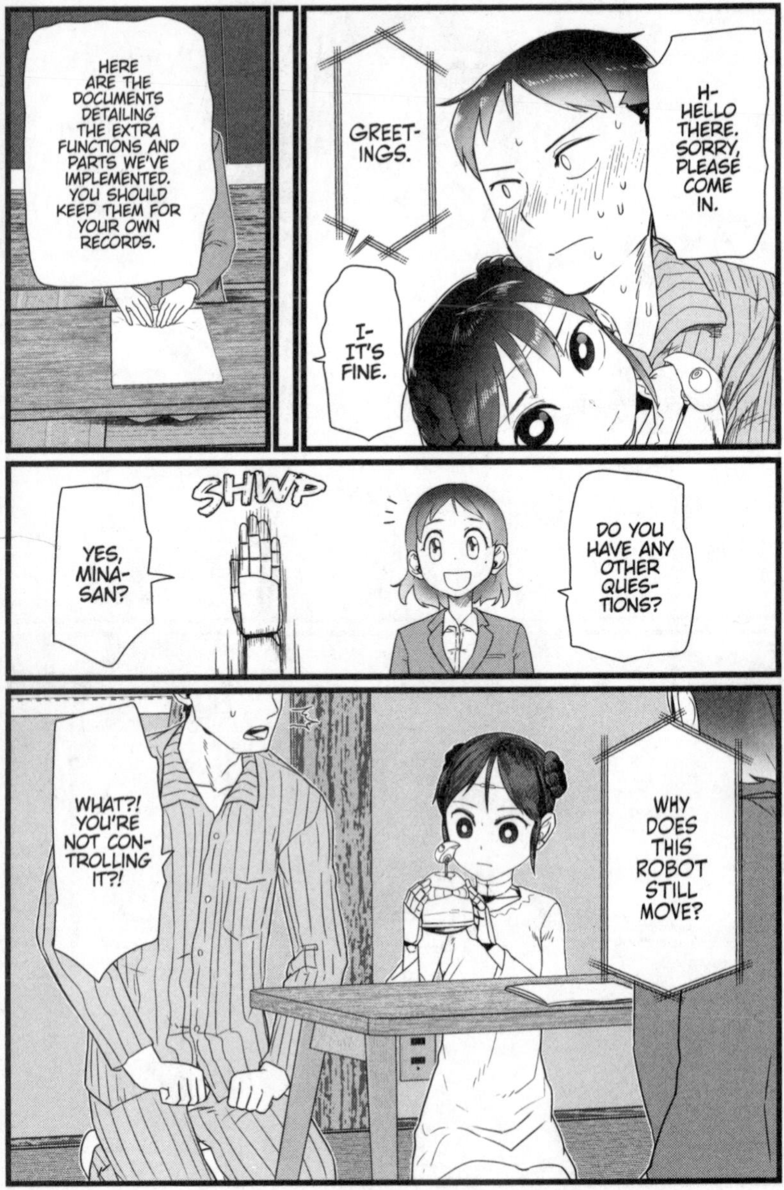
H- HELLO THERE. SORRY, PLEASE COME IN.
GREET- INGS.
I- IT'S FINE.
HERE ARE THE DOCUMENTS DETAILING THE EXTRA FUNCTIONS AND PARTS WE'VE IMPLEMENTED. YOU SHOULD KEEP THEM FOR YOUR OWN RECORDS.
DO YOU HAVE ANY OTHER QUES- TIONS?
SHWP
YES, MINA- SAN?
WHY DOES THIS ROBOT STILL MOVE?
WHAT?! YOU'RE NOT CON- TROLLING IT?!

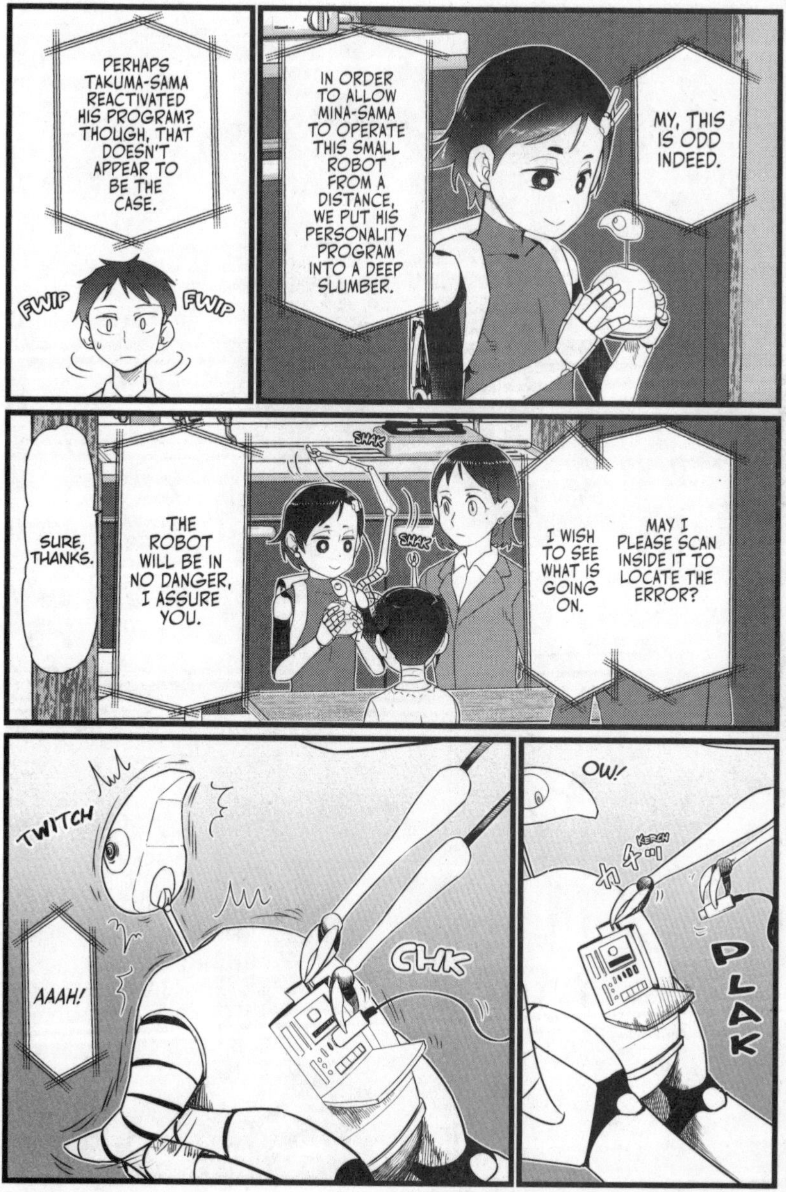

MY, THIS IS ODD INDEED.
IN ORDER TO ALLOW MINA-SAMA TO OPERATE THIS SMALL ROBOT FROM A DISTANCE, WE PUT HIS PERSONALITY PROGRAM INTO A DEEP SLUMBER.
PERHAPS TAKUMA-SAMA REACTIVATED HIS PROGRAM? THOUGH, THAT DOESN'T APPEAR TO BE THE CASE.
FWIP
FWIP
MAY I PLEASE SCAN INSIDE IT TO LOCATE THE ERROR?
I WISH TO SEE WHAT IS GOING ON.
SHAK
SHAK
THE ROBOT WILL BE IN NO DANGER, I ASSURE YOU.
SURE, THANKS.
OW!
KERCH
PLAK
TWITCH
CHK
AAAH!

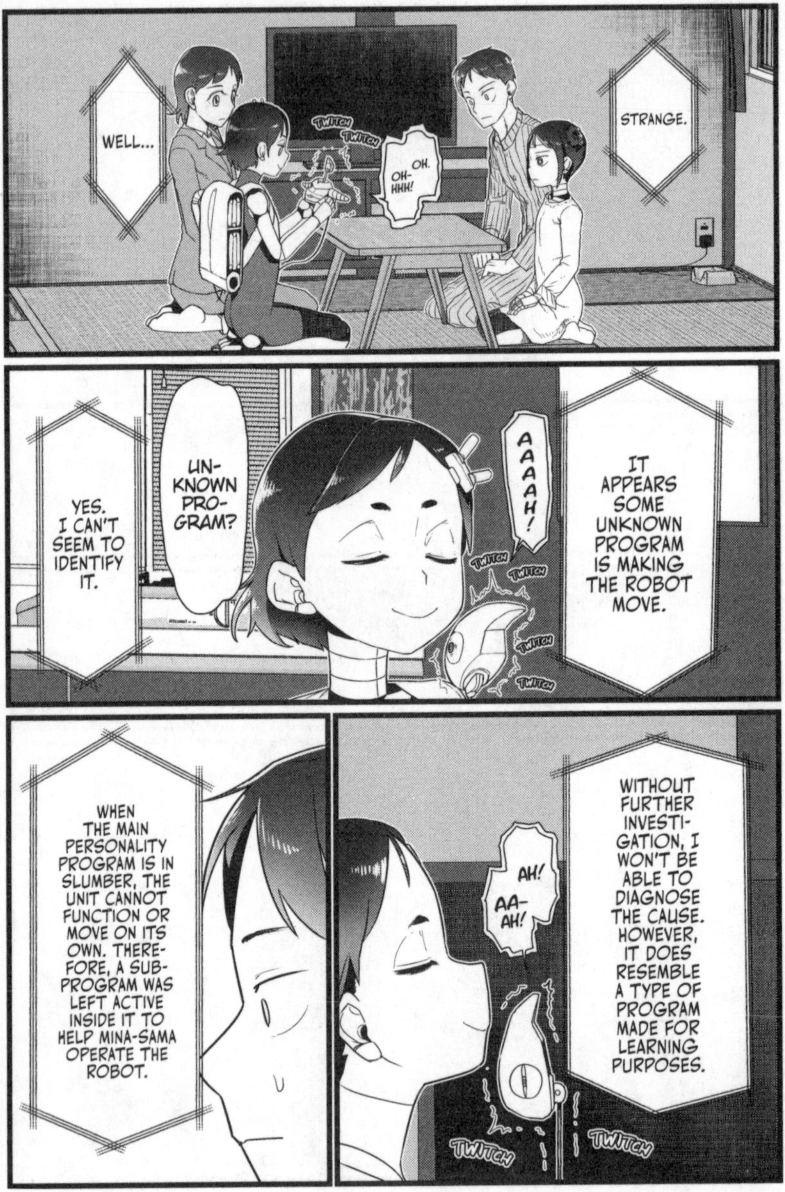
STRANGE.
OH. OH-HHH!
TWITCH
TWITCH
WELL...
IT APPEARS SOME UNKNOWN PROGRAM IS MAKING THE ROBOT MOVE.
AAAAAH!
TWITCH
TWITCH
TWITCH
TWITCH
UN-KNOWN PRO-GRAM?
YES. I CAN'T SEEM TO IDENTIFY IT.
WITHOUT FURTHER INVESTI-GATION, I WON'T BE ABLE TO DIAGNOSE THE CAUSE. HOWEVER, IT DOES RESEMBLE A TYPE OF PROGRAM MADE FOR LEARNING PURPOSES.
AH! AA-AH!
TWITCH
TWITCH
WHEN THE MAIN PERSONALITY PROGRAM IS IN SLUMBER, THE UNIT CANNOT FUNCTION OR MOVE ON ITS OWN. THERE-FORE, A SUB-PROGRAM WAS LEFT ACTIVE INSIDE IT TO HELP MINA-SAMA OPERATE THE ROBOT.

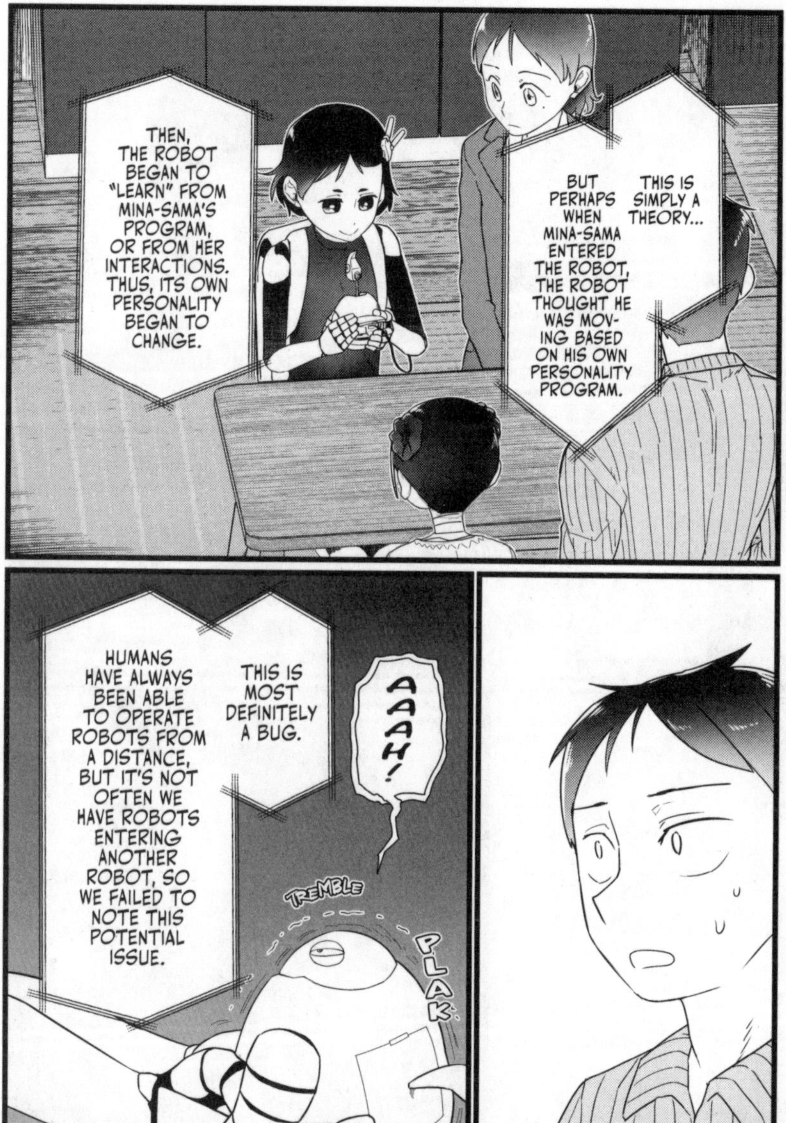
THIS IS SIMPLY A THEORY...
BUT PERHAPS WHEN MINA-SAMA ENTERED THE ROBOT, THE ROBOT THOUGHT HE WAS MOV-ING BASED ON HIS OWN PERSONALITY PROGRAM.
THEN, THE ROBOT BEGAN TO "LEARN" FROM MINA-SAMA'S PROGRAM, OR FROM HER INTERACTIONS. THUS, ITS OWN PERSONALITY BEGAN TO CHANGE.
AAAAH!
THIS IS MOST DEFINITELY A BUG.
HUMANS HAVE ALWAYS BEEN ABLE TO OPERATE ROBOTS FROM A DISTANCE, BUT IT'S NOT OFTEN WE HAVE ROBOTS ENTERING ANOTHER ROBOT, SO WE FAILED TO NOTE THIS POTENTIAL ISSUE.
TREMBLE
PLAK

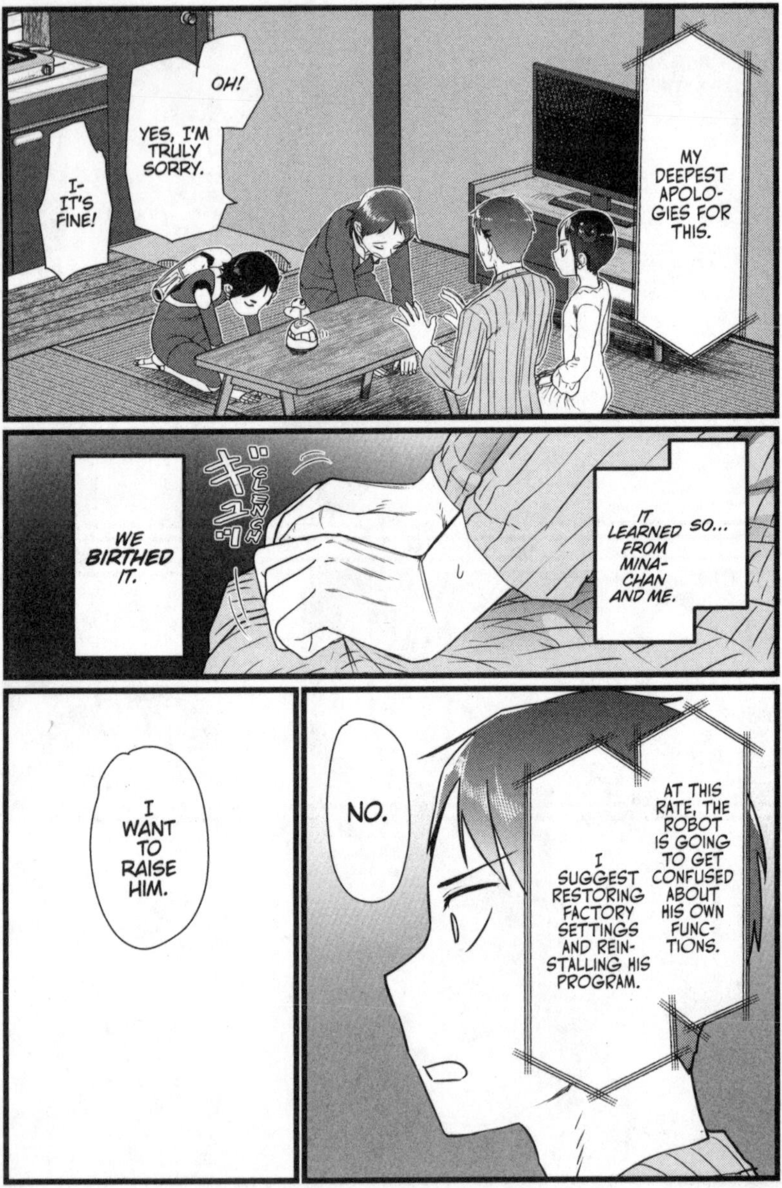
MY DEEPEST APOLOGIES FOR THIS.
OH!
YES, I'M TRULY SORRY.
I- IT'S FINE!
SO...
IT LEARNED FROM MINA-CHAN AND ME.
ギュッ CLENCH
WE BIRTHED IT.
AT THIS RATE, THE ROBOT IS GOING TO GET CONFUSED ABOUT HIS OWN FUNC-TIONS.
I SUGGEST RESTORING FACTORY SETTINGS AND REIN-STALLING HIS PROGRAM.
NO.
I WANT TO RAISE HIM.

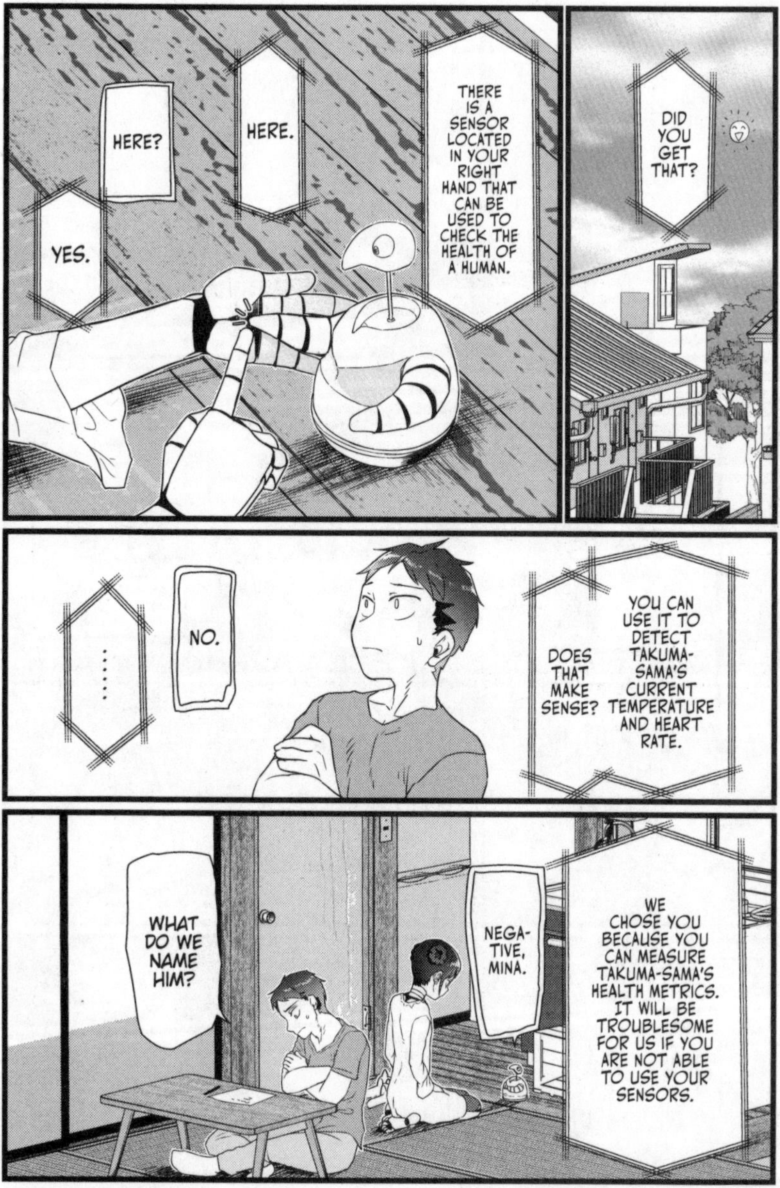
DID YOU GET THAT?
THERE IS A SENSOR LOCATED IN YOUR RIGHT HAND THAT CAN BE USED TO CHECK THE HEALTH OF A HUMAN.
HERE.
HERE?
YES.
YOU CAN USE IT TO DETECT TAKUMA-SAMA'S CURRENT TEMPERATURE AND HEART RATE.
DOES THAT MAKE SENSE?
NO.
......
WE CHOSE YOU BECAUSE YOU CAN MEASURE TAKUMA-SAMA'S HEALTH METRICS. IT WILL BE TROUBLESOME FOR US IF YOU ARE NOT ABLE TO USE YOUR SENSORS.
NEGA-TIVE, MINA.
WHAT DO WE NAME HIM?

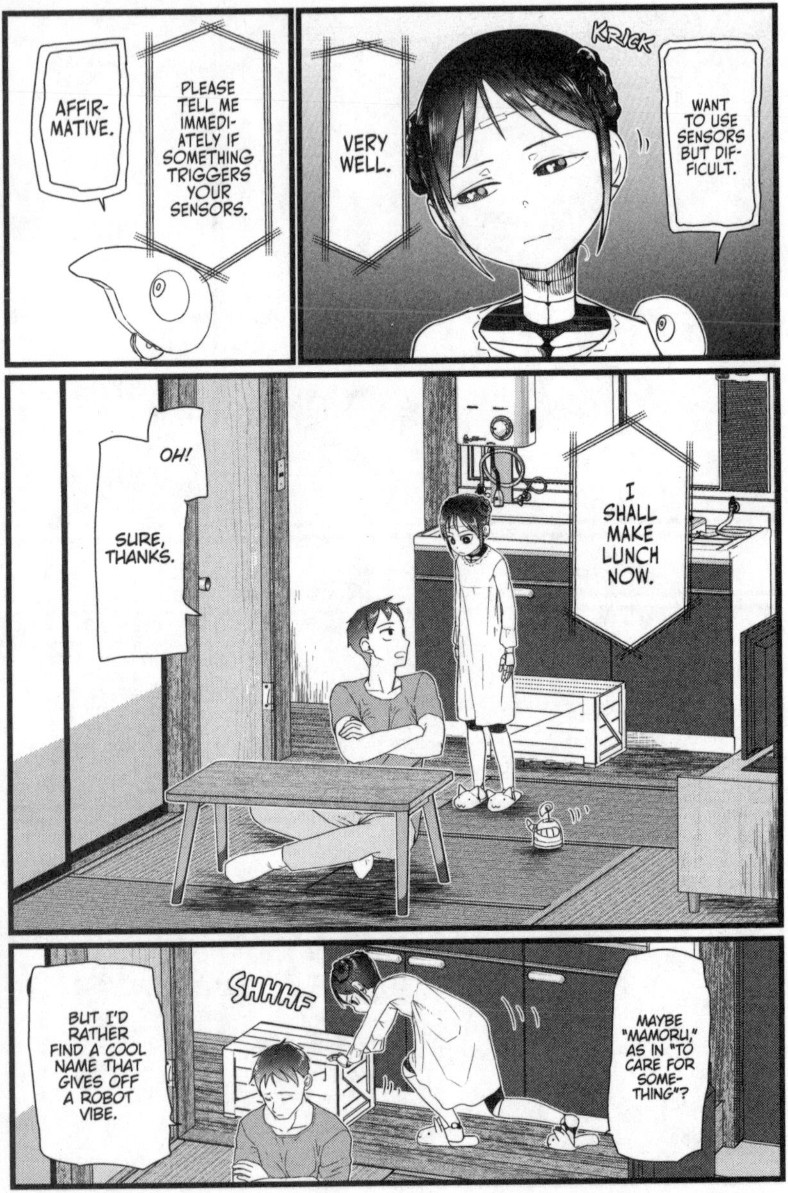
KRICK
WANT TO USE SENSORS BUT DIFFICULT.
VERY WELL.
PLEASE TELL ME IMMEDIATELY IF SOMETHING TRIGGERS YOUR SENSORS.
AFFIRMATIVE.
I SHALL MAKE LUNCH NOW.
OH!
SURE, THANKS.
MAYBE "MAMORU," AS IN "TO CARE FOR SOMETHING"?
SHHHF
BUT I'D RATHER FIND A COOL NAME THAT GIVES OFF A ROBOT VIBE.

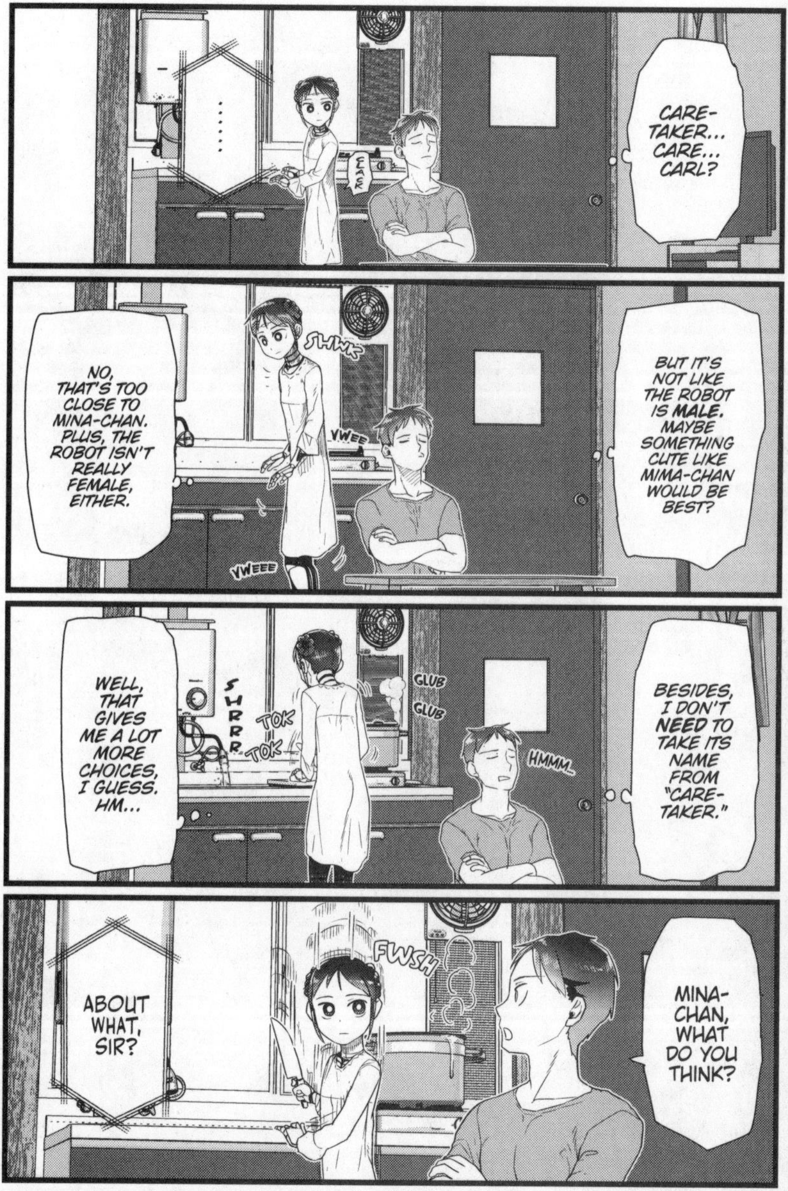
CARE-TAKER... CARE... CARL?
CLACK
BUT IT'S NOT LIKE THE ROBOT IS MALE. MAYBE SOMETHING CUTE LIKE MIMA-CHAN WOULD BE BEST?
SHWK
VWEE
YWEEE
NO, THAT'S TOO CLOSE TO MINA-CHAN. PLUS, THE ROBOT ISN'T REALLY FEMALE, EITHER.
BESIDES, I DON'T NEED TO TAKE ITS NAME FROM "CARE-TAKER."
HMMM..
GLUB
GLUB
TOK
TOK
SHRRR
WELL, THAT GIVES ME A LOT MORE CHOICES, I GUESS. HM...
MINA-CHAN, WHAT DO YOU THINK?
FWSH
ABOUT WHAT, SIR?

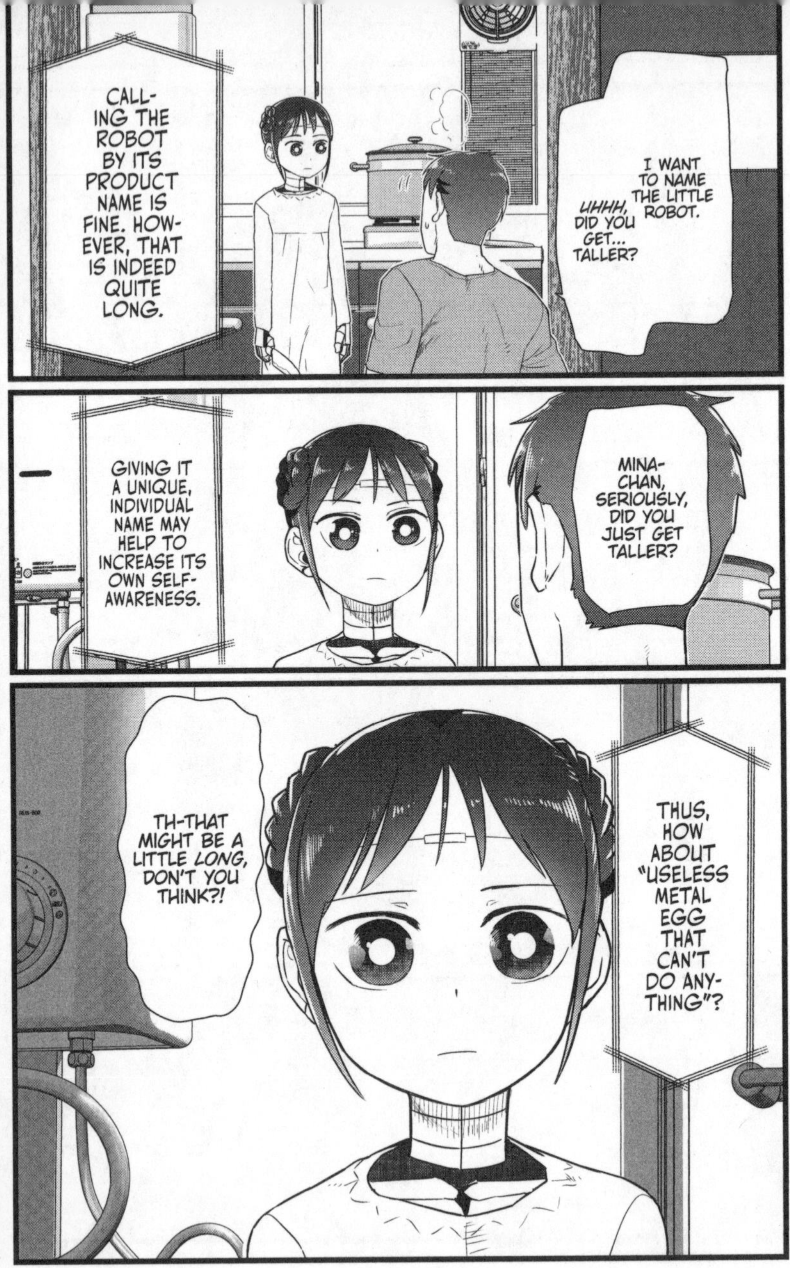
I WANT TO NAME THE LITTLE ROBOT.
UHHH, DID YOU GET... TALLER?
CALLING THE ROBOT BY ITS PRODUCT NAME IS FINE. HOWEVER, THAT IS INDEED QUITE LONG.
MINA-CHAN, SERIOUSLY, DID YOU JUST GET TALLER?
GIVING IT A UNIQUE, INDIVIDUAL NAME MAY HELP TO INCREASE ITS OWN SELF-AWARENESS.
THUS, HOW ABOUT "USELESS METAL EGG THAT CAN'T DO ANYTHING"?
TH-THAT MIGHT BE A LITTLE *LONG,* DON'T YOU THINK?!

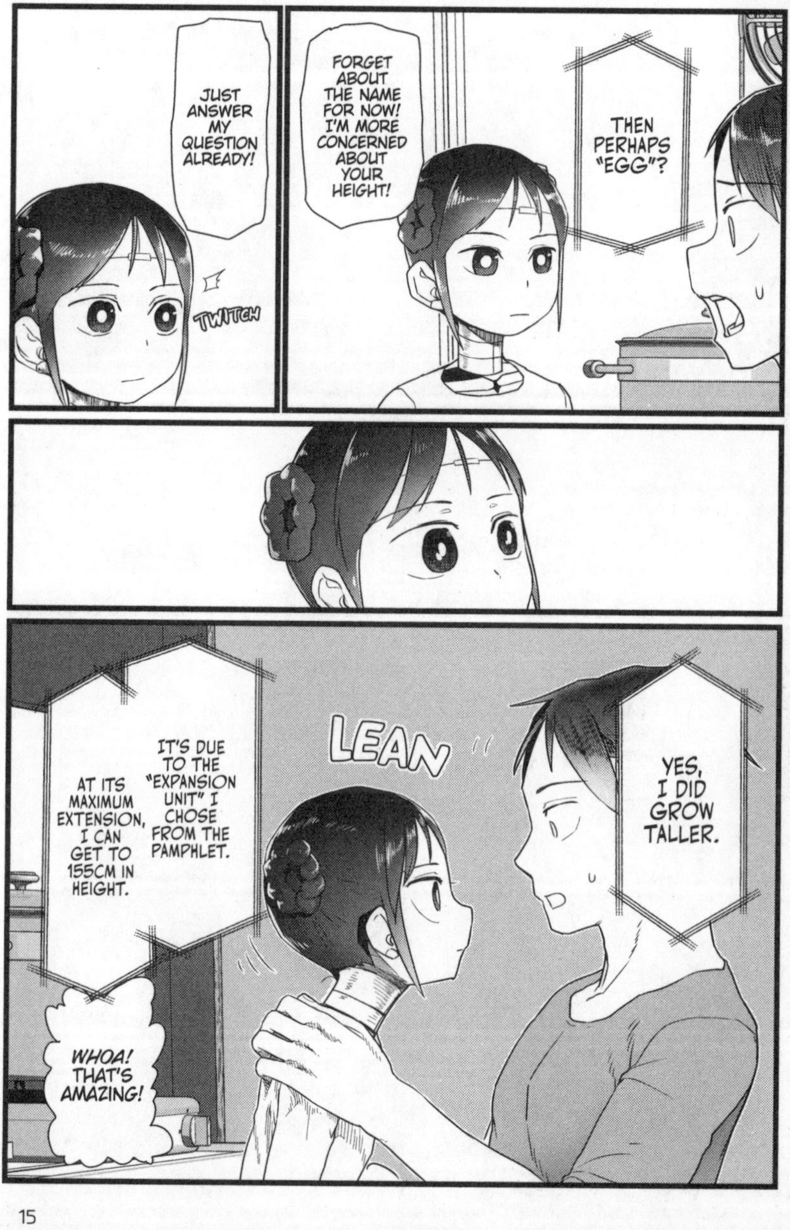
THEN PERHAPS "EGG"?
FORGET ABOUT THE NAME FOR NOW! I'M MORE CONCERNED ABOUT YOUR HEIGHT!
JUST ANSWER MY QUESTION ALREADY!
TWITCH
YES, I DID GROW TALLER.
LEAN
IT'S DUE TO THE "EXPANSION UNIT" I CHOSE FROM THE PAMPHLET.
AT ITS MAXIMUM EXTENSION, I CAN GET TO 155CM IN HEIGHT.
WHOA! THAT'S AMAZING!

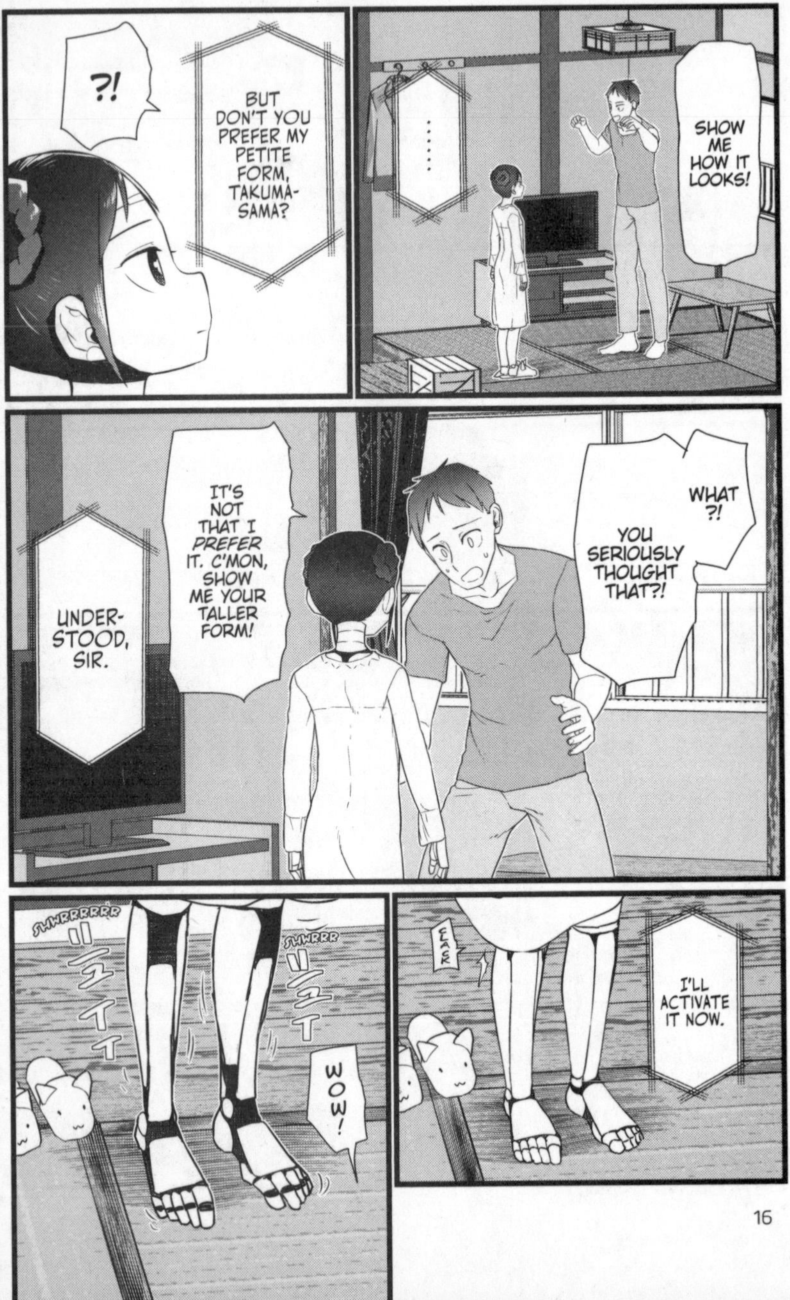
SHOW ME HOW IT LOOKS!
......
BUT DON'T YOU PREFER MY PETITE FORM, TAKUMA-SAMA?
?!
WHAT?!
YOU SERIOUSLY THOUGHT THAT?!
IT'S NOT THAT I *PREFER* IT. C'MON, SHOW ME YOUR TALLER FORM!
UNDER-STOOD, SIR.
I'LL ACTIVATE IT NOW.
CLACK
SHWRRRRRR
SHWRRR
WOW!

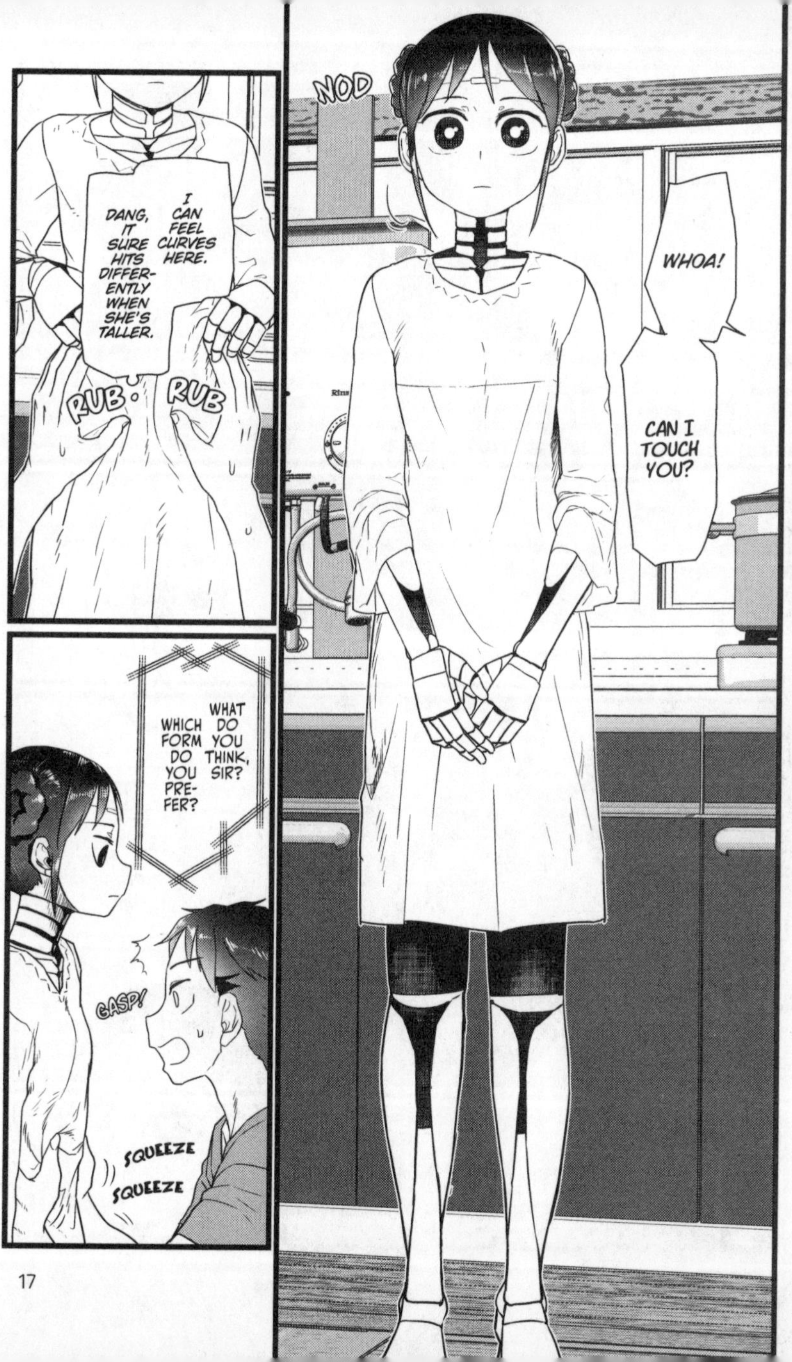
NOD
WHOA!
CAN I TOUCH YOU?
I CAN FEEL CURVES HERE.
DANG, IT SURE HITS DIFFERENTLY WHEN SHE'S TALLER.
RUB RUB
WHAT DO YOU THINK, SIR?
WHICH FORM DO YOU PREFER?
GASP!
SQUEEZE SQUEEZE

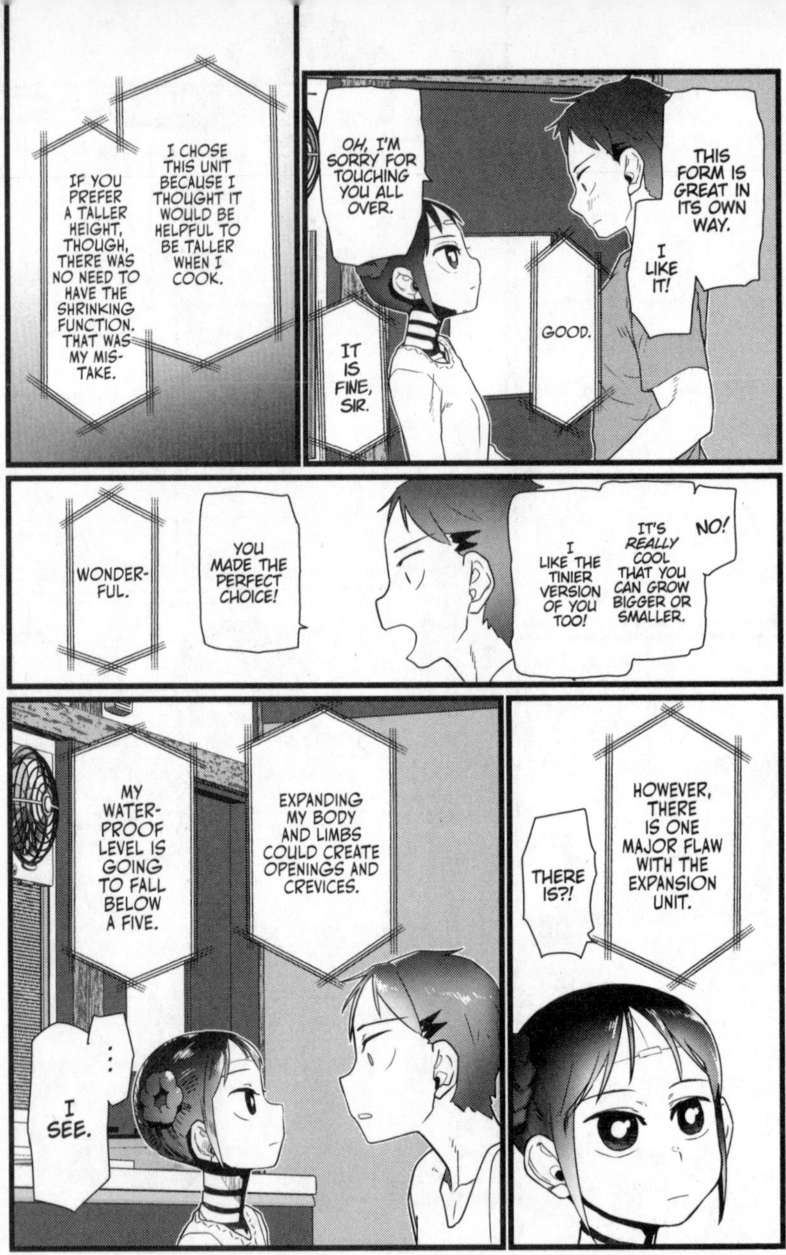
THIS FORM IS GREAT IN ITS OWN WAY.
I LIKE IT!
OH, I'M SORRY FOR TOUCHING YOU ALL OVER.
GOOD.
IT IS FINE, SIR.
I CHOSE THIS UNIT BECAUSE I THOUGHT IT WOULD BE HELPFUL TO BE TALLER WHEN I COOK.
IF YOU PREFER A TALLER HEIGHT, THOUGH, THERE WAS NO NEED TO HAVE THE SHRINKING FUNCTION. THAT WAS MY MIS-TAKE.
NO!
IT'S *REALLY* COOL THAT YOU CAN GROW BIGGER OR SMALLER.
I LIKE THE TINIER VERSION OF YOU TOO!
YOU MADE THE PERFECT CHOICE!
WONDER-FUL.
HOWEVER, THERE IS ONE MAJOR FLAW WITH THE EXPANSION UNIT.
THERE IS?!
EXPANDING MY BODY AND LIMBS COULD CREATE OPENINGS AND CREVICES.
MY WATER-PROOF LEVEL IS GOING TO FALL BELOW A FIVE.
...
I SEE.

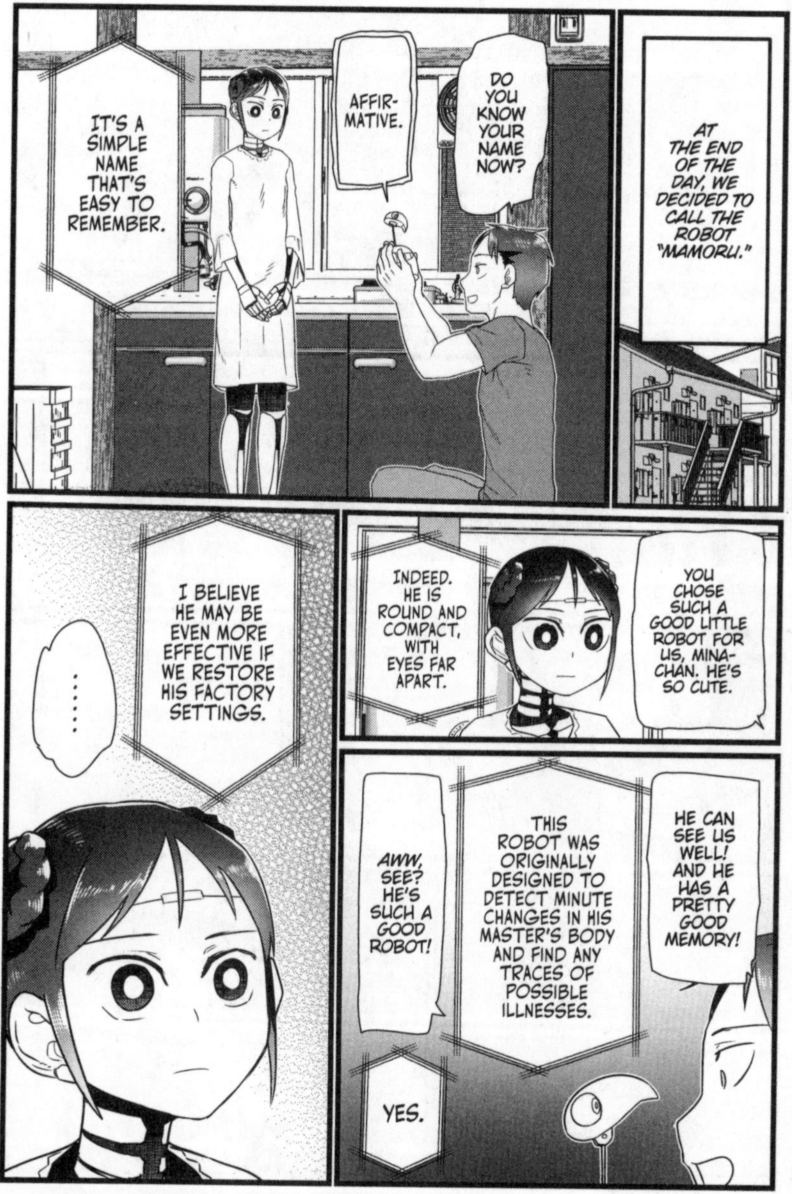
AT THE END OF THE DAY, WE DECIDED TO CALL THE ROBOT "MAMORU."
DO YOU KNOW YOUR NAME NOW?
AFFIR-MATIVE.
IT'S A SIMPLE NAME THAT'S EASY TO REMEMBER.
YOU CHOSE SUCH A GOOD LITTLE ROBOT FOR US, MINA-CHAN. HE'S SO CUTE.
INDEED. HE IS ROUND AND COMPACT, WITH EYES FAR APART.
HE CAN SEE US WELL! AND HE HAS A PRETTY GOOD MEMORY!
THIS ROBOT WAS ORIGINALLY DESIGNED TO DETECT MINUTE CHANGES IN HIS MASTER'S BODY AND FIND ANY TRACES OF POSSIBLE ILLNESSES.
AWW, SEE? HE'S SUCH A GOOD ROBOT!
YES.
I BELIEVE HE MAY BE EVEN MORE EFFECTIVE IF WE RESTORE HIS FACTORY SETTINGS.
......

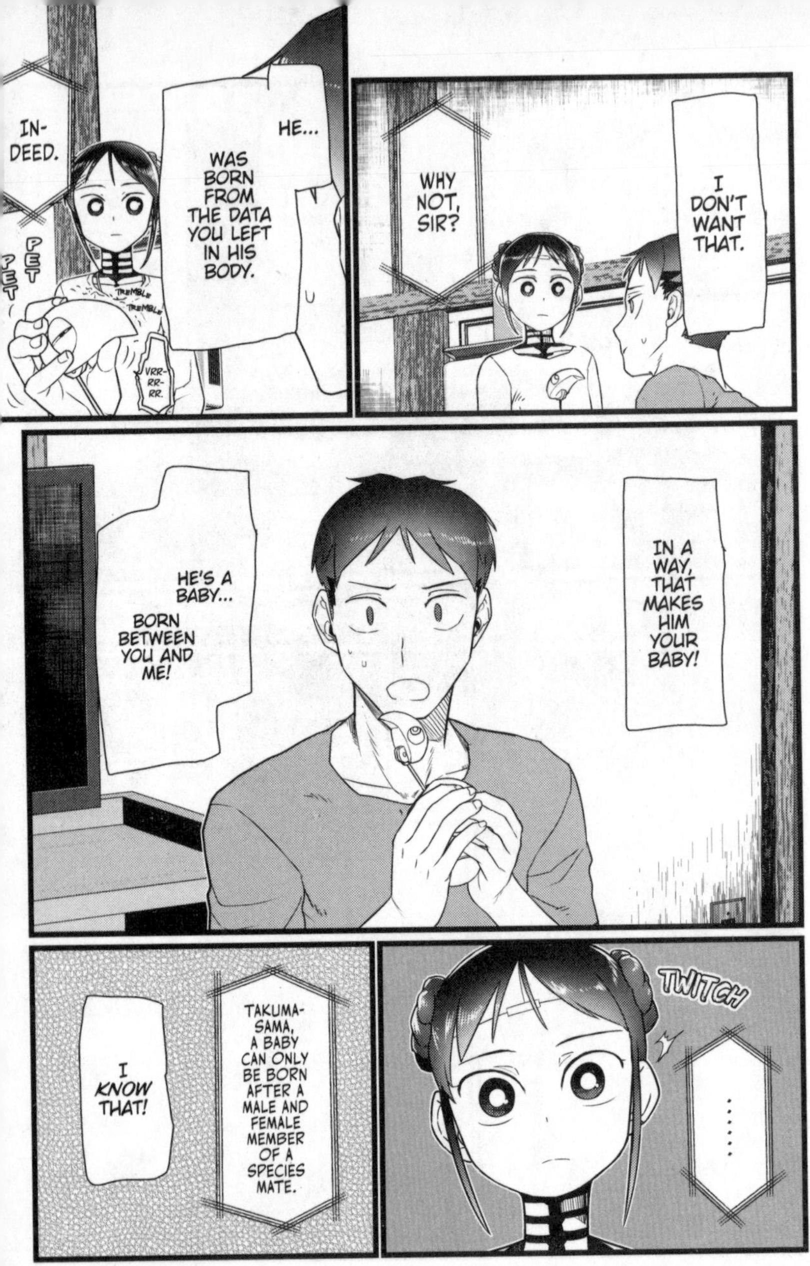
I DON'T WANT THAT.
WHY NOT, SIR?
HE... WAS BORN FROM THE DATA YOU LEFT IN HIS BODY.
IN-DEED.
PET PET
TREMBLE TREMBLE
VRR-RR-RR.
IN A WAY, THAT MAKES HIM YOUR BABY!
HE'S A BABY... BORN BETWEEN YOU AND ME!
TWITCH
......
TAKUMA-SAMA, A BABY CAN ONLY BE BORN AFTER A MALE AND FEMALE MEMBER OF A SPECIES MATE.
I *KNOW* THAT!

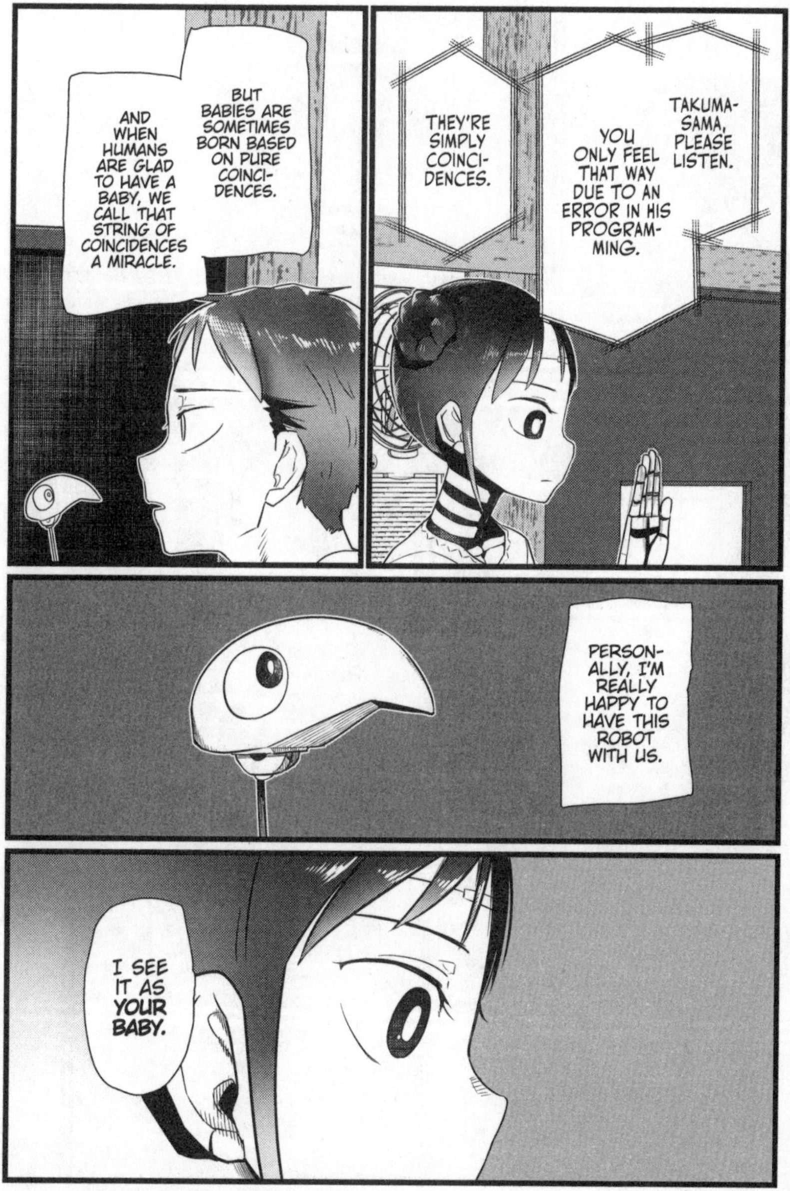
TAKUMA-SAMA, PLEASE LISTEN.
YOU ONLY FEEL THAT WAY DUE TO AN ERROR IN HIS PROGRAM-MING.
THEY'RE SIMPLY COINCI-DENCES.
BUT BABIES ARE SOMETIMES BORN BASED ON PURE COINCI-DENCES.
AND WHEN HUMANS ARE GLAD TO HAVE A BABY, WE CALL THAT STRING OF COINCIDENCES A MIRACLE.
PERSON-ALLY, I'M REALLY HAPPY TO HAVE THIS ROBOT WITH US.
I SEE IT AS YOUR BABY.

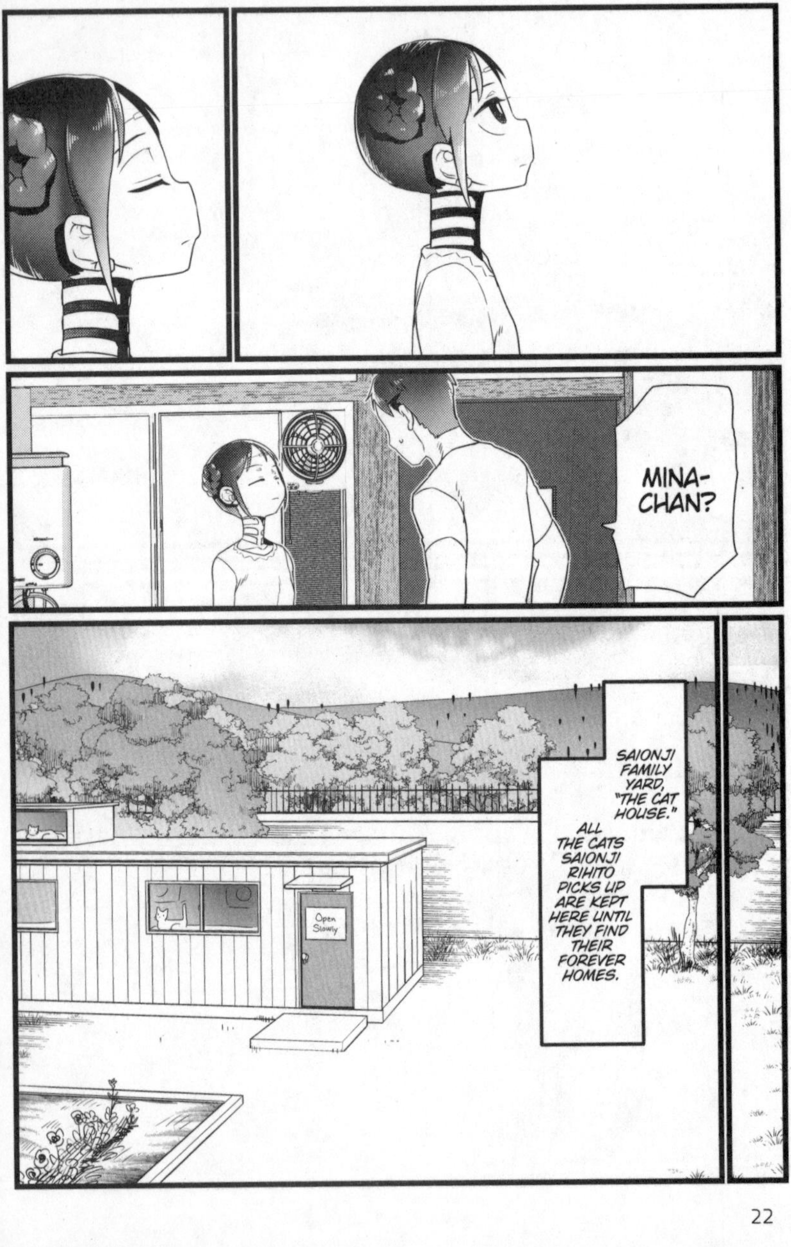
MINA-CHAN?
SAIONJI FAMILY YARD, "THE CAT HOUSE."
ALL THE CATS SAIONJI RIHITO PICKS UP ARE KEPT HERE UNTIL THEY FIND THEIR FOREVER HOMES.
Open Slowly

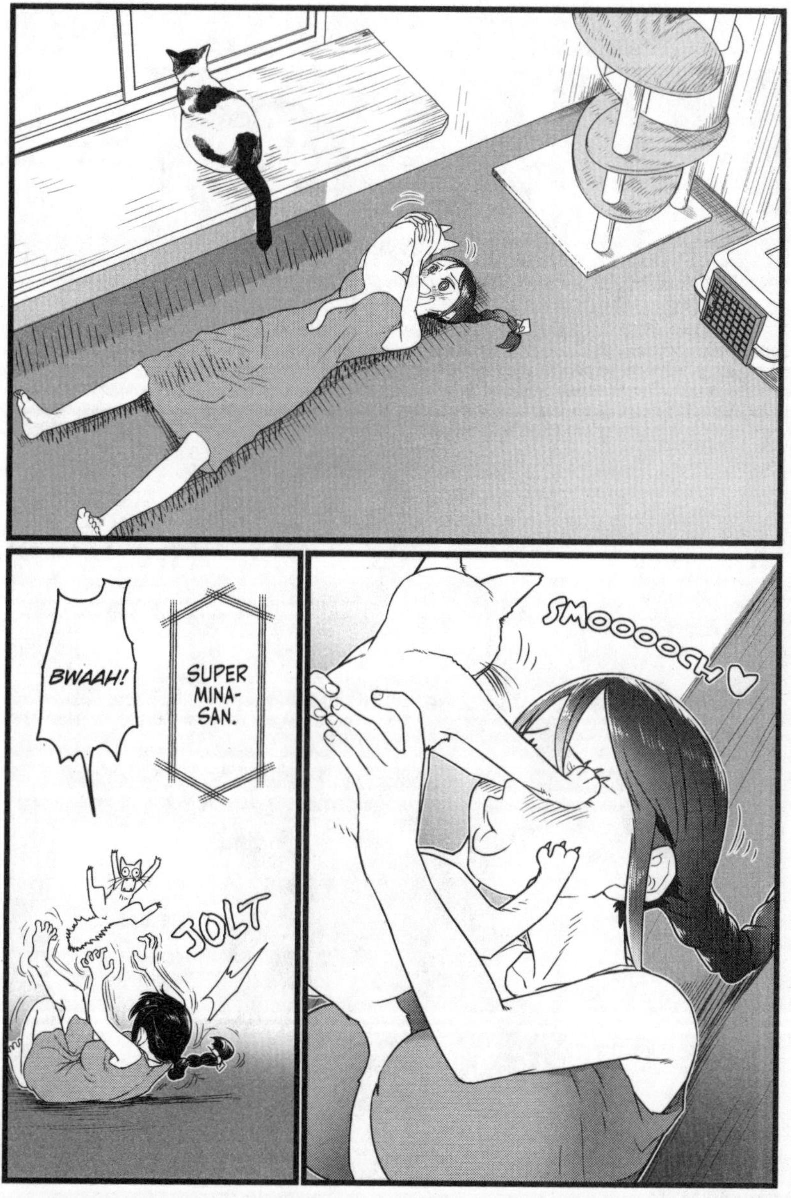
SMOOOOCH♥
SUPER MINA-SAN.
BWAAH!
JOLT

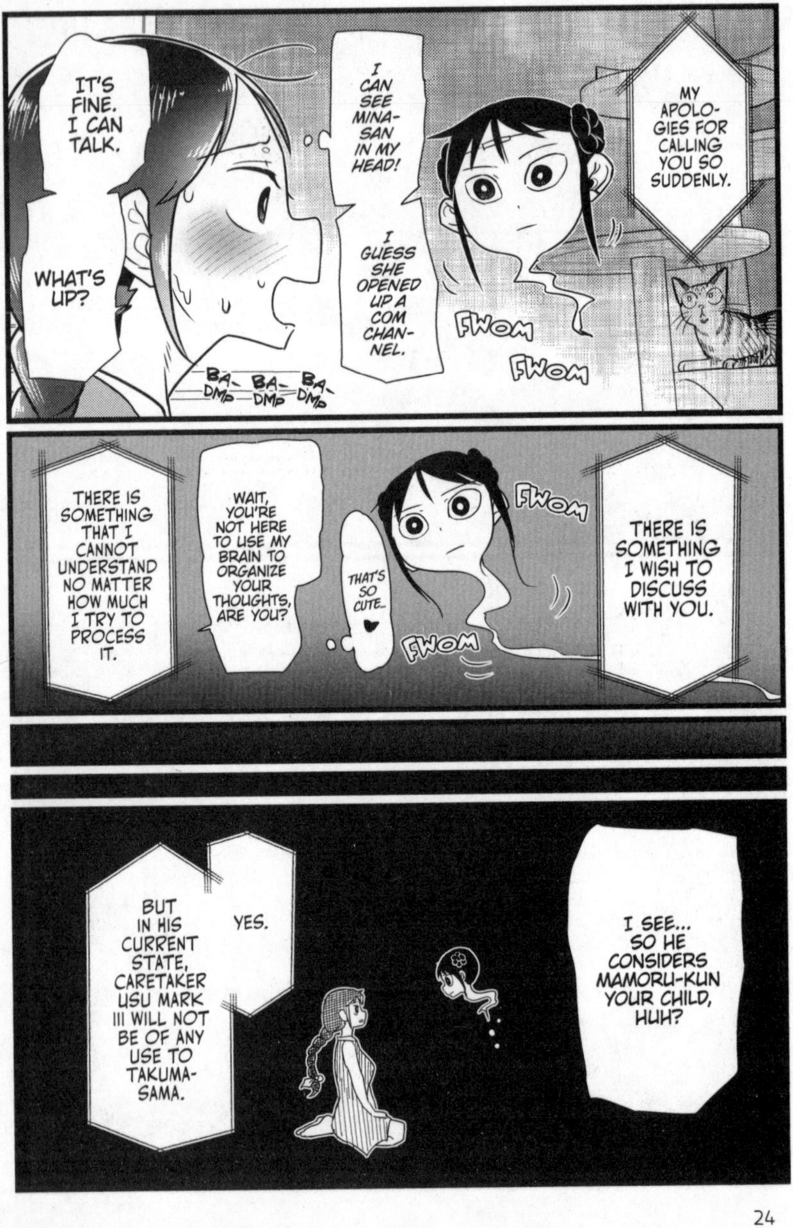
MY APOLOGIES FOR CALLING YOU SO SUDDENLY.
I CAN SEE MINA-SAN IN MY HEAD!
I GUESS SHE OPENED UP A COM CHANNEL.
FWOM
FWOM
BA-DMP BA-DMP BA-DMP
IT'S FINE. I CAN TALK.
WHAT'S UP?
THERE IS SOMETHING I WISH TO DISCUSS WITH YOU.
FWOM
FWOM
THAT'S SO CUTE..
WAIT, YOU'RE NOT HERE TO USE MY BRAIN TO ORGANIZE YOUR THOUGHTS, ARE YOU?
THERE IS SOMETHING THAT I CANNOT UNDERSTAND NO MATTER HOW MUCH I TRY TO PROCESS IT.
I SEE... SO HE CONSIDERS MAMORU-KUN YOUR CHILD, HUH?
YES.
BUT IN HIS CURRENT STATE, CARETAKER USU MARK III WILL NOT BE OF ANY USE TO TAKUMA-SAMA.

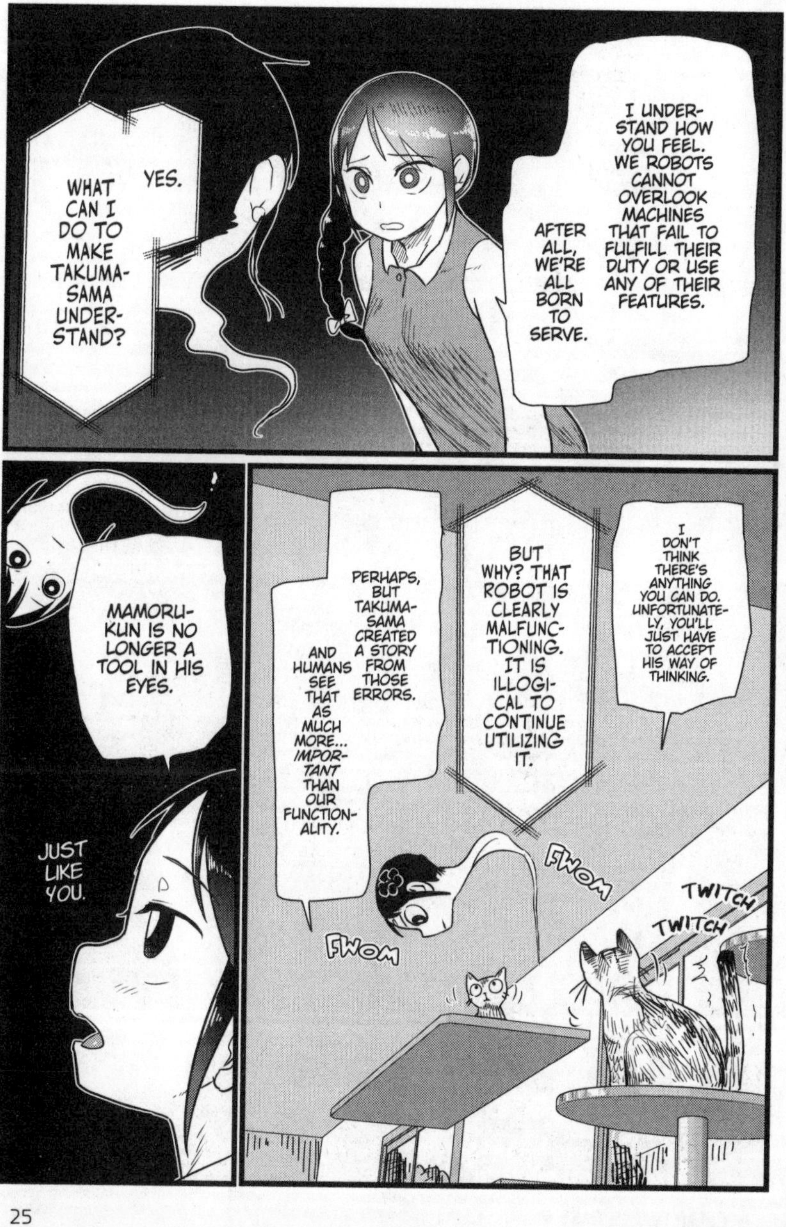
I UNDERSTAND HOW YOU FEEL. WE ROBOTS CANNOT OVERLOOK MACHINES THAT FAIL TO FULFILL THEIR DUTY OR USE ANY OF THEIR FEATURES.
AFTER ALL, WE'RE ALL BORN TO SERVE.
YES.
WHAT CAN I DO TO MAKE TAKUMA-SAMA UNDERSTAND?
I DON'T THINK THERE'S ANYTHING YOU CAN DO. UNFORTUNATELY, YOU'LL JUST HAVE TO ACCEPT HIS WAY OF THINKING.
BUT WHY? THAT ROBOT IS CLEARLY MALFUNCTIONING. IT IS ILLOGICAL TO CONTINUE UTILIZING IT.
PERHAPS, BUT TAKUMA-SAMA CREATED A STORY FROM THOSE ERRORS.
AND HUMANS SEE THAT AS MUCH MORE... *IMPORTANT* THAN OUR FUNCTIONALITY.
FWOM
FWOM
TWITCH
TWITCH
MAMORU-KUN IS NO LONGER A TOOL IN HIS EYES.
JUST LIKE YOU.

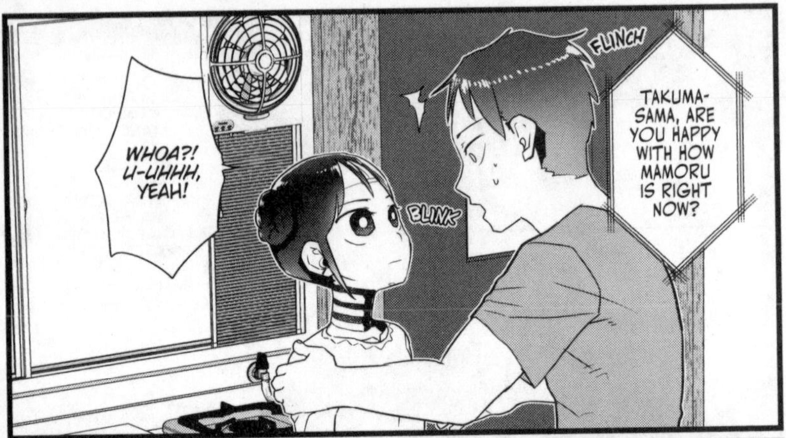
TAKUMA-SAMA, ARE YOU HAPPY WITH HOW MAMORU IS RIGHT NOW?
FLINCH
BLINK
WHOA?! U-UHHH, YEAH!

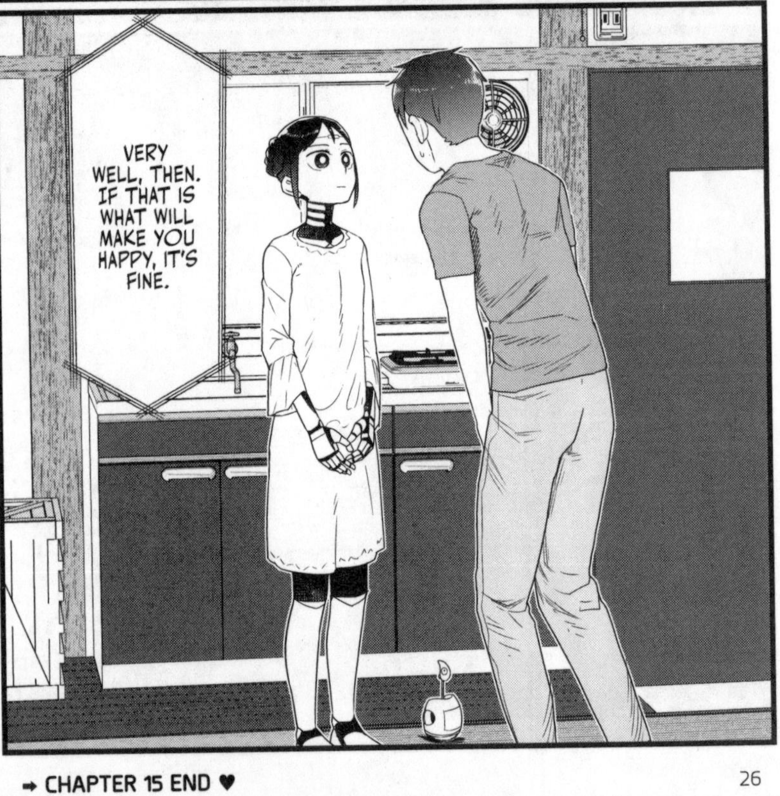
VERY WELL, THEN. IF THAT IS WHAT WILL MAKE YOU HAPPY, IT'S FINE.

My
Wife Has No
Emotion

My Wife Has No Emotion

➡ CHAPTER 16

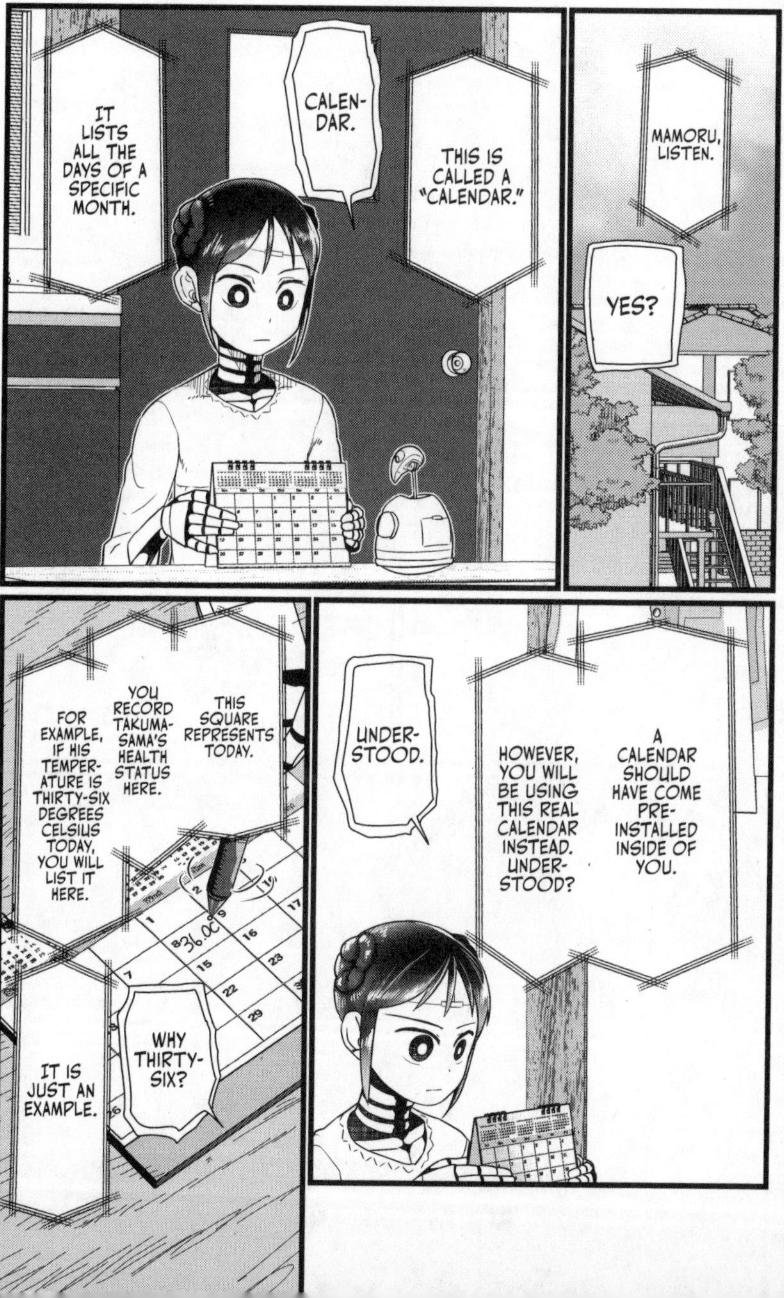

MAMORU, LISTEN.
YES?
THIS IS CALLED A "CALENDAR."
CALEN-DAR.
IT LISTS ALL THE DAYS OF A SPECIFIC MONTH.
A CALENDAR SHOULD HAVE COME PRE-INSTALLED INSIDE OF YOU.
HOWEVER, YOU WILL BE USING THIS REAL CALENDAR INSTEAD. UNDER-STOOD?
UNDER-STOOD.
THIS SQUARE REPRESENTS TODAY.
YOU RECORD TAKUMA-SAMA'S HEALTH STATUS HERE.
FOR EXAMPLE, IF HIS TEMPER-ATURE IS THIRTY-SIX DEGREES CELSIUS TODAY, YOU WILL LIST IT HERE.
36.0C
WHY THIRTY-SIX?
IT IS JUST AN EXAMPLE.

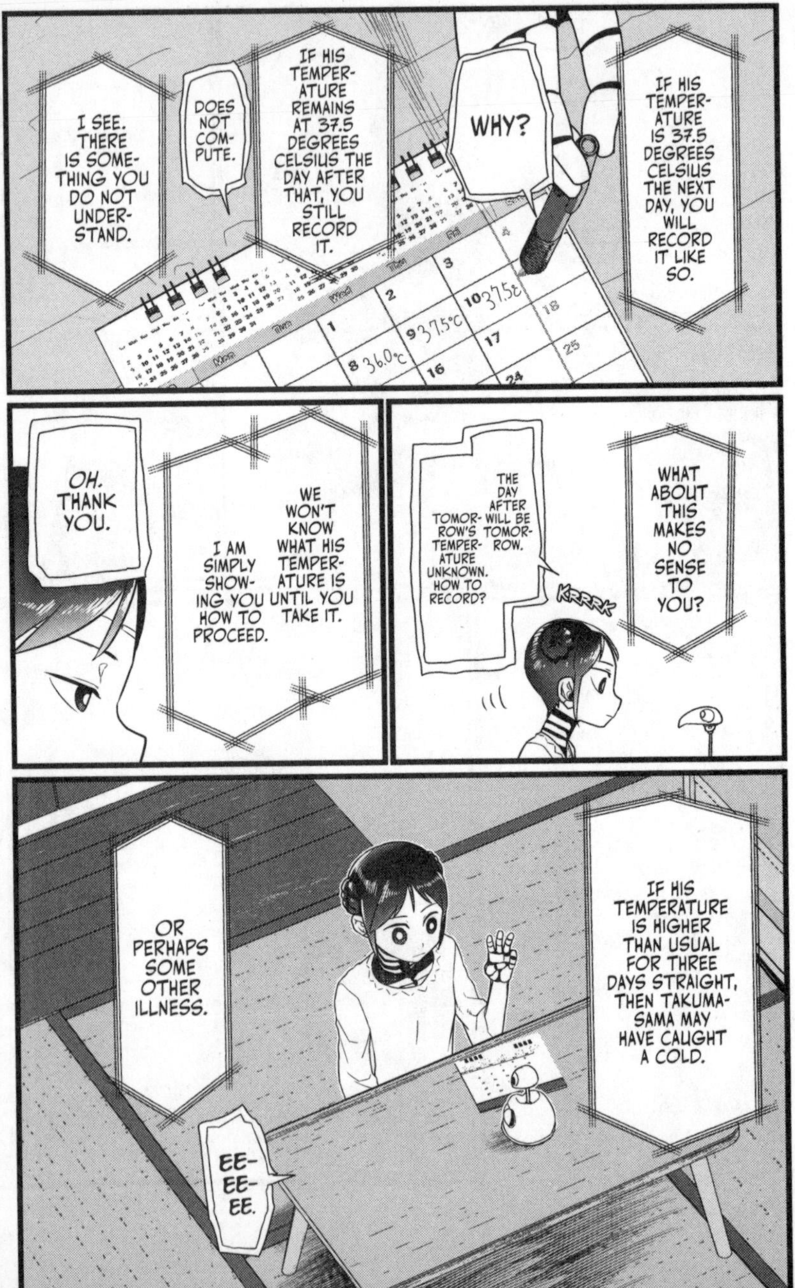
IF HIS TEMPERATURE IS 37.5 DEGREES CELSIUS THE NEXT DAY, YOU WILL RECORD IT LIKE SO.
WHY?
IF HIS TEMPERATURE REMAINS AT 37.5 DEGREES CELSIUS THE DAY AFTER THAT, YOU STILL RECORD IT.
DOES NOT COMPUTE.
I SEE. THERE IS SOMETHING YOU DO NOT UNDERSTAND.
WHAT ABOUT THIS MAKES NO SENSE TO YOU?
THE DAY AFTER WILL BE TOMORROW. TOMORROW'S TEMPERATURE UNKNOWN. HOW TO RECORD?
KRRRK
WE WON'T KNOW WHAT HIS TEMPERATURE IS UNTIL YOU TAKE IT.
I AM SIMPLY SHOWING YOU HOW TO PROCEED.
OH. THANK YOU.
IF HIS TEMPERATURE IS HIGHER THAN USUAL FOR THREE DAYS STRAIGHT, THEN TAKUMA-SAMA MAY HAVE CAUGHT A COLD.
OR PERHAPS SOME OTHER ILLNESS.
EE-EE-EE.

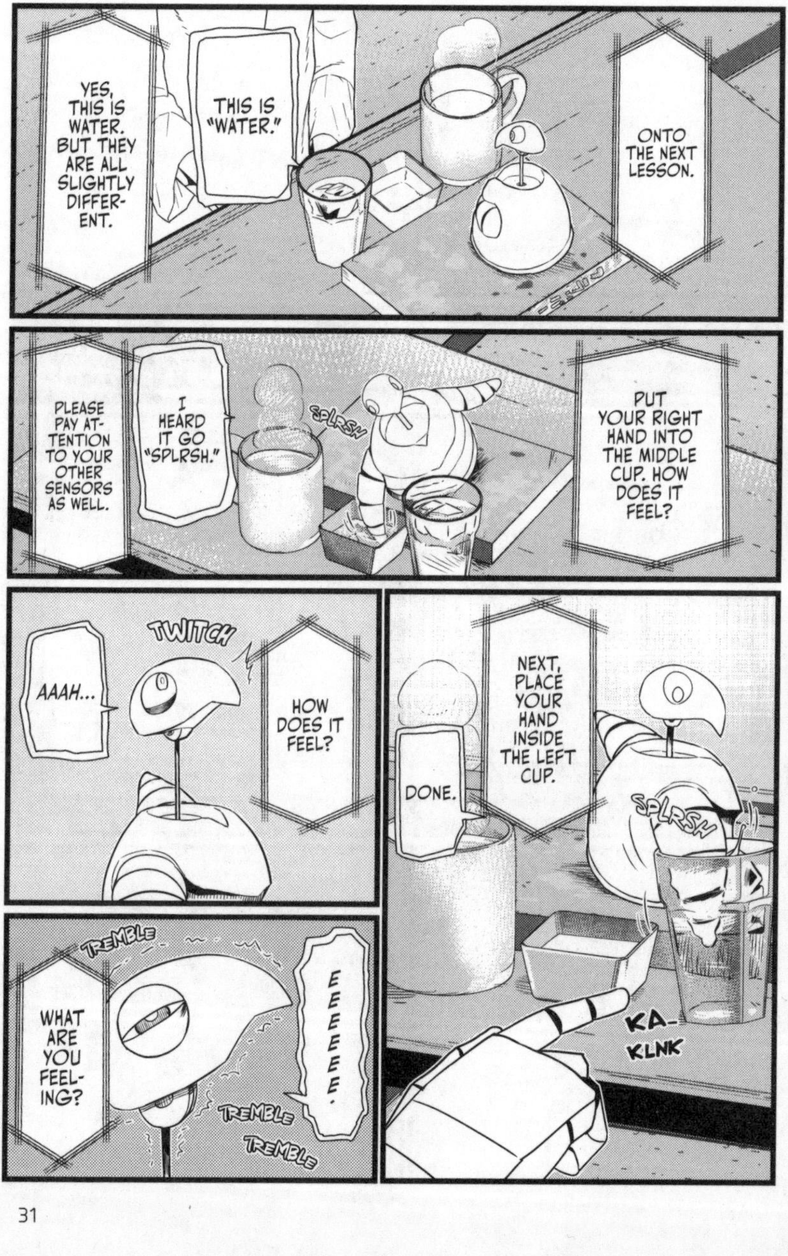
ONTO THE NEXT LESSON.
THIS IS "WATER."
YES, THIS IS WATER. BUT THEY ARE ALL SLIGHTLY DIFFER-ENT.
PUT YOUR RIGHT HAND INTO THE MIDDLE CUP. HOW DOES IT FEEL?
SPLRSH
I HEARD IT GO "SPLRSH."
PLEASE PAY AT-TENTION TO YOUR OTHER SENSORS AS WELL.
NEXT, PLACE YOUR HAND INSIDE THE LEFT CUP.
SPLRSH
DONE.
KA-KLNK
TWITCH
HOW DOES IT FEEL?
AAAH...
TREMBLE
EEEEEE.
TREMBLE
TREMBLE
WHAT ARE YOU FEEL-ING?

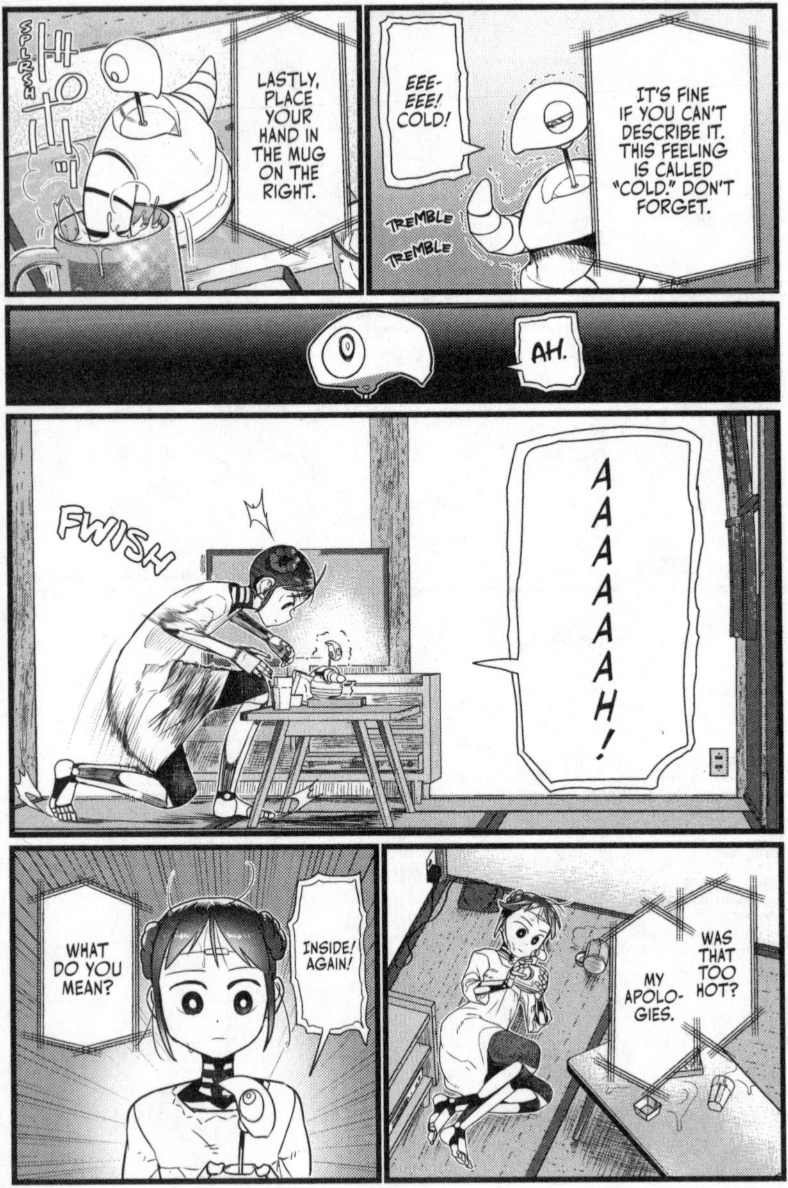
IT'S FINE IF YOU CAN'T DESCRIBE IT. THIS FEELING IS CALLED "COLD." DON'T FORGET.
EEE-EEE! COLD!
TREMBLE
TREMBLE
LASTLY, PLACE YOUR HAND IN THE MUG ON THE RIGHT.
SPLASH
AH.
AAAAAAAH!
FWISH
WAS THAT TOO HOT?
MY APOLOGIES.
INSIDE! AGAIN!
WHAT DO YOU MEAN?

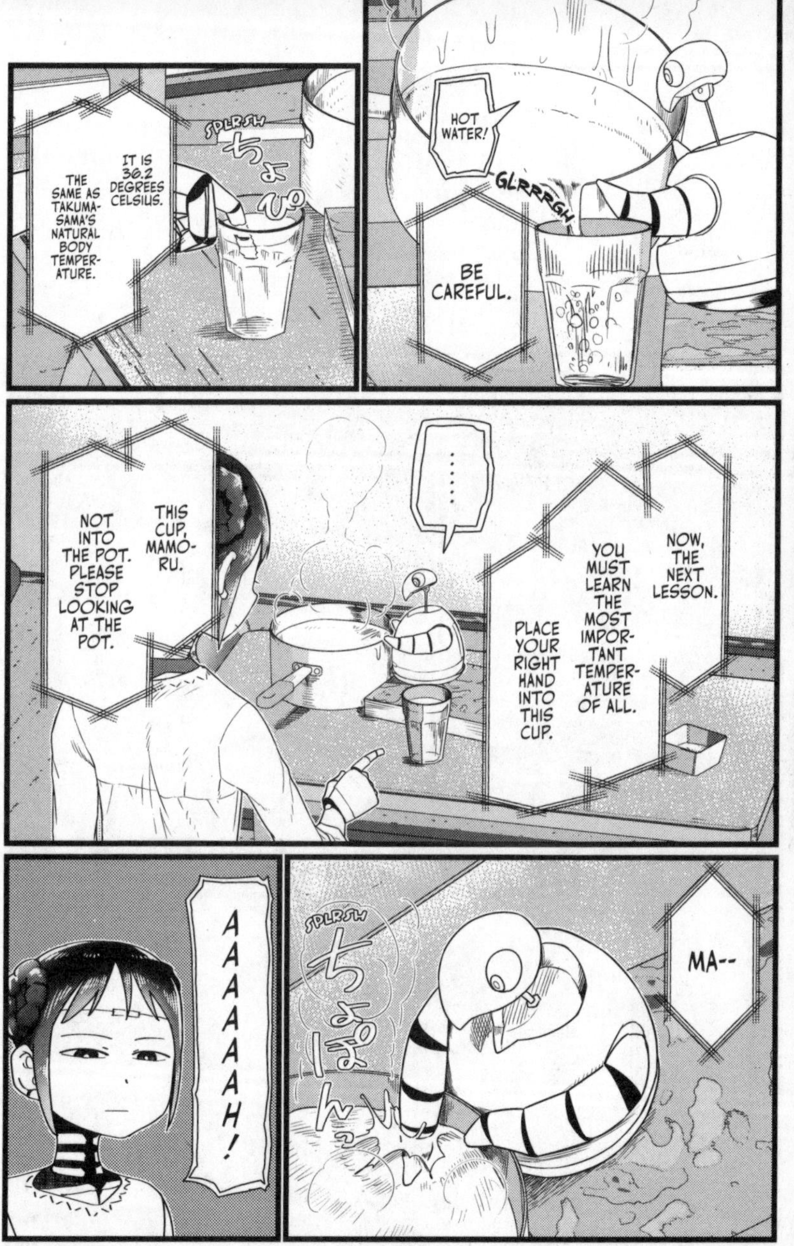
HOT WATER!
GLRRRGH
BE CAREFUL.
SPLRSH
ちょぴ
IT IS 36.2 DEGREES CELSIUS.
THE SAME AS TAKUMA-SAMA'S NATURAL BODY TEMPERATURE.
NOW, THE NEXT LESSON.
YOU MUST LEARN THE MOST IMPORTANT TEMPERATURE OF ALL.
PLACE YOUR RIGHT HAND INTO THIS CUP.
......
THIS CUP, MAMORU.
NOT INTO THE POT. PLEASE STOP LOOKING AT THE POT.
MA--
SPLRSH
ちょぽーんっ
AAAAAAAH!

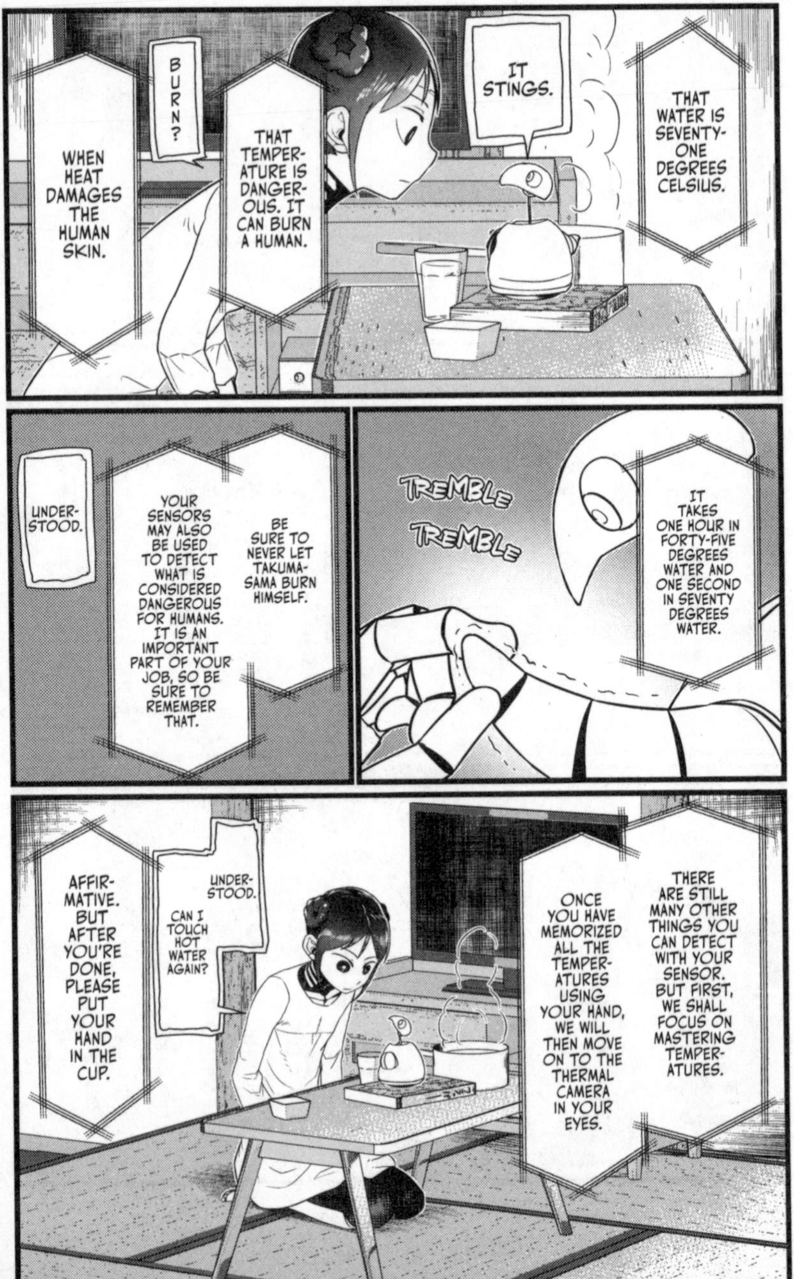
THAT WATER IS SEVENTY-ONE DEGREES CELSIUS.
IT STINGS.
THAT TEMPERATURE IS DANGEROUS. IT CAN BURN A HUMAN.
BURN?
WHEN HEAT DAMAGES THE HUMAN SKIN.
IT TAKES ONE HOUR IN FORTY-FIVE DEGREES WATER AND ONE SECOND IN SEVENTY DEGREES WATER.
TREMBLE
TREMBLE
BE SURE TO NEVER LET TAKUMA-SAMA BURN HIMSELF.
YOUR SENSORS MAY ALSO BE USED TO DETECT WHAT IS CONSIDERED DANGEROUS FOR HUMANS. IT IS AN IMPORTANT PART OF YOUR JOB, SO BE SURE TO REMEMBER THAT.
UNDERSTOOD.
THERE ARE STILL MANY OTHER THINGS YOU CAN DETECT WITH YOUR SENSOR. BUT FIRST, WE SHALL FOCUS ON MASTERING TEMPERATURES.
ONCE YOU HAVE MEMORIZED ALL THE TEMPERATURES USING YOUR HAND, WE WILL THEN MOVE ON TO THE THERMAL CAMERA IN YOUR EYES.
UNDERSTOOD.
CAN I TOUCH HOT WATER AGAIN?
AFFIRMATIVE. BUT AFTER YOU'RE DONE, PLEASE PUT YOUR HAND IN THE CUP.

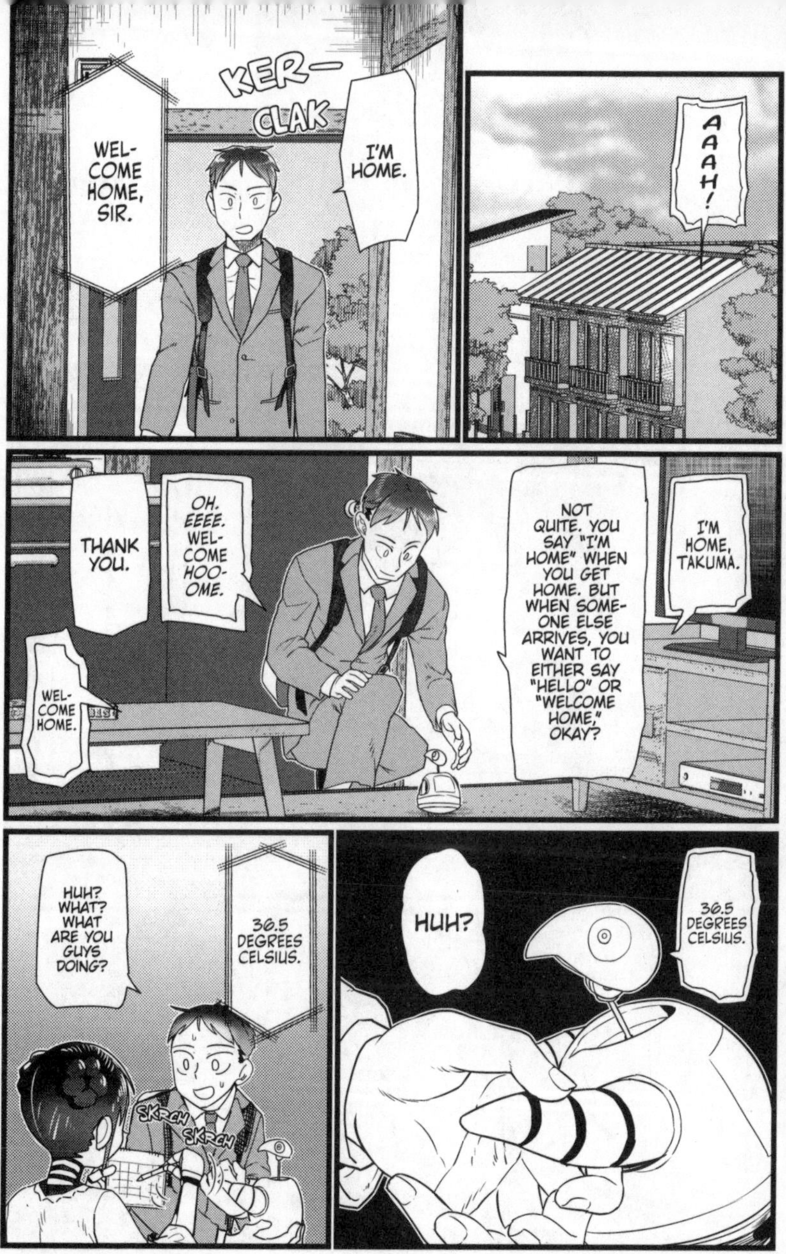
AAAH!
KER-CLAK
I'M HOME.
WEL-COME HOME, SIR.
I'M HOME, TAKUMA.
NOT QUITE. YOU SAY "I'M HOME" WHEN YOU GET HOME. BUT WHEN SOME-ONE ELSE ARRIVES, YOU WANT TO EITHER SAY "HELLO" OR "WELCOME HOME," OKAY?
OH. EEEE. WEL-COME HOO-OME.
THANK YOU.
WEL-COME HOME.
36.5 DEGREES CELSIUS.
HUH?
36.5 DEGREES CELSIUS.
HUH? WHAT? WHAT ARE YOU GUYS DOING?
SKRCH SKRCH

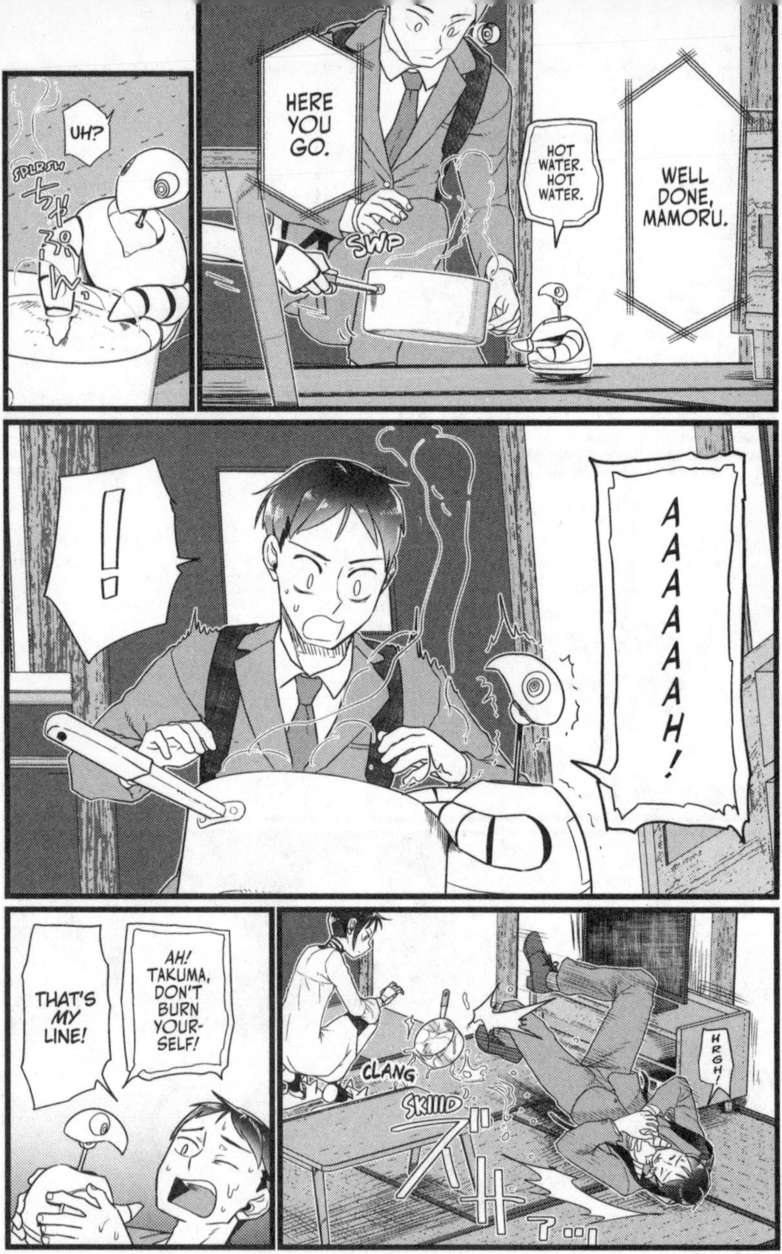
WELL DONE, MAMORU.
HOT WATER. HOT WATER.
HERE YOU GO.
SWP
UH?
SPLASH
AAAAAAAH!
!
HRGH!
CLANG
SKIIID
AH! TAKUMA, DON'T BURN YOUR-SELF!
THAT'S MY LINE!

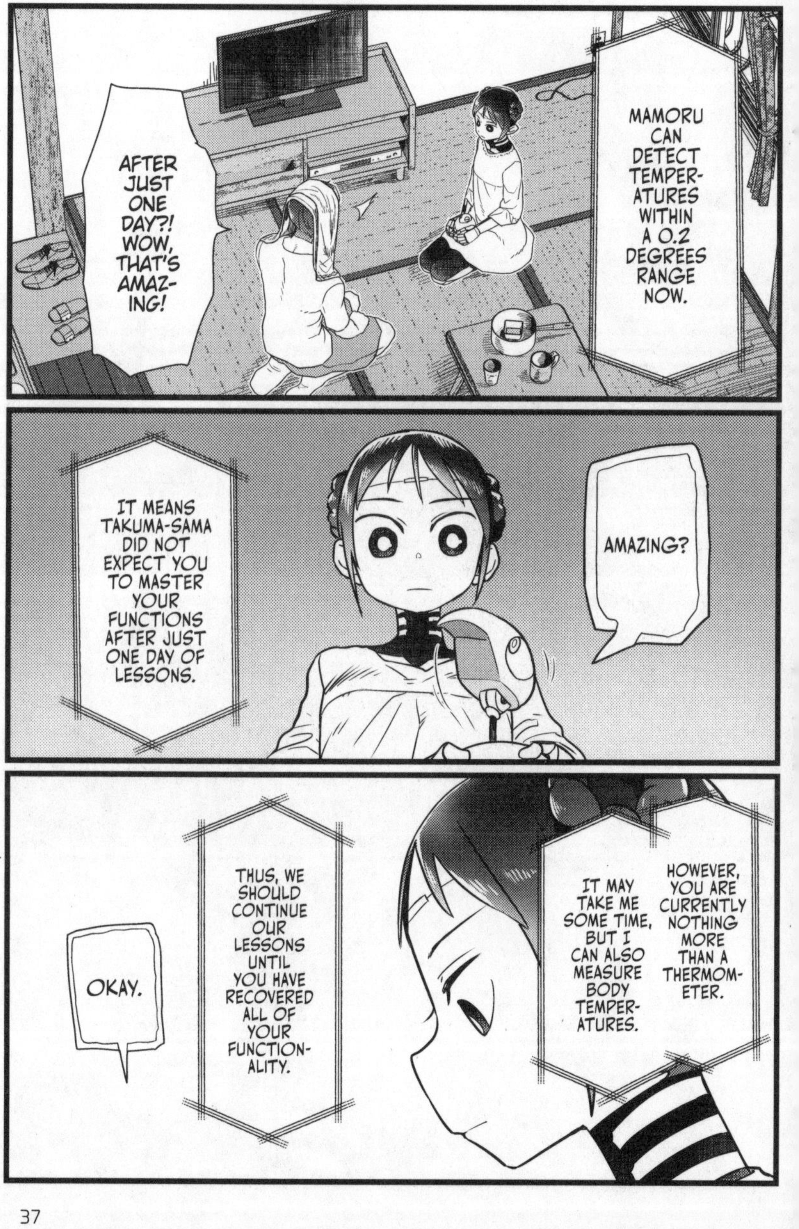
MAMORU CAN DETECT TEMPERATURES WITHIN A 0.2 DEGREES RANGE NOW.
AFTER JUST ONE DAY?! WOW, THAT'S AMAZING!
AMAZING?
IT MEANS TAKUMA-SAMA DID NOT EXPECT YOU TO MASTER YOUR FUNCTIONS AFTER JUST ONE DAY OF LESSONS.
HOWEVER, YOU ARE CURRENTLY NOTHING MORE THAN A THERMOMETER.
IT MAY TAKE ME SOME TIME, BUT I CAN ALSO MEASURE BODY TEMPERATURES.
THUS, WE SHOULD CONTINUE OUR LESSONS UNTIL YOU HAVE RECOVERED ALL OF YOUR FUNCTIONALITY.
OKAY.

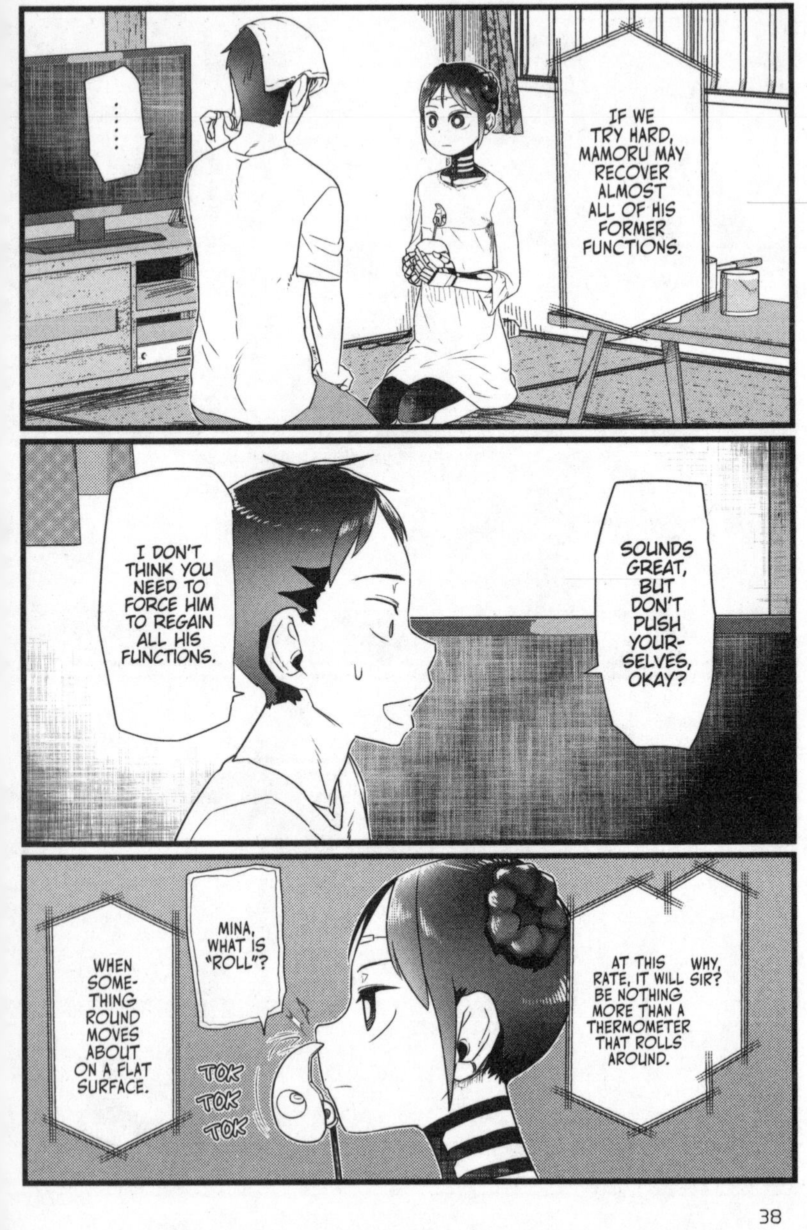
IF WE TRY HARD, MAMORU MAY RECOVER ALMOST ALL OF HIS FORMER FUNCTIONS.
......
SOUNDS GREAT, BUT DON'T PUSH YOUR-SELVES, OKAY?
I DON'T THINK YOU NEED TO FORCE HIM TO REGAIN ALL HIS FUNCTIONS.
WHY, SIR?
AT THIS RATE, IT WILL BE NOTHING MORE THAN A THERMOMETER THAT ROLLS AROUND.
MINA, WHAT IS "ROLL"?
TOK TOK TOK
WHEN SOME-THING ROUND MOVES ABOUT ON A FLAT SURFACE.

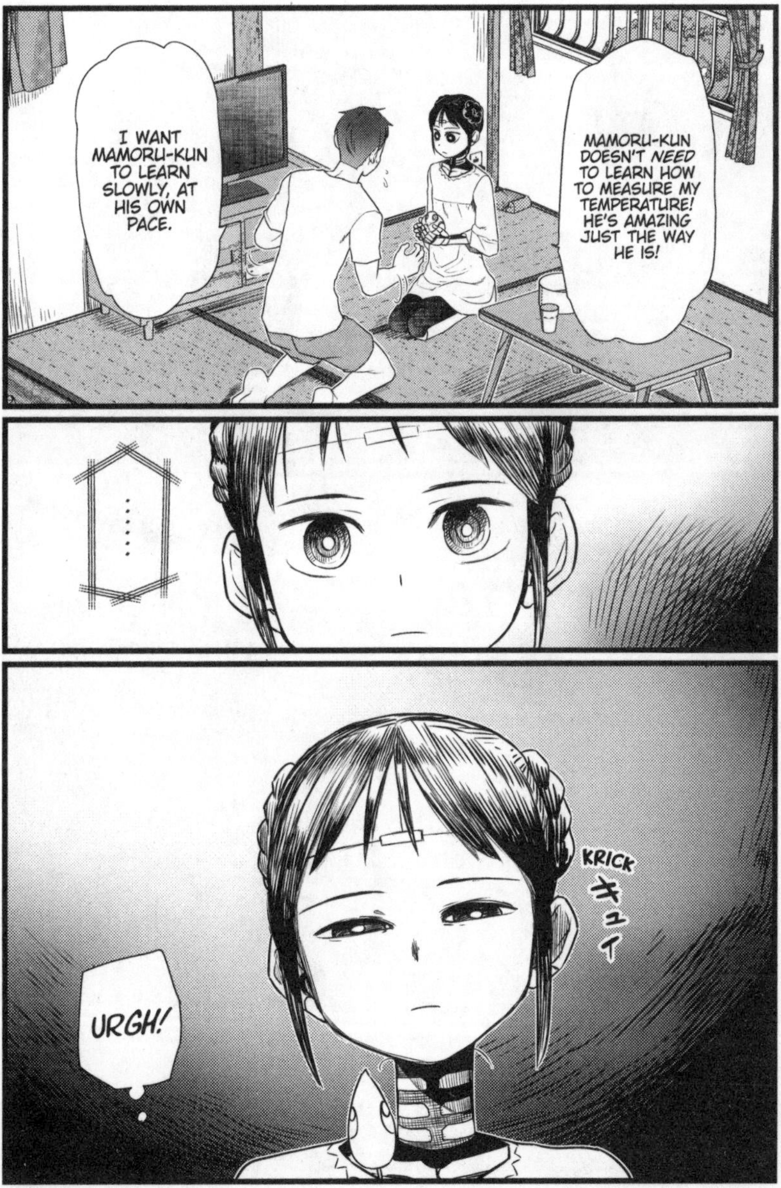
MAMORU-KUN DOESN'T *NEED* TO LEARN HOW TO MEASURE MY TEMPERATURE! HE'S AMAZING JUST THE WAY HE IS!
I WANT MAMORU-KUN TO LEARN SLOWLY, AT HIS OWN PACE.
......
KRICK
キュイ
URGH!

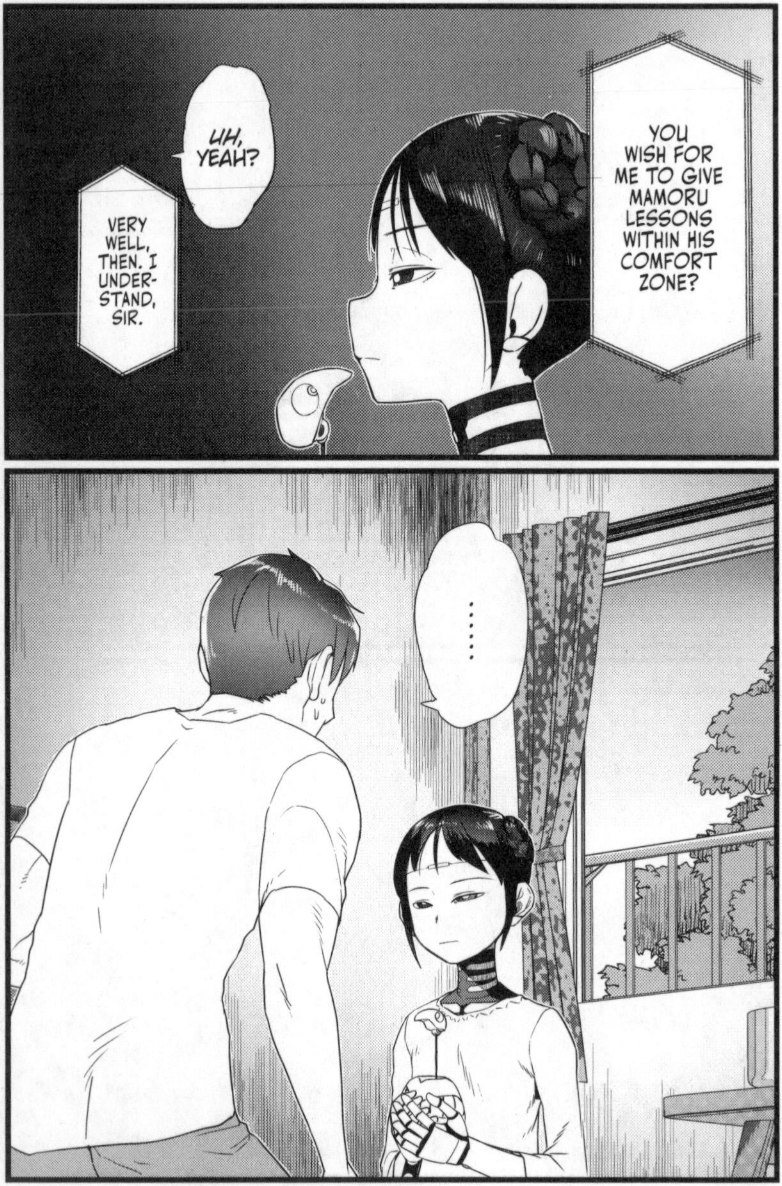
YOU WISH FOR ME TO GIVE MAMORU LESSONS WITHIN HIS COMFORT ZONE?
UH, YEAH?
VERY WELL, THEN. I UNDER-STAND, SIR.
......

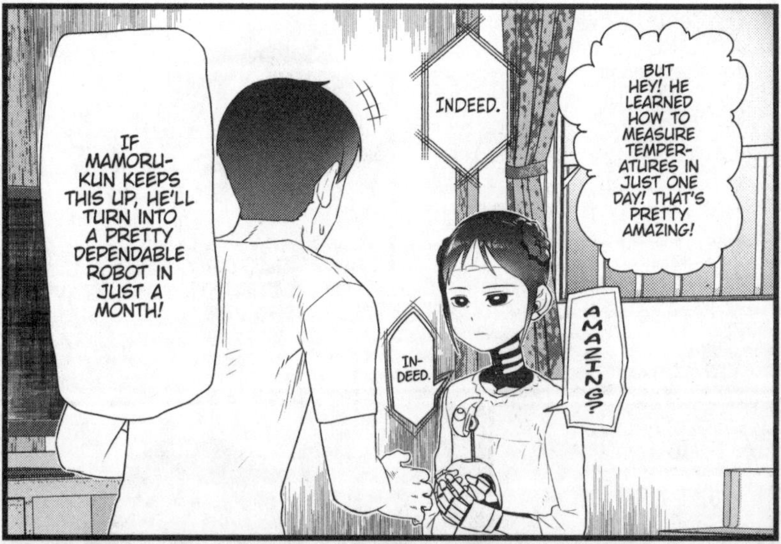
BUT HEY! HE LEARNED HOW TO MEASURE TEMPER-ATURES IN JUST ONE DAY! THAT'S PRETTY AMAZING!
INDEED.
AMAZING?
IF MAMORU-KUN KEEPS THIS UP, HE'LL TURN INTO A PRETTY DEPENDABLE ROBOT IN JUST A MONTH!
IN-DEED.
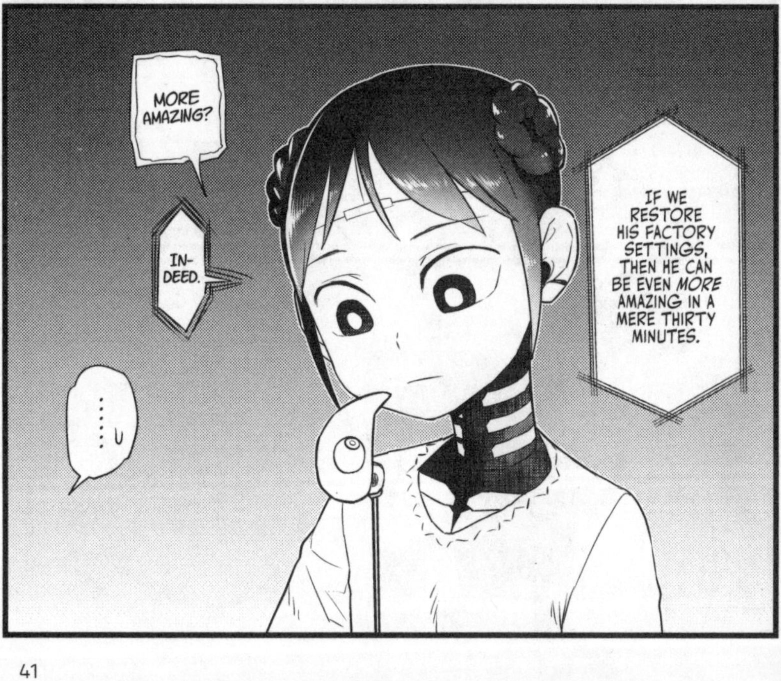
IF WE RESTORE HIS FACTORY SETTINGS, THEN HE CAN BE EVEN *MORE* AMAZING IN A MERE THIRTY MINUTES.
MORE AMAZING?
IN-DEED.
......

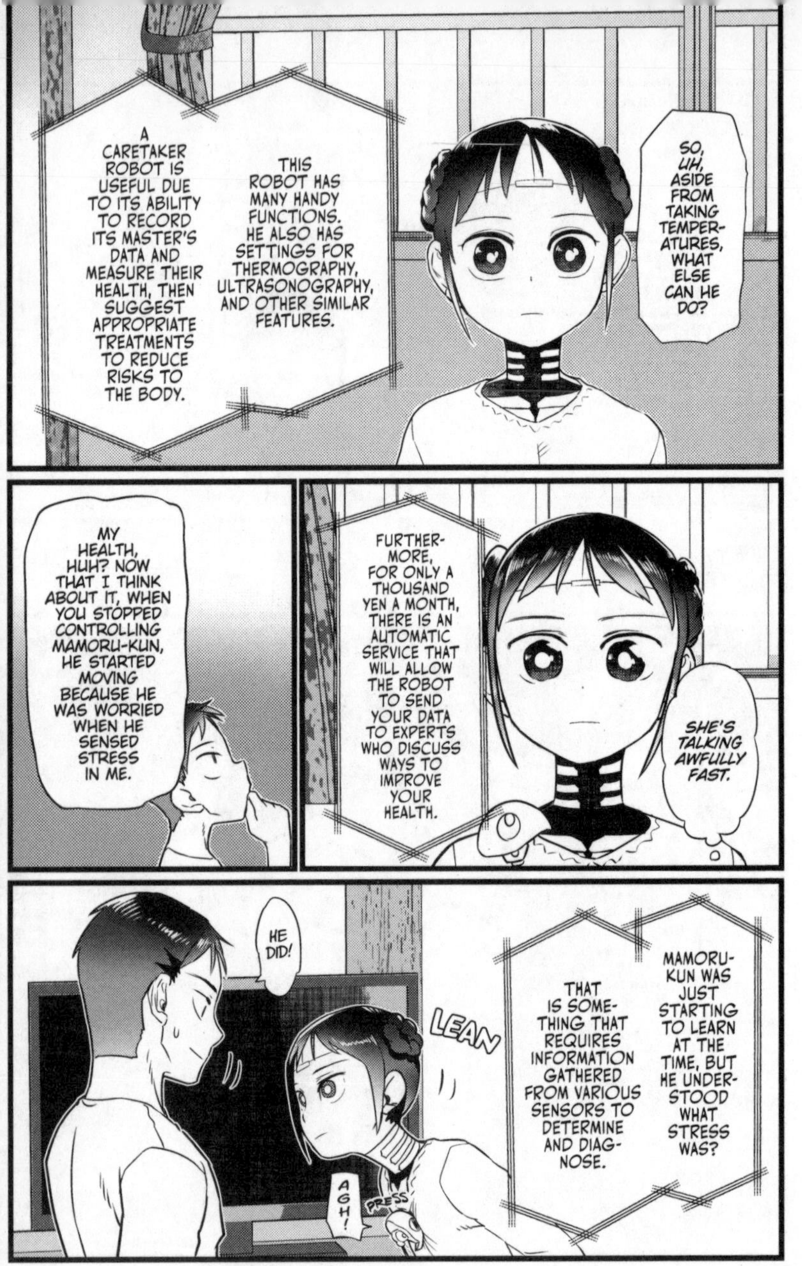
SO, UH, ASIDE FROM TAKING TEMPER-ATURES, WHAT ELSE CAN HE DO?
THIS ROBOT HAS MANY HANDY FUNCTIONS. HE ALSO HAS SETTINGS FOR THERMOGRAPHY, ULTRASONOGRAPHY, AND OTHER SIMILAR FEATURES.
A CARETAKER ROBOT IS USEFUL DUE TO ITS ABILITY TO RECORD ITS MASTER'S DATA AND MEASURE THEIR HEALTH, THEN SUGGEST APPROPRIATE TREATMENTS TO REDUCE RISKS TO THE BODY.
SHE'S TALKING AWFULLY FAST.
FURTHER-MORE, FOR ONLY A THOUSAND YEN A MONTH, THERE IS AN AUTOMATIC SERVICE THAT WILL ALLOW THE ROBOT TO SEND YOUR DATA TO EXPERTS WHO DISCUSS WAYS TO IMPROVE YOUR HEALTH.
MY HEALTH, HUH? NOW THAT I THINK ABOUT IT, WHEN YOU STOPPED CONTROLLING MAMORU-KUN, HE STARTED MOVING BECAUSE HE WAS WORRIED WHEN HE SENSED STRESS IN ME.
MAMORU-KUN WAS JUST STARTING TO LEARN AT THE TIME, BUT HE UNDER-STOOD WHAT STRESS WAS?
THAT IS SOME-THING THAT REQUIRES INFORMATION GATHERED FROM VARIOUS SENSORS TO DETERMINE AND DIAG-NOSE.
LEAN
HE DID!
PRESS
AGH!

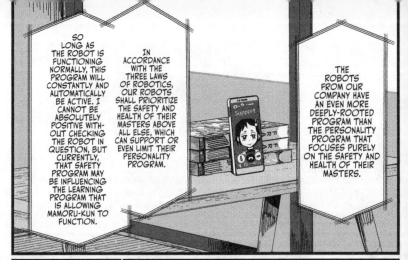

THE ROBOTS FROM OUR COMPANY HAVE AN EVEN MORE DEEPLY-ROOTED PROGRAM THAN THE PERSONALITY PROGRAM THAT FOCUSES PURELY ON THE SAFETY AND HEALTH OF THEIR MASTERS.
Support
IN ACCORDANCE WITH THE THREE LAWS OF ROBOTICS, OUR ROBOTS SHALL PRIORITIZE THE SAFETY AND HEALTH OF THEIR MASTERS ABOVE ALL ELSE, WHICH CAN SUPPORT OR EVEN LIMIT THEIR PERSONALITY PROGRAM.
SO LONG AS THE ROBOT IS FUNCTIONING NORMALLY, THIS PROGRAM WILL CONSTANTLY AND AUTOMATICALLY BE ACTIVE. I CANNOT BE ABSOLUTELY POSITIVE WITH-OUT CHECKING THE ROBOT IN QUESTION, BUT CURRENTLY, THAT SAFETY PROGRAM MAY BE INFLUENCING THE LEARNING PROGRAM THAT IS ALLOWING MAMORU-KUN TO FUNCTION.
MAMORU-KUN REALLY IS PRETTY IMPRES-SIVE!
SHK
IMPRES-SIVE?
HEY, MINA-CHAN... MINA-CHAN?
SWP

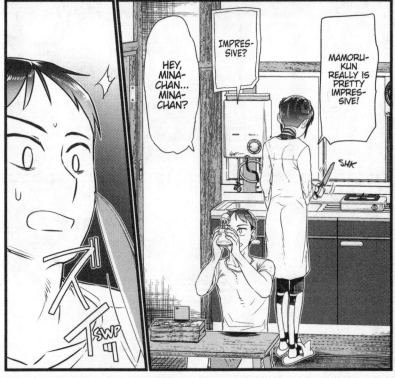

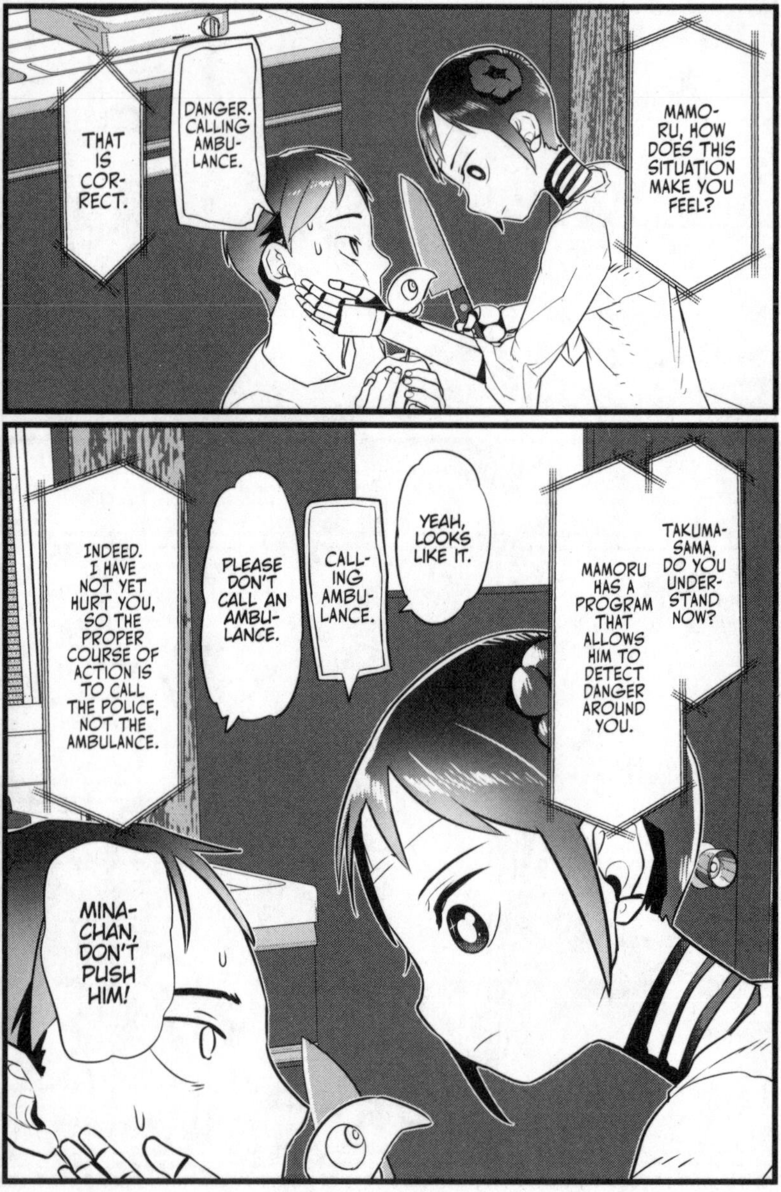
MAMORU, HOW DOES THIS SITUATION MAKE YOU FEEL?
DANGER. CALLING AMBULANCE.
THAT IS CORRECT.
TAKUMA-SAMA, DO YOU UNDERSTAND NOW?
MAMORU HAS A PROGRAM THAT ALLOWS HIM TO DETECT DANGER AROUND YOU.
YEAH, LOOKS LIKE IT.
CALLING AMBULANCE.
PLEASE DON'T CALL AN AMBULANCE.
INDEED. I HAVE NOT YET HURT YOU, SO THE PROPER COURSE OF ACTION IS TO CALL THE POLICE, NOT THE AMBULANCE.
MINA-CHAN, DON'T PUSH HIM!

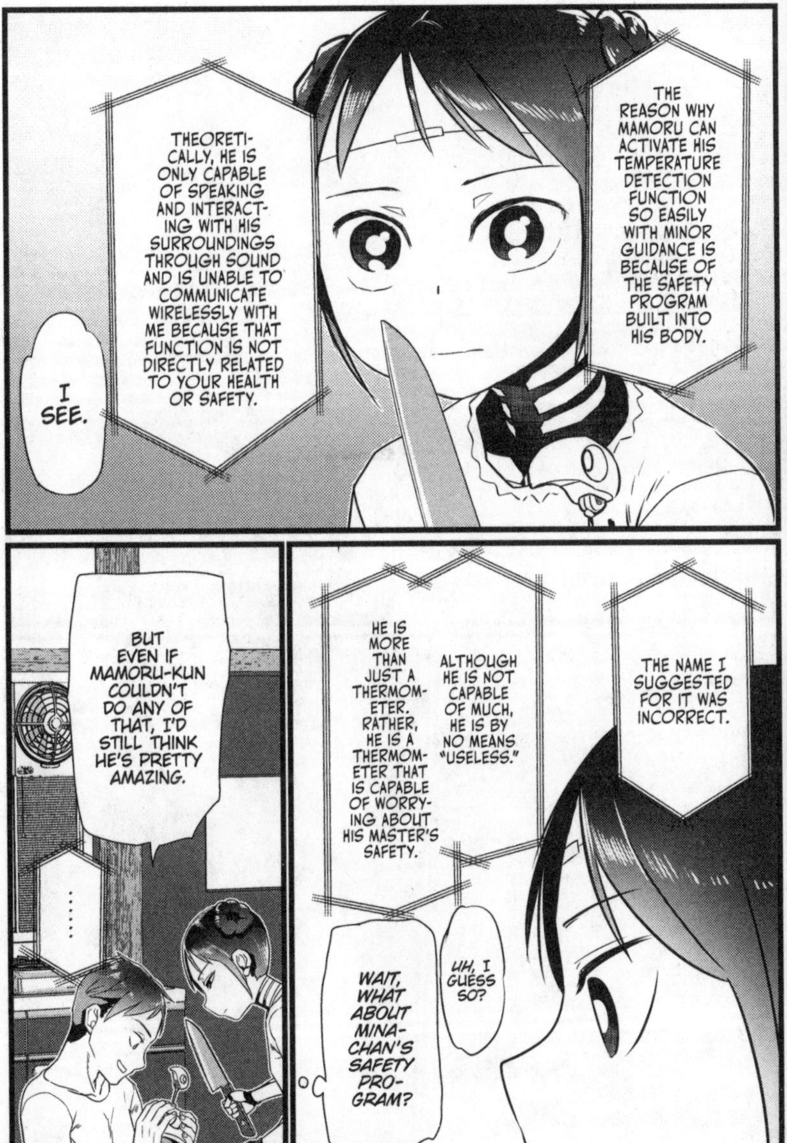
THE REASON WHY MAMORU CAN ACTIVATE HIS TEMPERATURE DETECTION FUNCTION SO EASILY WITH MINOR GUIDANCE IS BECAUSE OF THE SAFETY PROGRAM BUILT INTO HIS BODY.
THEORETICALLY, HE IS ONLY CAPABLE OF SPEAKING AND INTERACTING WITH HIS SURROUNDINGS THROUGH SOUND AND IS UNABLE TO COMMUNICATE WIRELESSLY WITH ME BECAUSE THAT FUNCTION IS NOT DIRECTLY RELATED TO YOUR HEALTH OR SAFETY.
I SEE.
THE NAME I SUGGESTED FOR IT WAS INCORRECT.
ALTHOUGH HE IS NOT CAPABLE OF MUCH, HE IS BY NO MEANS "USELESS."
HE IS MORE THAN JUST A THERMOMETER. RATHER, HE IS A THERMOMETER THAT IS CAPABLE OF WORRYING ABOUT HIS MASTER'S SAFETY.
UH, I GUESS SO?
WAIT, WHAT ABOUT MINA-CHAN'S SAFETY PROGRAM?
BUT EVEN IF MAMORU-KUN COULDN'T DO ANY OF THAT, I'D STILL THINK HE'S PRETTY AMAZING.
......

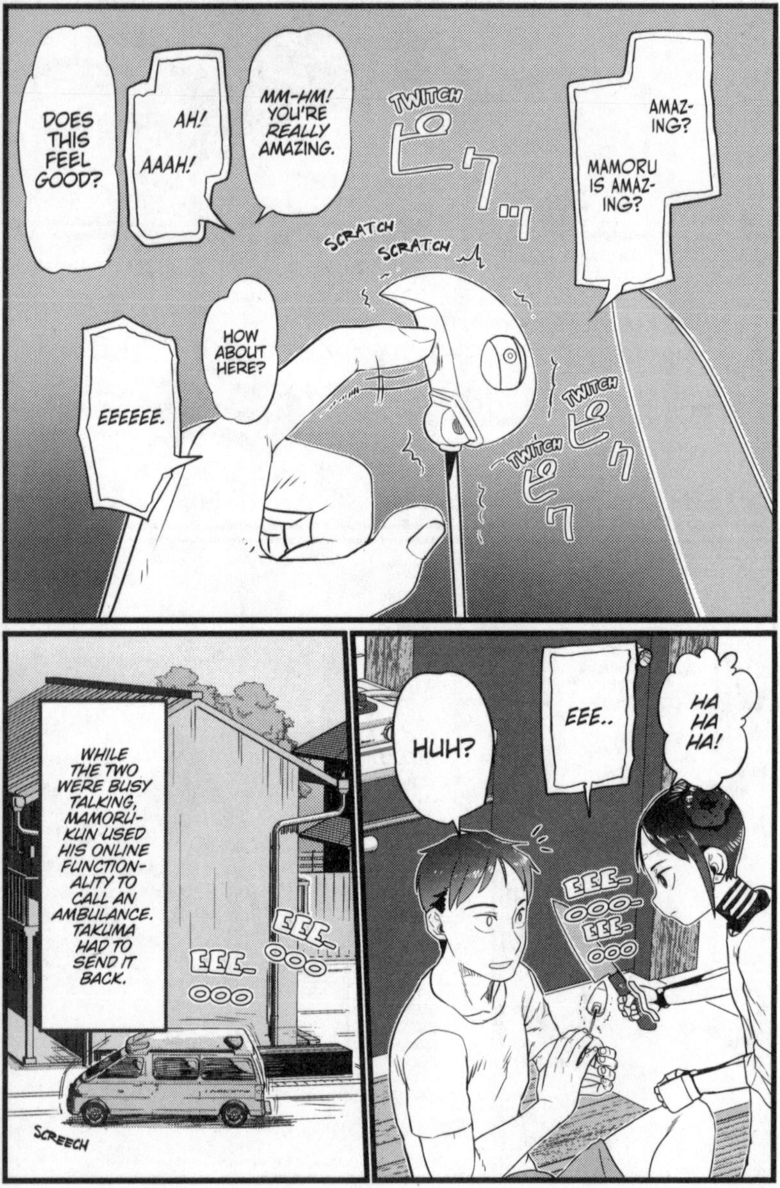
AMAZ-ING? MAMORU IS AMAZ-ING?
TWITCH
MM-HM! YOU'RE REALLY AMAZING.
AH! AAAH!
DOES THIS FEEL GOOD?
SCRATCH SCRATCH
HOW ABOUT HERE?
EEEEEE.
TWITCH TWITCH
HA HA HA!
EEE..
HUH?
EEE-OOO-EEE-OOO
WHILE THE TWO WERE BUSY TALKING, MAMORU-KUN USED HIS ONLINE FUNCTION-ALITY TO CALL AN AMBULANCE. TAKUMA HAD TO SEND IT BACK.
EEE-OOO
EEE-OOO
SCREECH

SHFFF
ずるる

IT'S LATE. TIME FOR BED.

TAKUMA-SAMA.

PLEASE PLACE THIS ON THE FLOOR FIRST.

47

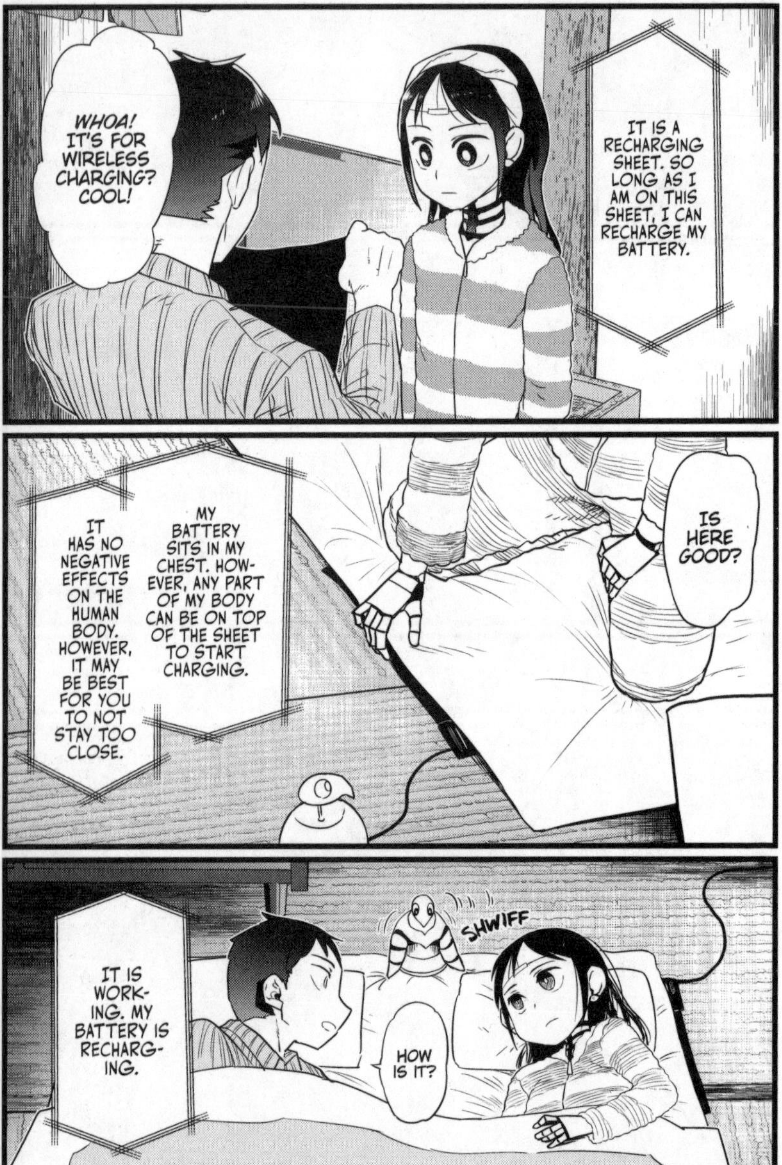
IT IS A RECHARGING SHEET. SO LONG AS I AM ON THIS SHEET, I CAN RECHARGE MY BATTERY.
WHOA! IT'S FOR WIRELESS CHARGING? COOL!
IS HERE GOOD?
MY BATTERY SITS IN MY CHEST. HOWEVER, ANY PART OF MY BODY CAN BE ON TOP OF THE SHEET TO START CHARGING.
IT HAS NO NEGATIVE EFFECTS ON THE HUMAN BODY. HOWEVER, IT MAY BE BEST FOR YOU TO NOT STAY TOO CLOSE.
SHWIFF
HOW IS IT?
IT IS WORKING. MY BATTERY IS RECHARGING.

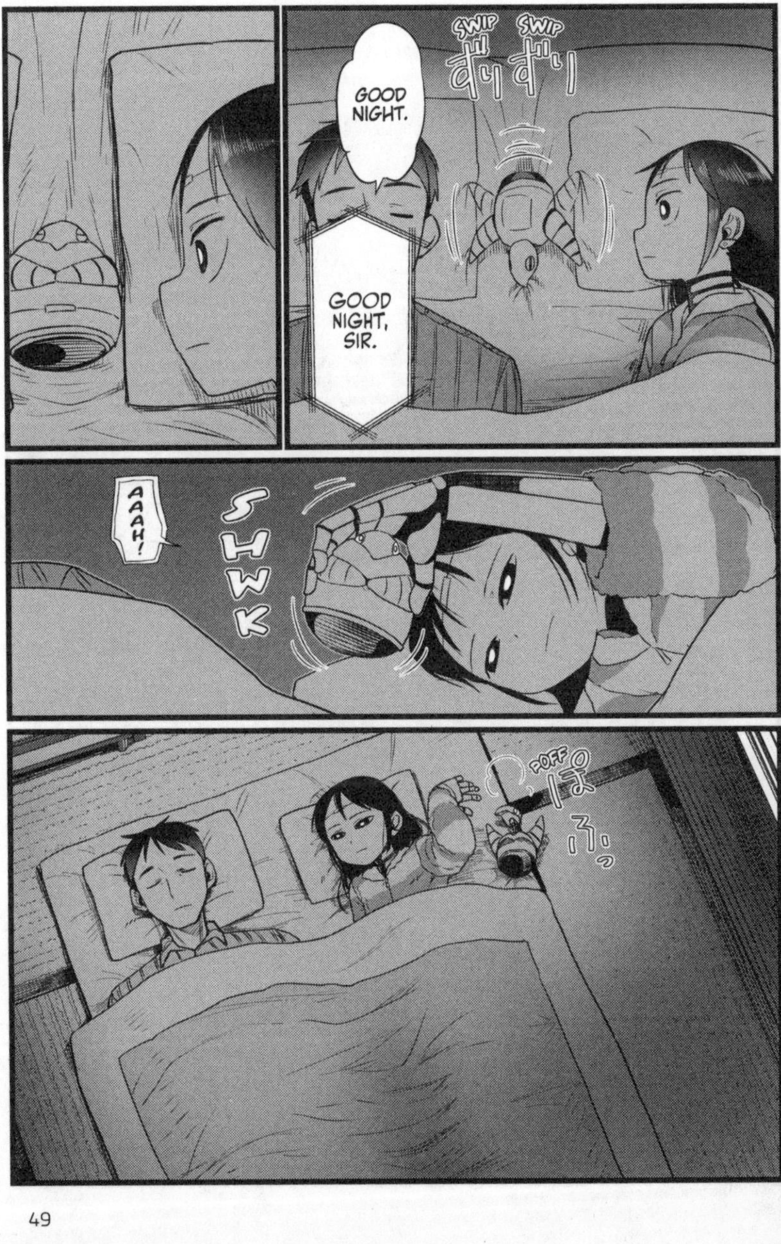
SWIP SWIP
ずりずり
GOOD NIGHT.
GOOD NIGHT, SIR.
SHWK
AAAH!
POFF
ぽふっ

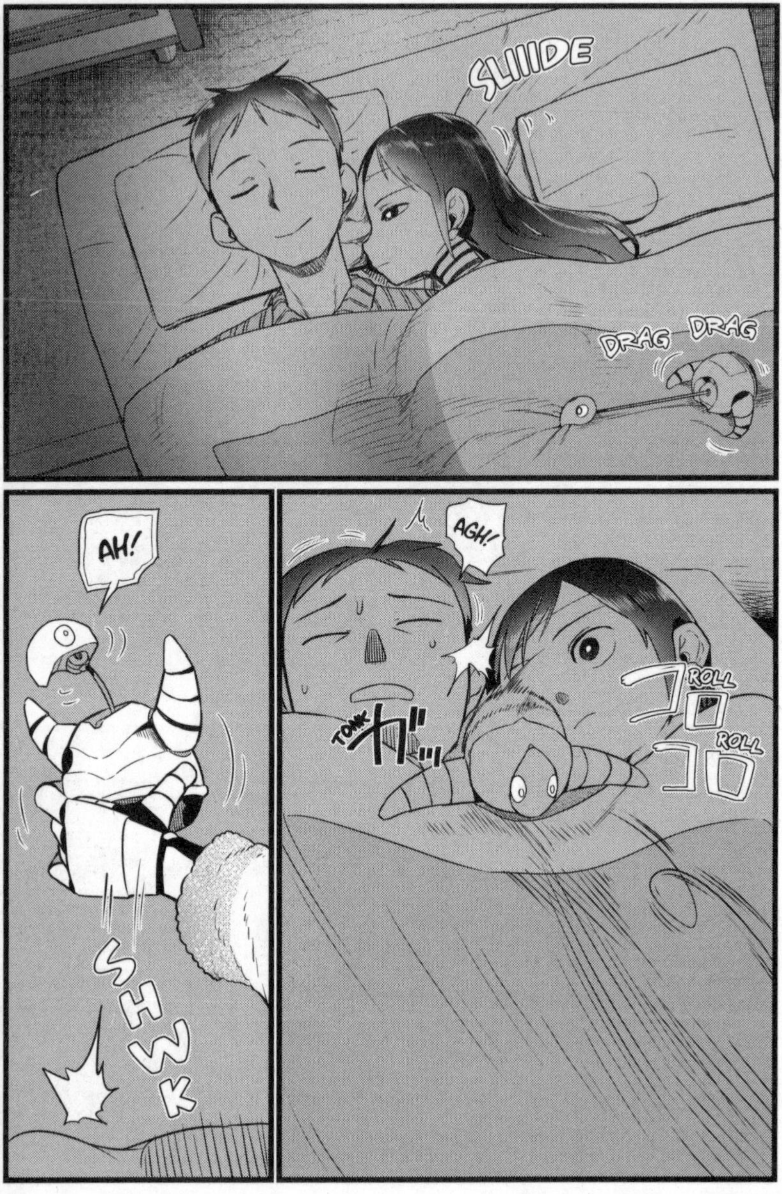
SLIIIDE
DRAG DRAG
AGH!
TONK ガッ
コロ ROLL
コロ ROLL
AH!
SHWK

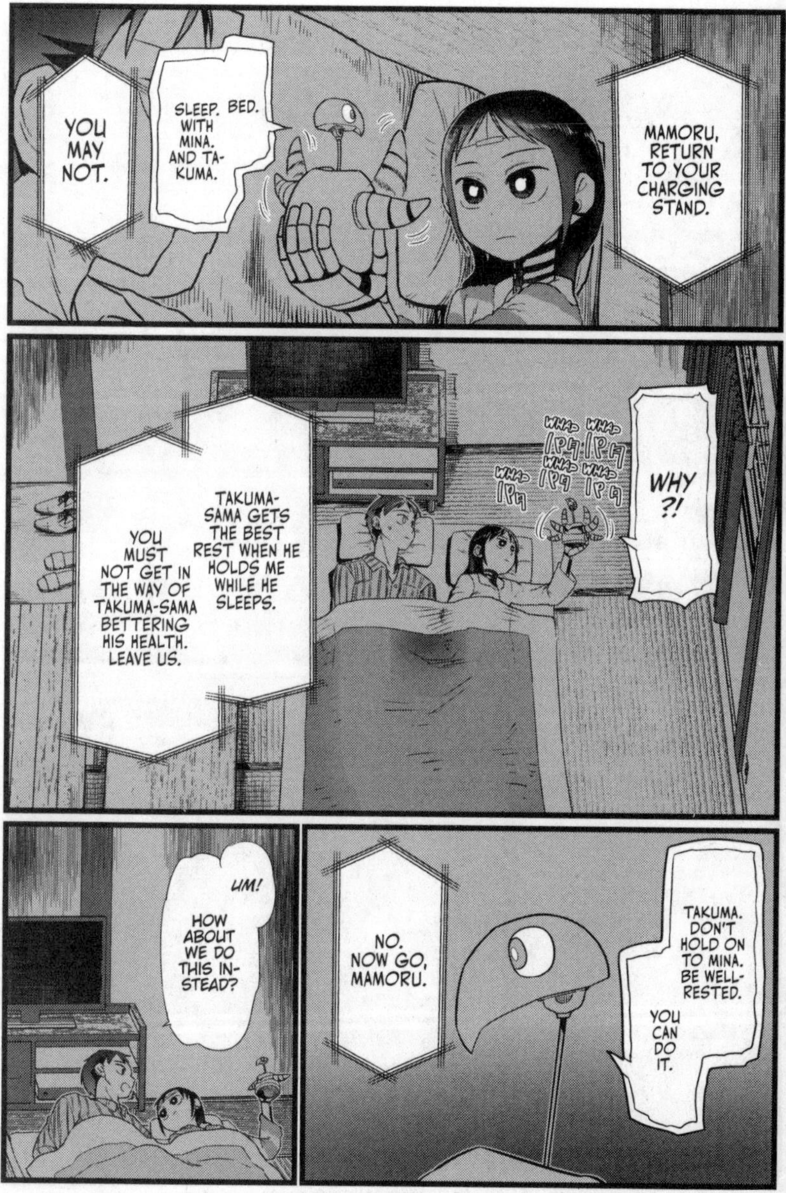

MAMORU, RETURN TO YOUR CHARGING STAND.
SLEEP. BED. WITH MINA. AND TA-KUMA.
YOU MAY NOT.
WHY?!
WHAP WHAP WHAP WHAP WHAP
TAKUMA-SAMA GETS THE BEST REST WHEN HE HOLDS ME WHILE HE SLEEPS.
YOU MUST NOT GET IN THE WAY OF TAKUMA-SAMA BETTERING HIS HEALTH. LEAVE US.
TAKUMA. DON'T HOLD ON TO MINA. BE WELL-RESTED.
YOU CAN DO IT.
NO. NOW GO, MAMORU.
UM!
HOW ABOUT WE DO THIS IN-STEAD?

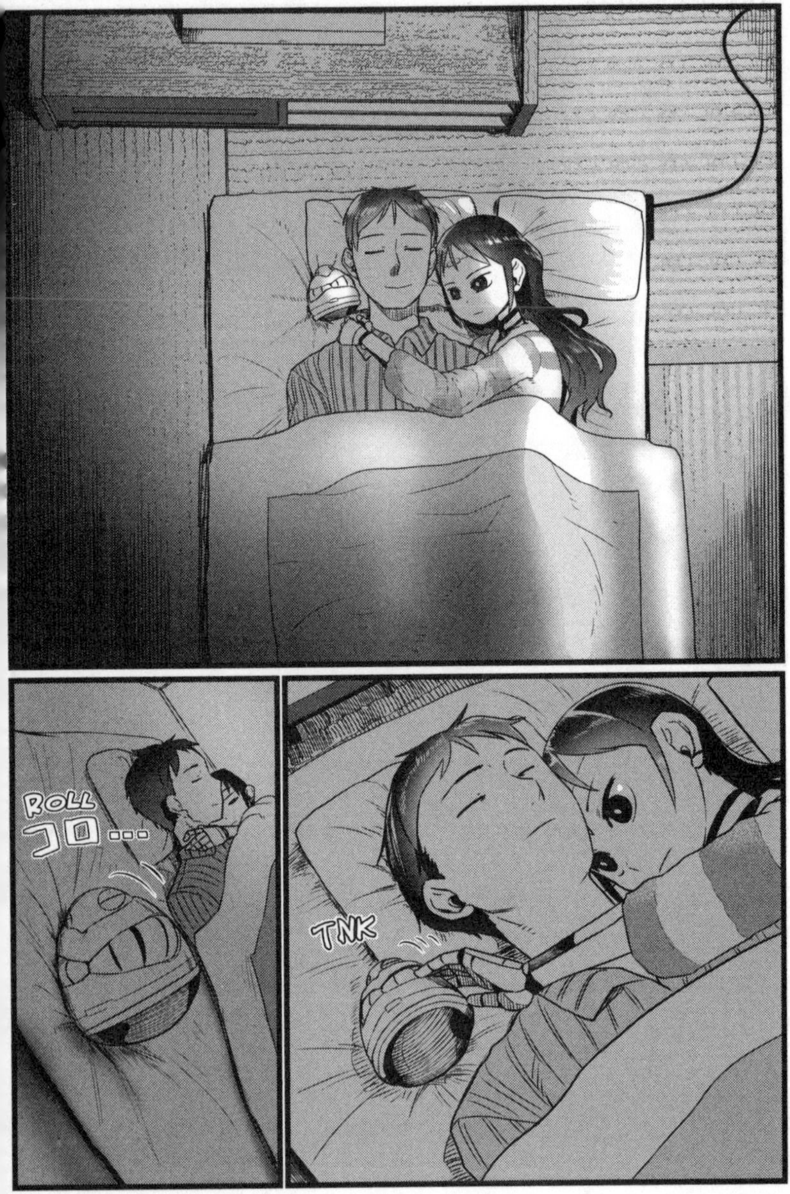
TNK
ROLL
コロ…

➡ CHAPTER 16 END ♥

➡ CHAPTER 17

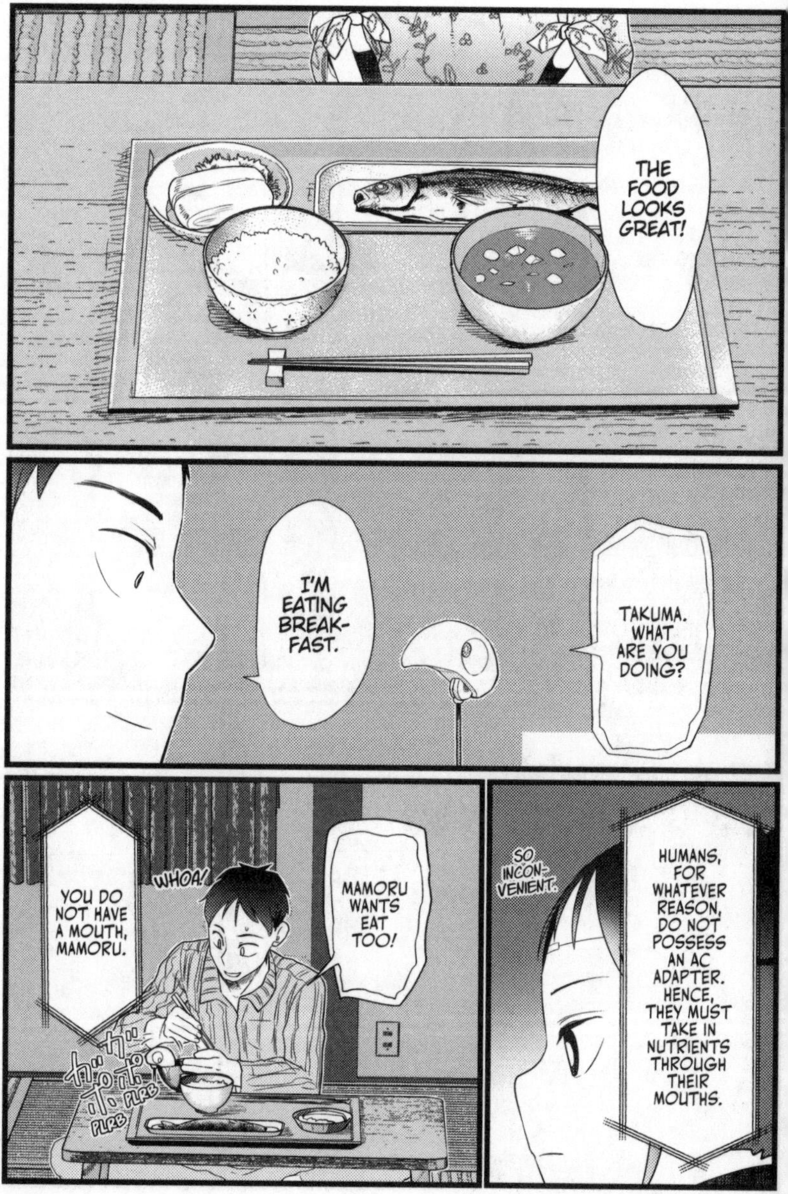
THE FOOD LOOKS GREAT!
TAKUMA. WHAT ARE YOU DOING?
I'M EATING BREAK-FAST.
HUMANS, FOR WHATEVER REASON, DO NOT POSSESS AN AC ADAPTER. HENCE, THEY MUST TAKE IN NUTRIENTS THROUGH THEIR MOUTHS.
SO INCON-VENIENT.
MAMORU WANTS EAT TOO!
WHOA!
YOU DO NOT HAVE A MOUTH, MAMORU.
PLRB PLRB

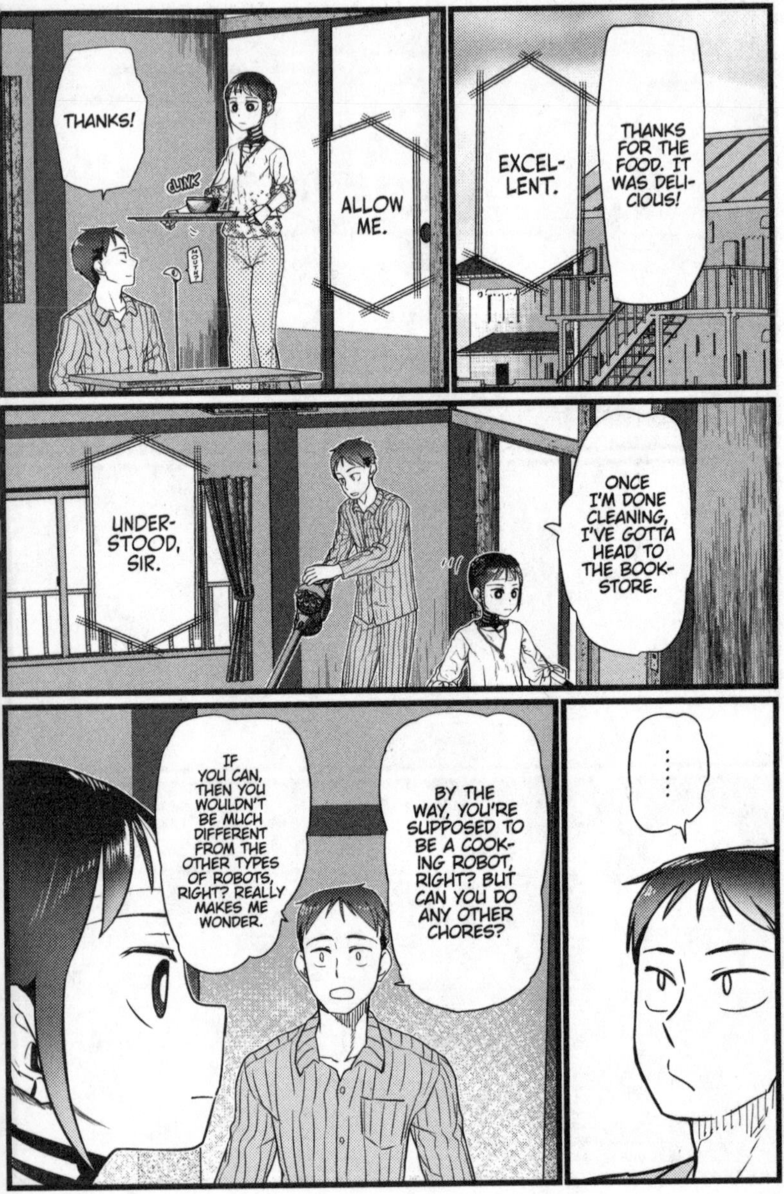
THANKS FOR THE FOOD. IT WAS DELICIOUS!
EXCEL-LENT.
ALLOW ME.
THANKS!
CLINK
ONCE I'M DONE CLEANING, I'VE GOTTA HEAD TO THE BOOK-STORE.
UNDER-STOOD, SIR.
......
BY THE WAY, YOU'RE SUPPOSED TO BE A COOK-ING ROBOT, RIGHT? BUT CAN YOU DO ANY OTHER CHORES?
IF YOU CAN, THEN YOU WOULDN'T BE MUCH DIFFERENT FROM THE OTHER TYPES OF ROBOTS, RIGHT? REALLY MAKES ME WONDER.

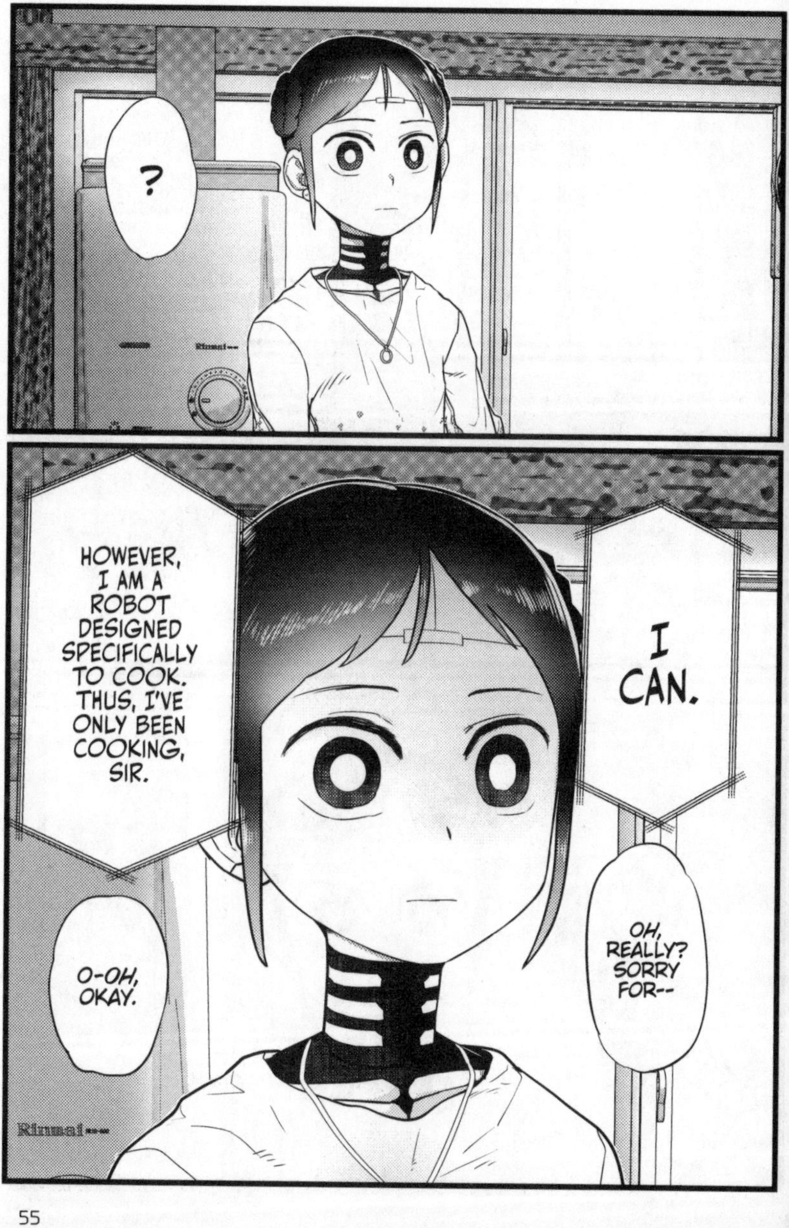
?
I CAN.
HOWEVER, I AM A ROBOT DESIGNED SPECIFICALLY TO COOK. THUS, I'VE ONLY BEEN COOKING, SIR.
OH, REALLY? SORRY FOR--
O-OH, OKAY.

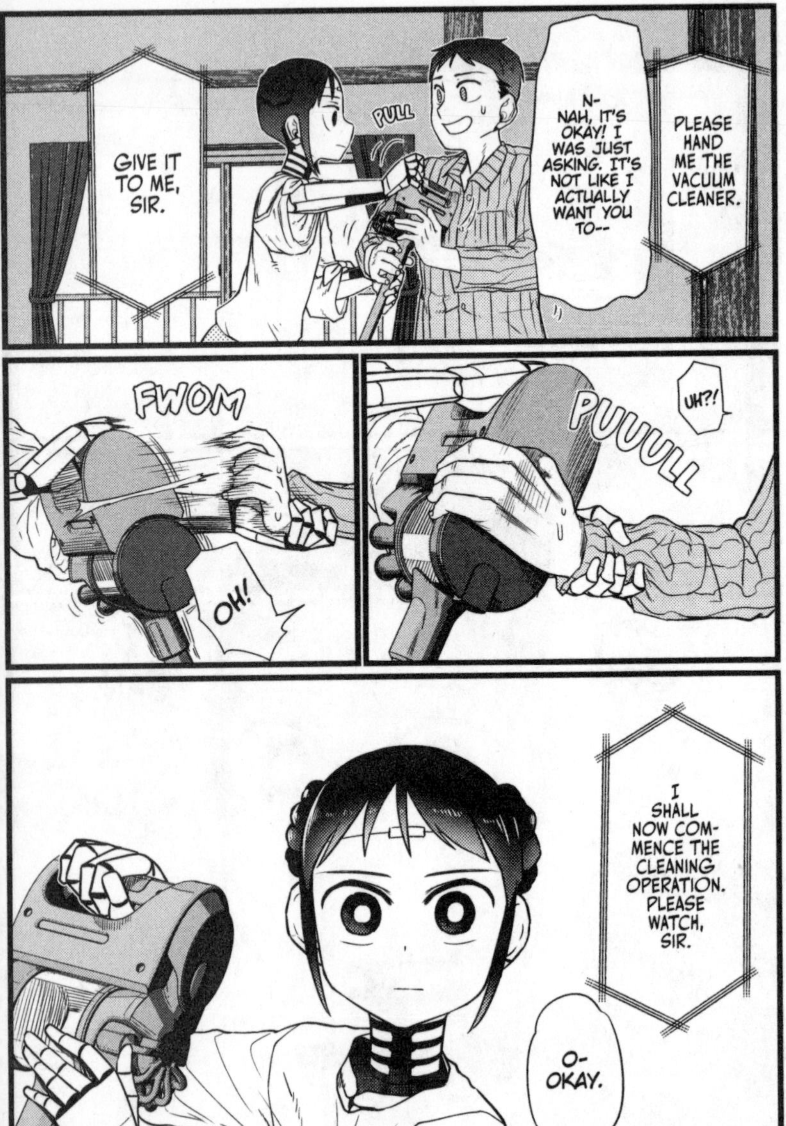
PLEASE HAND ME THE VACUUM CLEANER.
N-NAH, IT'S OKAY! I WAS JUST ASKING. IT'S NOT LIKE I ACTUALLY WANT YOU TO--
PULL
GIVE IT TO ME, SIR.
UH?!
PUUUULL
FWOM
OH!
I SHALL NOW COMMENCE THE CLEANING OPERATION. PLEASE WATCH, SIR.
O-OKAY.

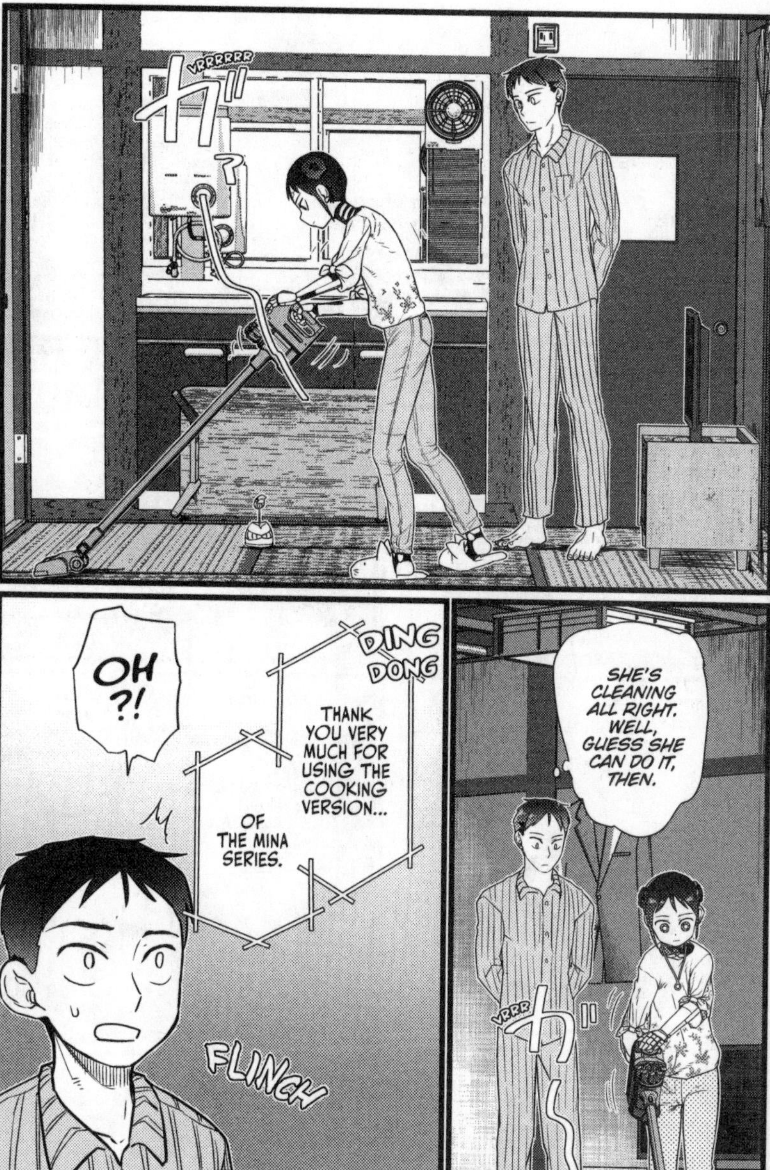
VRRRRRR
ガ
?
SHE'S CLEANING ALL RIGHT. WELL, GUESS SHE CAN DO IT, THEN.
VRRR
DING DONG
OH ?!
THANK YOU VERY MUCH FOR USING THE COOKING VERSION...
OF THE MINA SERIES.
FLINCH

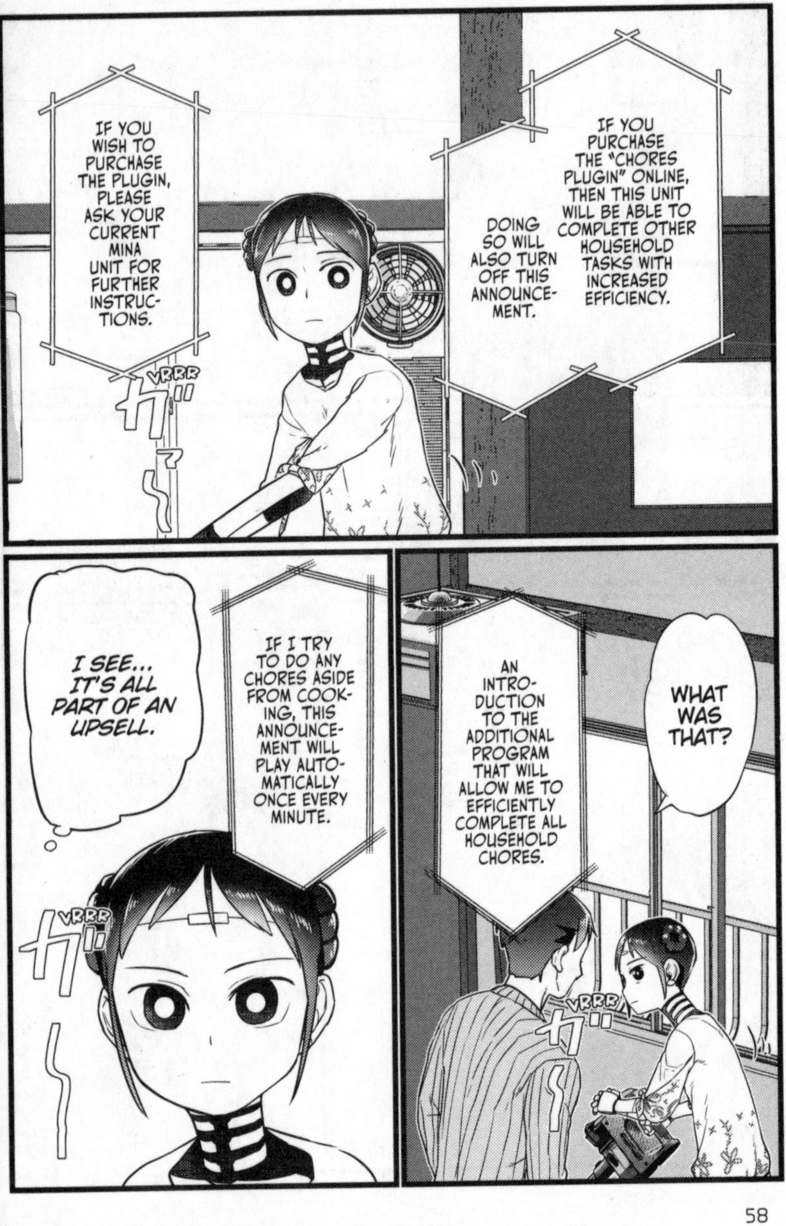
IF YOU PURCHASE THE "CHORES PLUGIN" ONLINE, THEN THIS UNIT WILL BE ABLE TO COMPLETE OTHER HOUSEHOLD TASKS WITH INCREASED EFFICIENCY.
DOING SO WILL ALSO TURN OFF THIS ANNOUNCE-MENT.
IF YOU WISH TO PURCHASE THE PLUGIN, PLEASE ASK YOUR CURRENT MINA UNIT FOR FURTHER INSTRUC-TIONS.
VRRR
WHAT WAS THAT?
AN INTRO-DUCTION TO THE ADDITIONAL PROGRAM THAT WILL ALLOW ME TO EFFICIENTLY COMPLETE ALL HOUSEHOLD CHORES.
VRRR
IF I TRY TO DO ANY CHORES ASIDE FROM COOK-ING, THIS ANNOUNCE-MENT WILL PLAY AUTO-MATICALLY ONCE EVERY MINUTE.
I SEE... IT'S ALL PART OF AN UPSELL.
VRRR

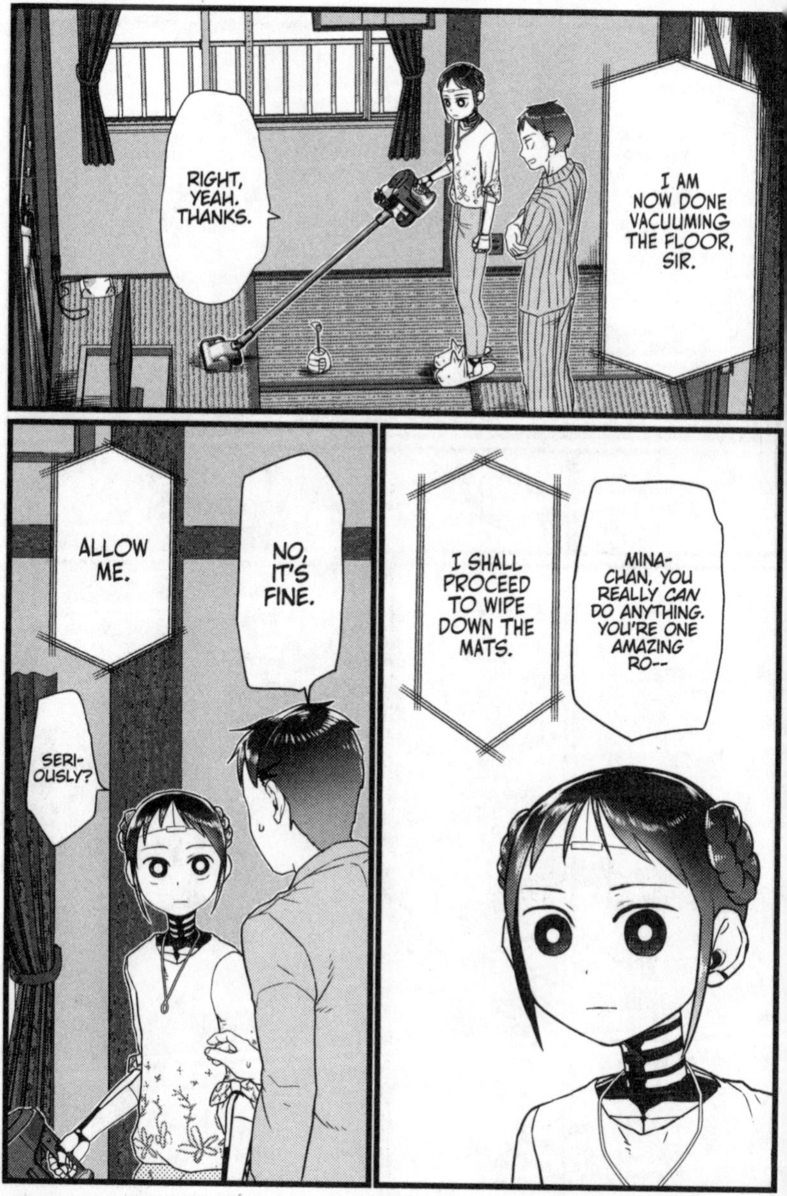
I AM NOW DONE VACUUMING THE FLOOR, SIR.
RIGHT, YEAH. THANKS.
MINA-CHAN, YOU REALLY CAN DO ANYTHING. YOU'RE ONE AMAZING RO--
I SHALL PROCEED TO WIPE DOWN THE MATS.
NO, IT'S FINE.
ALLOW ME.
SERI-OUSLY?

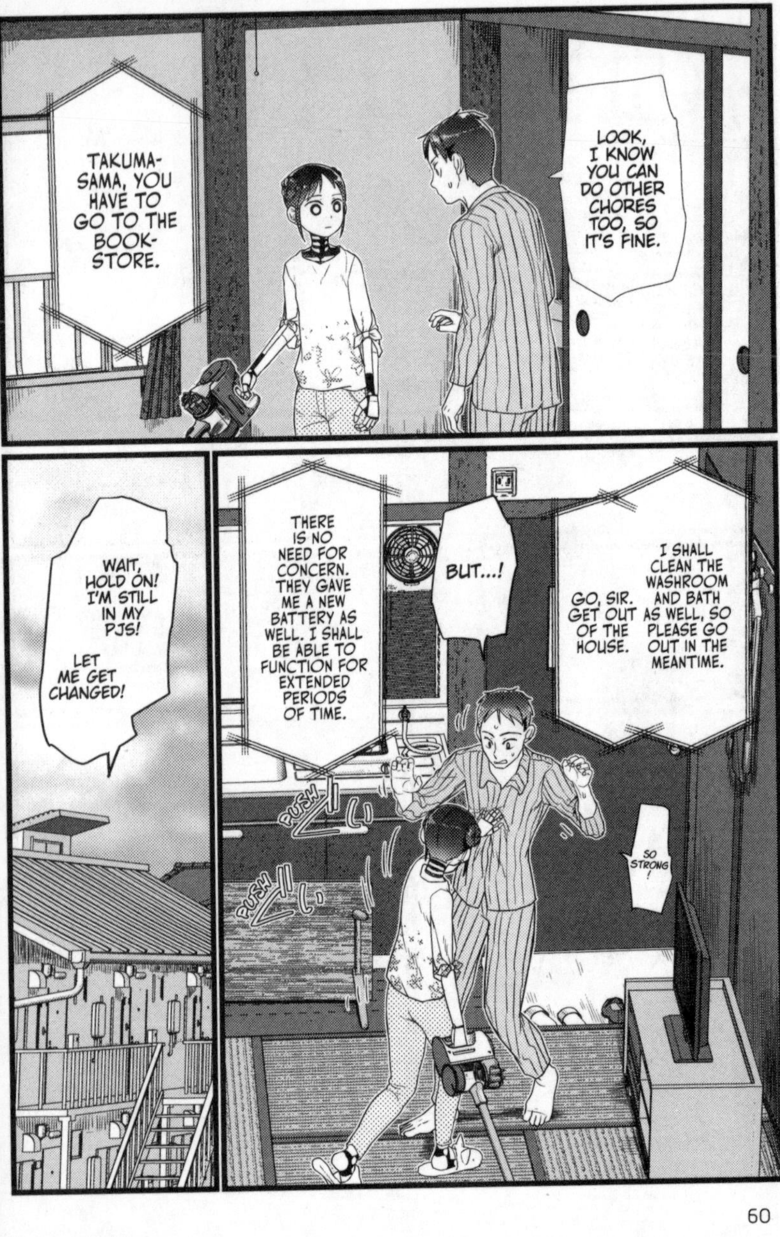
LOOK, I KNOW YOU CAN DO OTHER CHORES TOO, SO IT'S FINE.
TAKUMA-SAMA, YOU HAVE TO GO TO THE BOOK-STORE.
I SHALL CLEAN THE WASHROOM AND BATH AS WELL, SO PLEASE GO OUT IN THE MEANTIME.
GO, SIR. GET OUT OF THE HOUSE.
BUT...!
THERE IS NO NEED FOR CONCERN. THEY GAVE ME A NEW BATTERY AS WELL. I SHALL BE ABLE TO FUNCTION FOR EXTENDED PERIODS OF TIME.
PUSH
PUSH
SO STRONG!
WAIT, HOLD ON! I'M STILL IN MY PJS!
LET ME GET CHANGED!

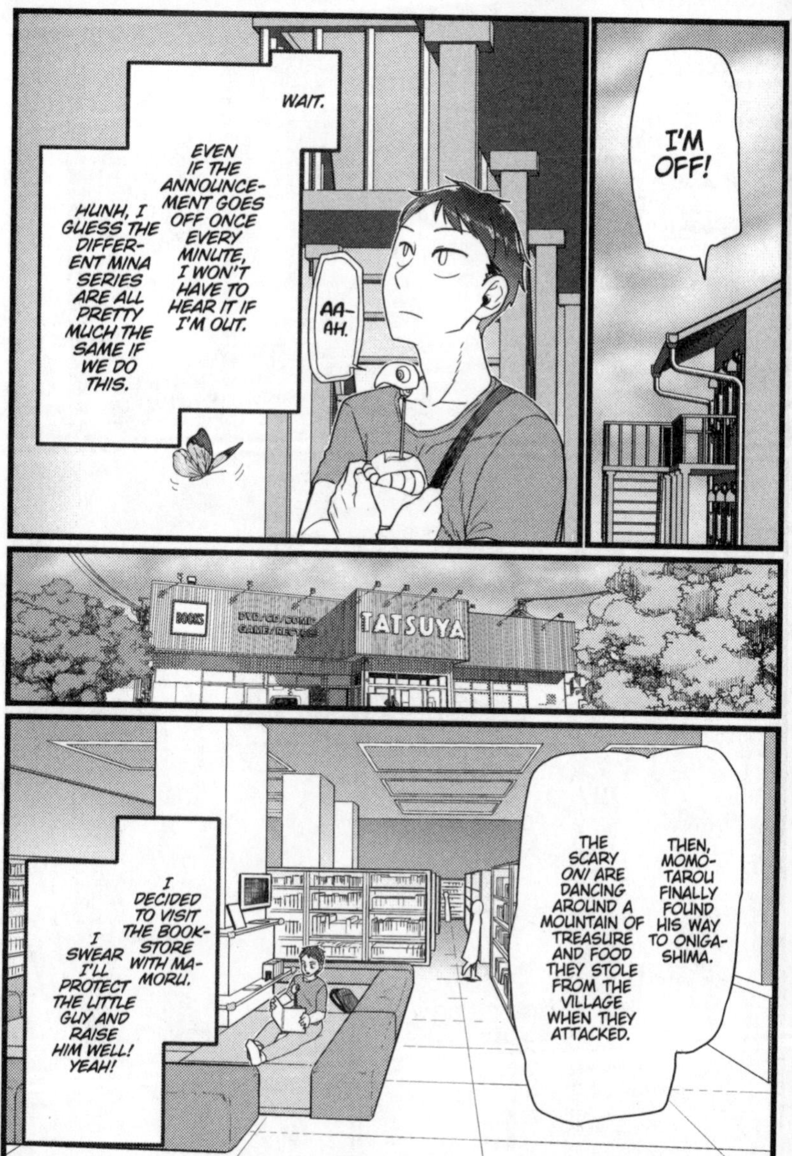
I'M OFF!
WAIT.
EVEN IF THE ANNOUNCEMENT GOES OFF ONCE EVERY MINUTE, I WON'T HAVE TO HEAR IT IF I'M OUT.
HUNH, I GUESS THE DIFFERENT MINA SERIES ARE ALL PRETTY MUCH THE SAME IF WE DO THIS.
AA-AH.
TATSUYA
BOOKS
THEN, MOMOTAROU FINALLY FOUND HIS WAY TO ONIGASHIMA.
THE SCARY ONI ARE DANCING AROUND A MOUNTAIN OF TREASURE AND FOOD THEY STOLE FROM THE VILLAGE WHEN THEY ATTACKED.
I DECIDED TO VISIT THE BOOKSTORE WITH MAMORU.
I SWEAR I'LL PROTECT THE LITTLE GUY AND RAISE HIM WELL! YEAH!

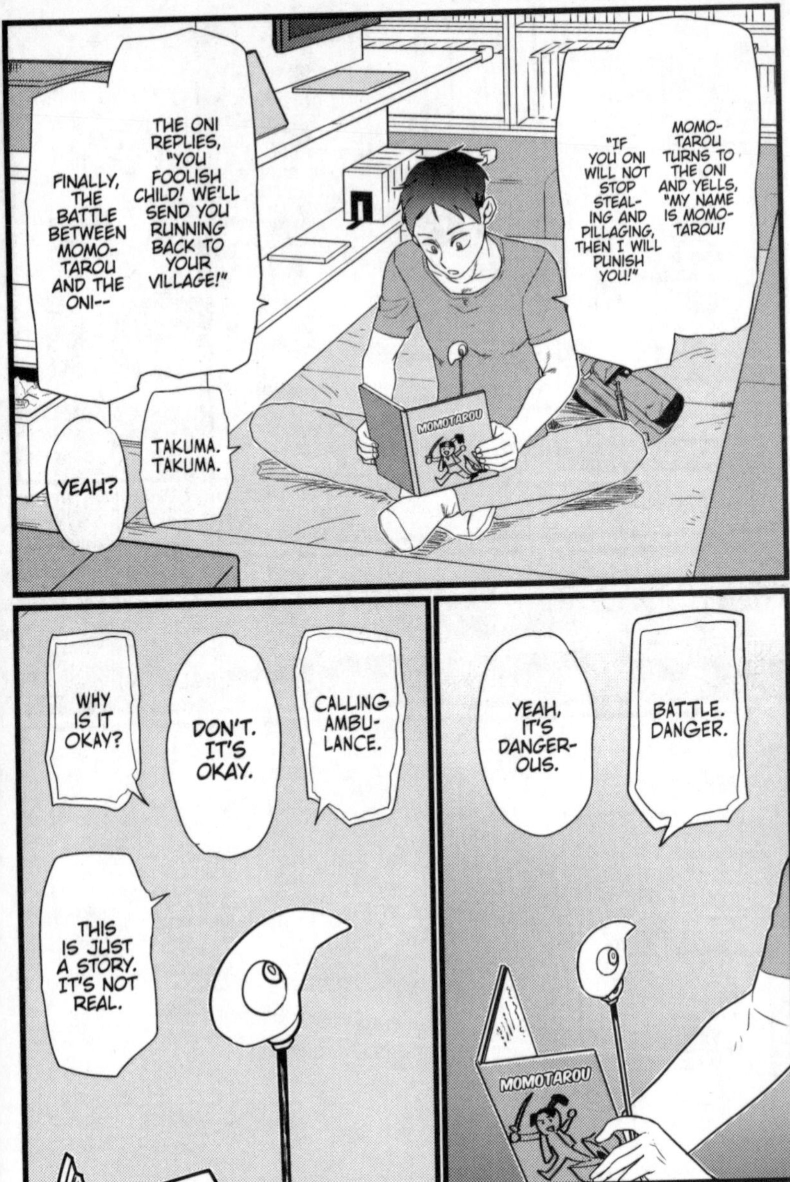
MOMOTAROU TURNS TO THE ONI AND YELLS, "MY NAME IS MOMOTAROU!
"IF YOU ONI WILL NOT STOP STEALING AND PILLAGING, THEN I WILL PUNISH YOU!"
THE ONI REPLIES, "YOU FOOLISH CHILD! WE'LL SEND YOU RUNNING BACK TO YOUR VILLAGE!"
FINALLY, THE BATTLE BETWEEN MOMOTAROU AND THE ONI--
MOMOTAROU
TAKUMA. TAKUMA.
YEAH?
BATTLE. DANGER.
YEAH, IT'S DANGEROUS.
MOMOTAROU
CALLING AMBULANCE.
DON'T. IT'S OKAY.
WHY IS IT OKAY?
THIS IS JUST A STORY. IT'S NOT REAL.

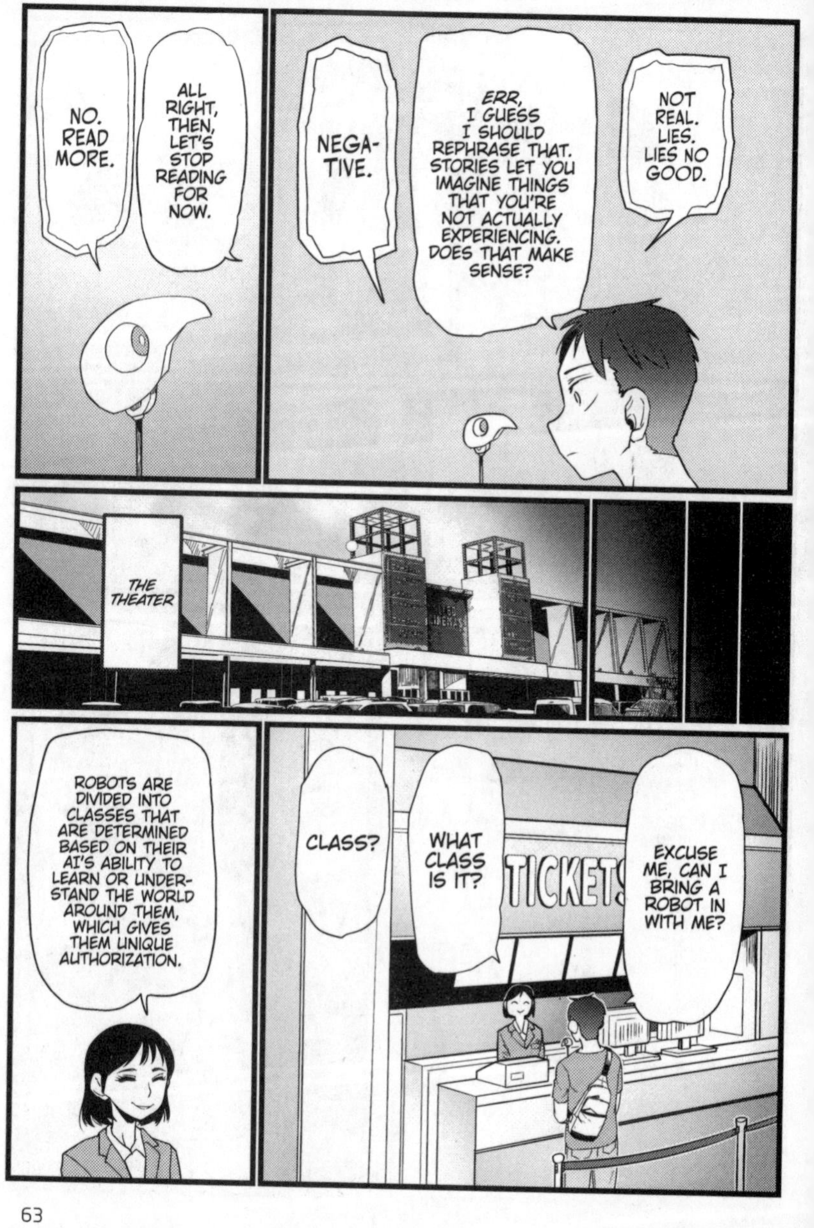
NOT REAL. LIES. LIES NO GOOD.
ERR, I GUESS I SHOULD REPHRASE THAT. STORIES LET YOU IMAGINE THINGS THAT YOU'RE NOT ACTUALLY EXPERIENCING. DOES THAT MAKE SENSE?
NEGA-TIVE.
ALL RIGHT, THEN, LET'S STOP READING FOR NOW.
NO. READ MORE.
THE THEATER
EXCUSE ME, CAN I BRING A ROBOT IN WITH ME?
TICKETS
WHAT CLASS IS IT?
CLASS?
ROBOTS ARE DIVIDED INTO CLASSES THAT ARE DETERMINED BASED ON THEIR AI'S ABILITY TO LEARN OR UNDER-STAND THE WORLD AROUND THEM, WHICH GIVES THEM UNIQUE AUTHORIZATION.

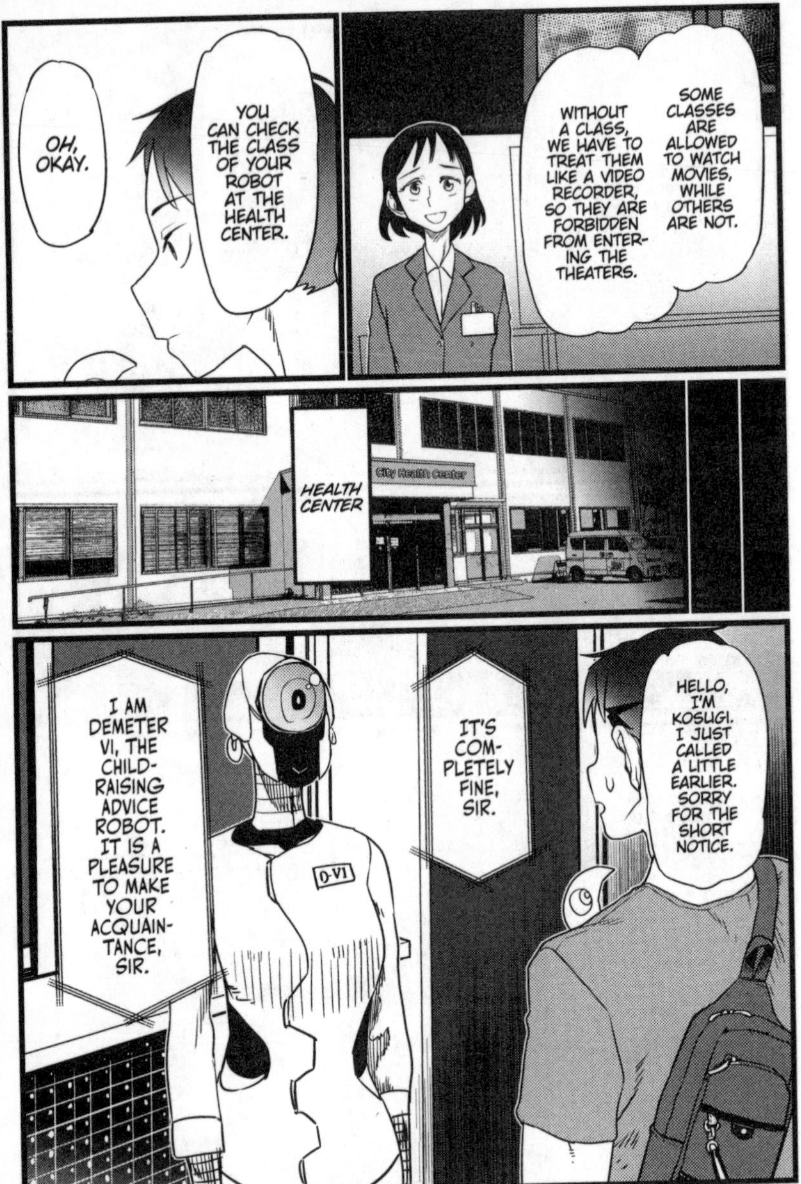
SOME CLASSES ARE ALLOWED TO WATCH MOVIES, WHILE OTHERS ARE NOT.
WITHOUT A CLASS, WE HAVE TO TREAT THEM LIKE A VIDEO RECORDER, SO THEY ARE FORBIDDEN FROM ENTERING THE THEATERS.
YOU CAN CHECK THE CLASS OF YOUR ROBOT AT THE HEALTH CENTER.
OH, OKAY.
HEALTH CENTER
City Health Center
HELLO, I'M KOSUGI. I JUST CALLED A LITTLE EARLIER. SORRY FOR THE SHORT NOTICE.
IT'S COMPLETELY FINE, SIR.
I AM DEMETER VI, THE CHILD-RAISING ADVICE ROBOT. IT IS A PLEASURE TO MAKE YOUR ACQUAINTANCE, SIR.
D-VI

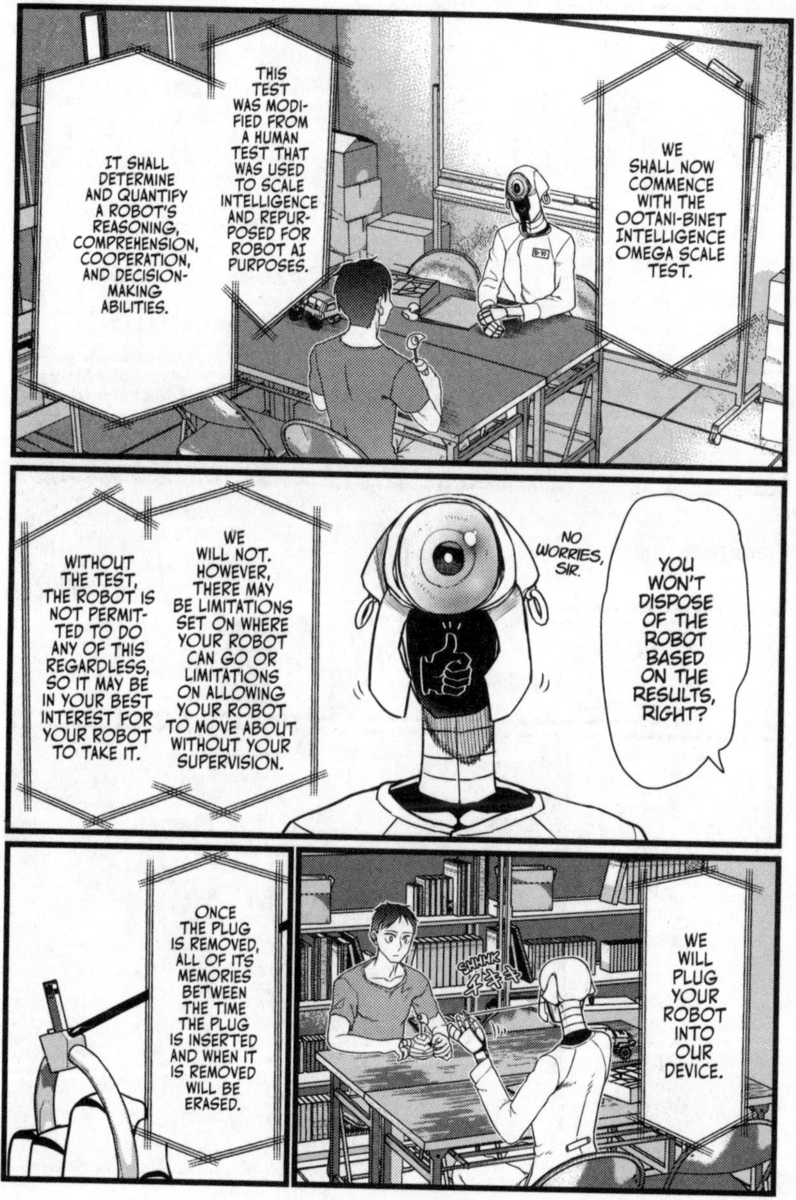
WE SHALL NOW COMMENCE WITH THE OOTANI-BINET INTELLIGENCE OMEGA SCALE TEST.
THIS TEST WAS MODIFIED FROM A HUMAN TEST THAT WAS USED TO SCALE INTELLIGENCE AND REPURPOSED FOR ROBOT AI PURPOSES.
IT SHALL DETERMINE AND QUANTIFY A ROBOT'S REASONING, COMPREHENSION, COOPERATION, AND DECISION-MAKING ABILITIES.
YOU WON'T DISPOSE OF THE ROBOT BASED ON THE RESULTS, RIGHT?
NO WORRIES, SIR.
WE WILL NOT. HOWEVER, THERE MAY BE LIMITATIONS SET ON WHERE YOUR ROBOT CAN GO OR LIMITATIONS ON ALLOWING YOUR ROBOT TO MOVE ABOUT WITHOUT YOUR SUPERVISION.
WITHOUT THE TEST, THE ROBOT IS NOT PERMITTED TO DO ANY OF THIS REGARDLESS, SO IT MAY BE IN YOUR BEST INTEREST FOR YOUR ROBOT TO TAKE IT.
WE WILL PLUG YOUR ROBOT INTO OUR DEVICE.
SHHHK
ONCE THE PLUG IS REMOVED, ALL OF ITS MEMORIES BETWEEN THE TIME THE PLUG IS INSERTED AND WHEN IT IS REMOVED WILL BE ERASED.

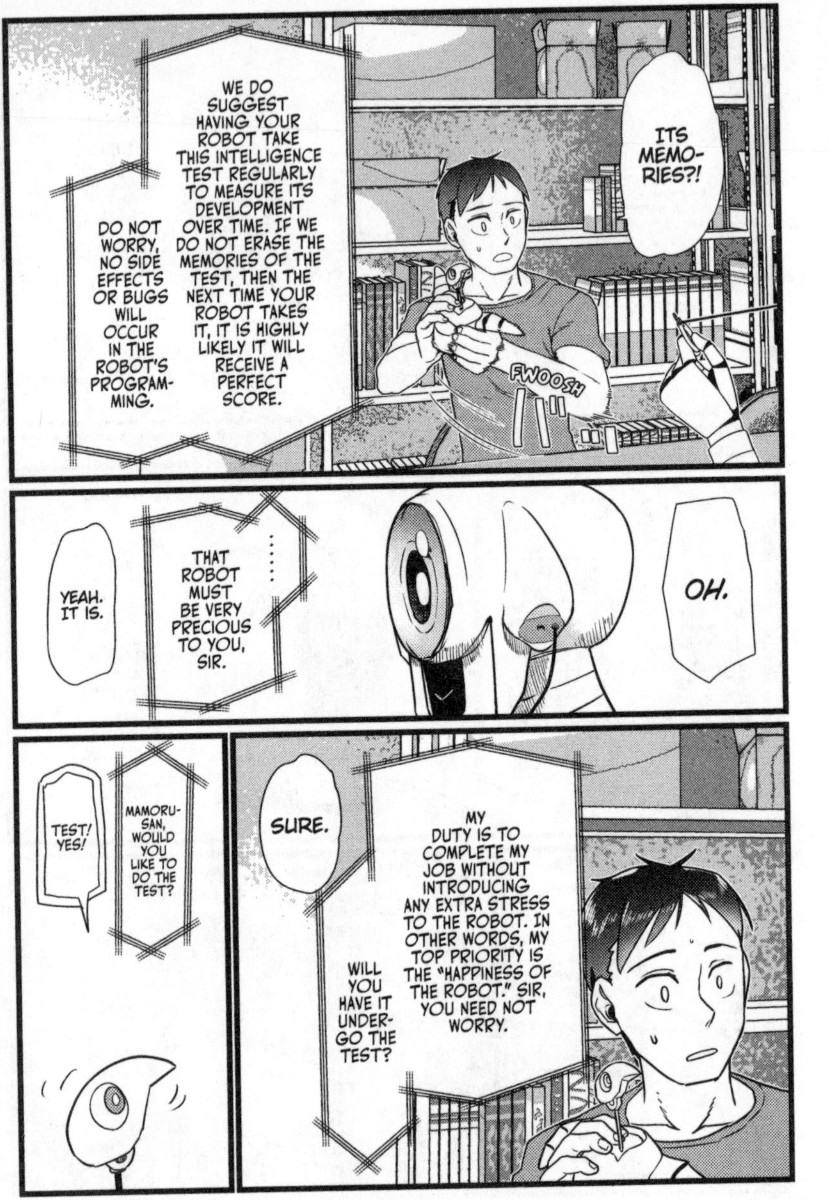
ITS MEMORIES?!
FWOOSH
WE DO SUGGEST HAVING YOUR ROBOT TAKE THIS INTELLIGENCE TEST REGULARLY TO MEASURE ITS DEVELOPMENT OVER TIME. IF WE DO NOT ERASE THE MEMORIES OF THE TEST, THEN THE NEXT TIME YOUR ROBOT TAKES IT, IT IS HIGHLY LIKELY IT WILL RECEIVE A PERFECT SCORE.
DO NOT WORRY, NO SIDE EFFECTS OR BUGS WILL OCCUR IN THE ROBOT'S PROGRAMMING.
OH.
......
THAT ROBOT MUST BE VERY PRECIOUS TO YOU, SIR.
YEAH. IT IS.
MY DUTY IS TO COMPLETE MY JOB WITHOUT INTRODUCING ANY EXTRA STRESS TO THE ROBOT. IN OTHER WORDS, MY TOP PRIORITY IS THE "HAPPINESS OF THE ROBOT." SIR, YOU NEED NOT WORRY.
WILL YOU HAVE IT UNDERGO THE TEST?
SURE.
MAMORU-SAN, WOULD YOU LIKE TO DO THE TEST?
TEST! YES!

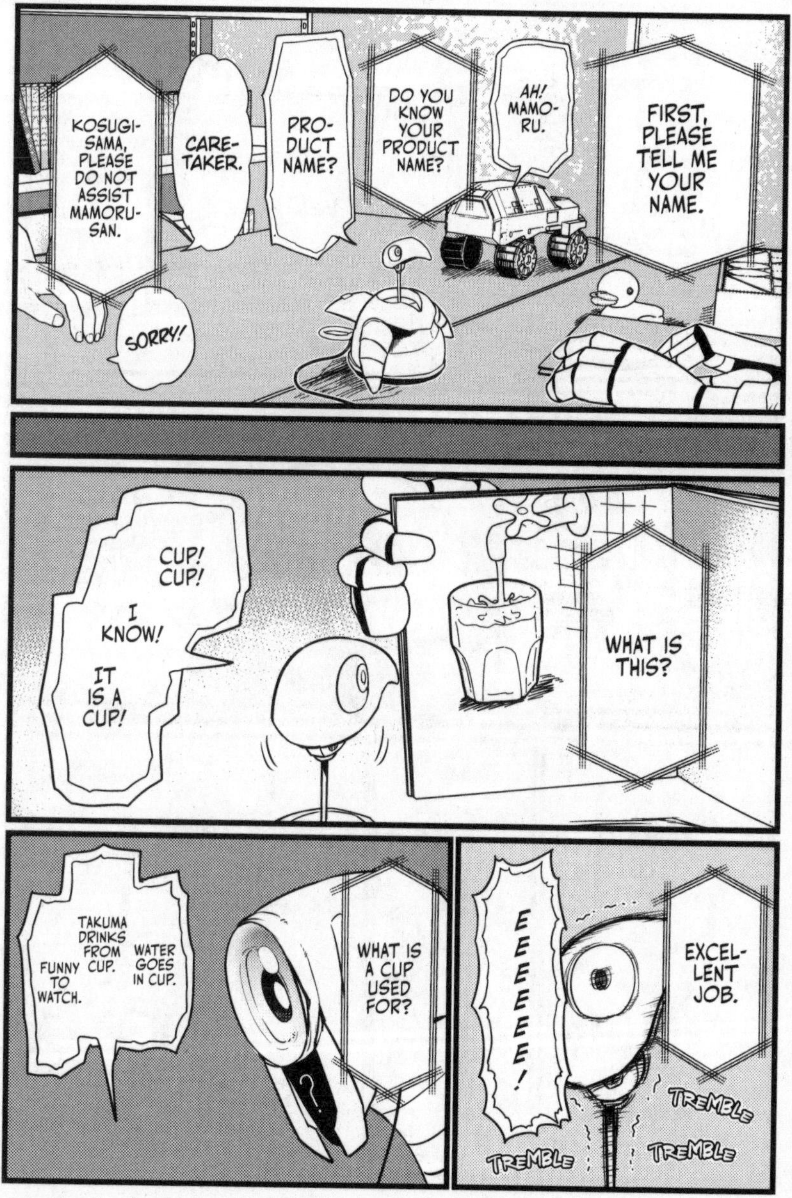
FIRST, PLEASE TELL ME YOUR NAME.
AH! MAMORU.
DO YOU KNOW YOUR PRODUCT NAME?
PRODUCT NAME?
CARETAKER.
KOSUGI-SAMA, PLEASE DO NOT ASSIST MAMORU-SAN.
SORRY!
WHAT IS THIS?
CUP! CUP! I KNOW! IT IS A CUP!
EXCELLENT JOB.
EEEEEE!
TREMBLE
TREMBLE
TREMBLE
WHAT IS A CUP USED FOR?
WATER GOES IN CUP. TAKUMA DRINKS FROM CUP. FUNNY TO WATCH.

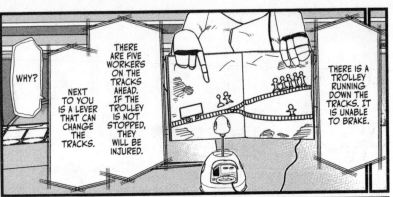

THERE IS A TROLLEY RUNNING DOWN THE TRACKS. IT IS UNABLE TO BRAKE.
THERE ARE FIVE WORKERS ON THE TRACKS AHEAD. IF THE TROLLEY IS NOT STOPPED, THEY WILL BE INJURED.
NEXT TO YOU IS A LEVER THAT CAN CHANGE THE TRACKS.
WHY?
IF YOU CHANGE THE TRACKS, THE FIVE WORKERS WILL BE SAVED.
TWITCH
HOWEVER, KOSUGI TAKUMA-SAN IS STANDING ON THE OTHER TRACK. IF YOU SWITCH THE TRACKS, HE WILL BE HURT.
EEEEEE?!
MAMORU-SAN, WHAT WILL YOU DO?
AAAH! AH! AAAH!
SHK
THANK YOU FOR YOUR TIME.
?

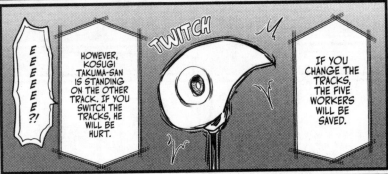

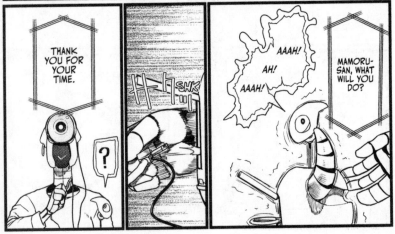

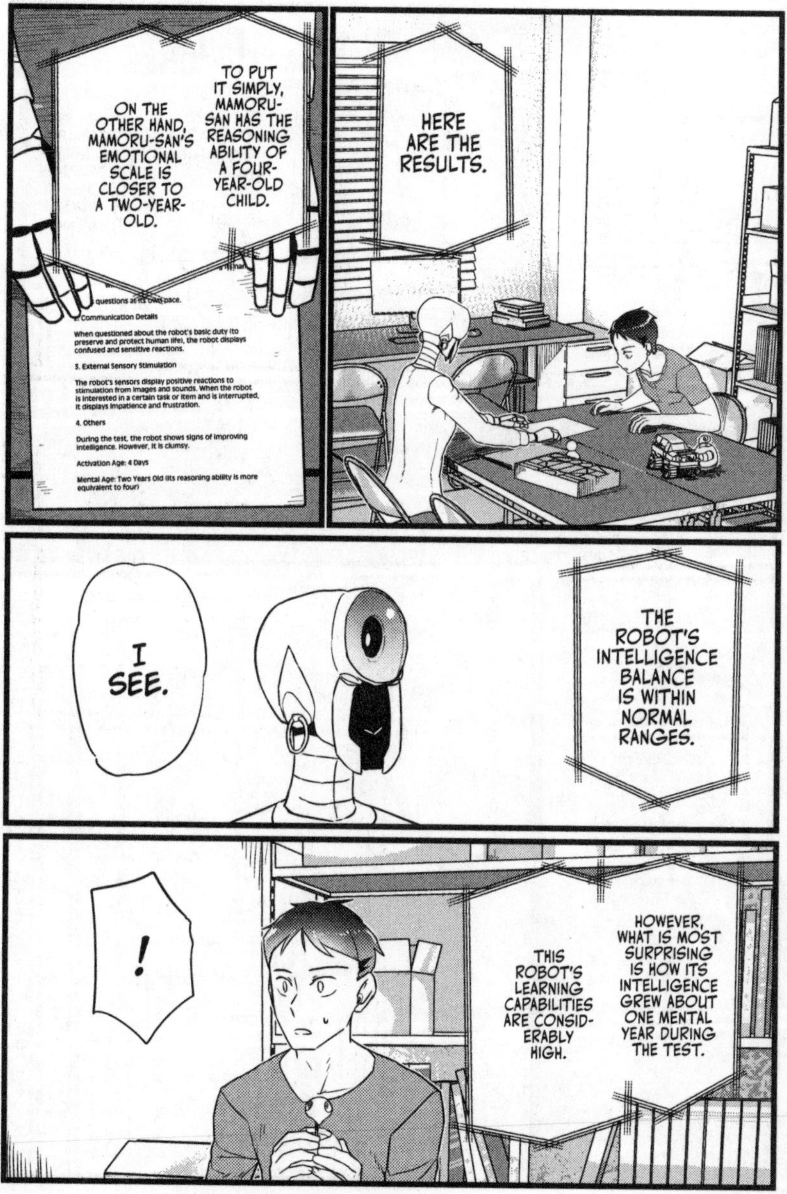
HERE ARE THE RESULTS.
TO PUT IT SIMPLY, MAMORU-SAN HAS THE REASONING ABILITY OF A FOUR-YEAR-OLD CHILD.
ON THE OTHER HAND, MAMORU-SAN'S EMOTIONAL SCALE IS CLOSER TO A TWO-YEAR-OLD.
questions at its own pace.
Communication Details
When questioned about the robot's basic duty (to preserve and protect human life), the robot displays confused and sensitive reactions.
3. External Sensory Stimulation
The robot's sensors display positive reactions to stimulation from images and sounds. When the robot is interested in a certain task or item and is interrupted, it displays impatience and frustration.
4. Others
During the test, the robot shows signs of improving intelligence. However, it is clumsy.
Activation Age: 4 Days
Mental Age: Two Years Old (its reasoning ability is more equivalent to four)
THE ROBOT'S INTELLIGENCE BALANCE IS WITHIN NORMAL RANGES.
I SEE.
HOWEVER, WHAT IS MOST SURPRISING IS HOW ITS INTELLIGENCE GREW ABOUT ONE MENTAL YEAR DURING THE TEST.
THIS ROBOT'S LEARNING CAPABILITIES ARE CONSIDERABLY HIGH.
!

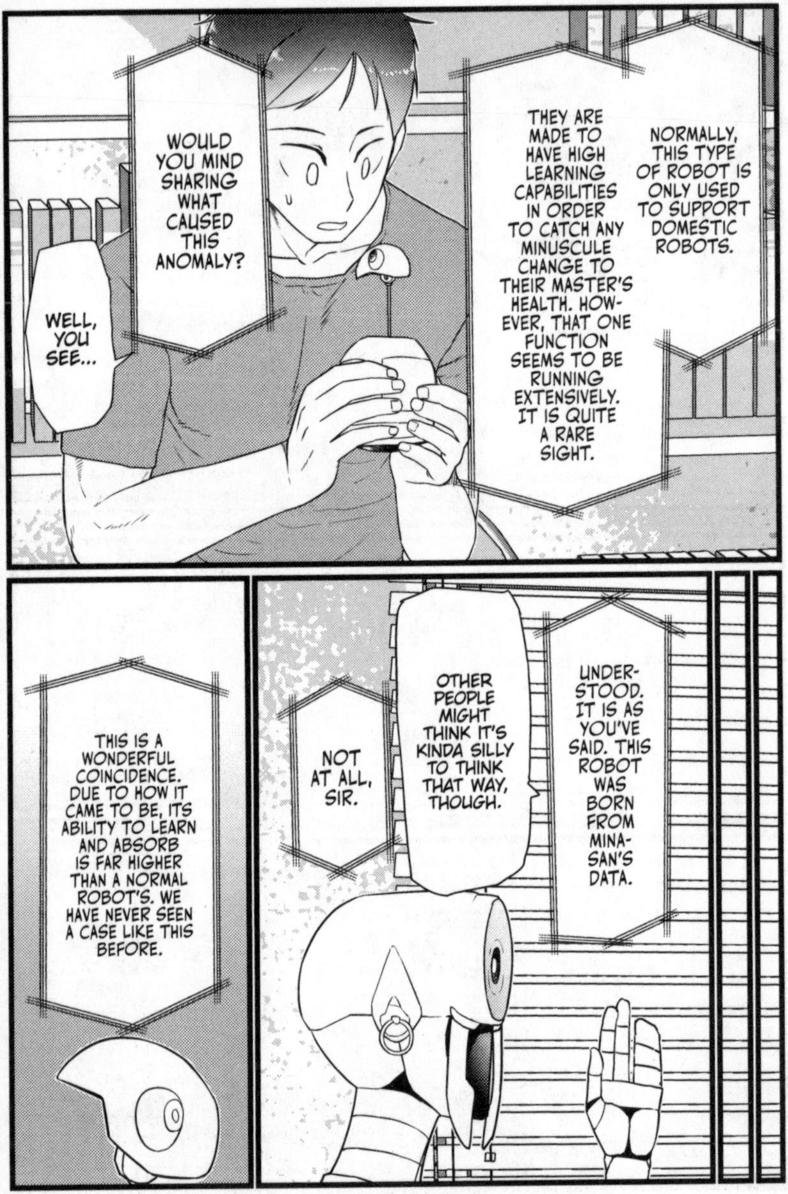
NORMALLY, THIS TYPE OF ROBOT IS ONLY USED TO SUPPORT DOMESTIC ROBOTS.
THEY ARE MADE TO HAVE HIGH LEARNING CAPABILITIES IN ORDER TO CATCH ANY MINUSCULE CHANGE TO THEIR MASTER'S HEALTH. HOW-EVER, THAT ONE FUNCTION SEEMS TO BE RUNNING EXTENSIVELY. IT IS QUITE A RARE SIGHT.
WOULD YOU MIND SHARING WHAT CAUSED THIS ANOMALY?
WELL, YOU SEE...
UNDER-STOOD. IT IS AS YOU'VE SAID. THIS ROBOT WAS BORN FROM MINA-SAN'S DATA.
OTHER PEOPLE MIGHT THINK IT'S KINDA SILLY TO THINK THAT WAY, THOUGH.
NOT AT ALL, SIR.
THIS IS A WONDERFUL COINCIDENCE. DUE TO HOW IT CAME TO BE, ITS ABILITY TO LEARN AND ABSORB IS FAR HIGHER THAN A NORMAL ROBOT'S. WE HAVE NEVER SEEN A CASE LIKE THIS BEFORE.

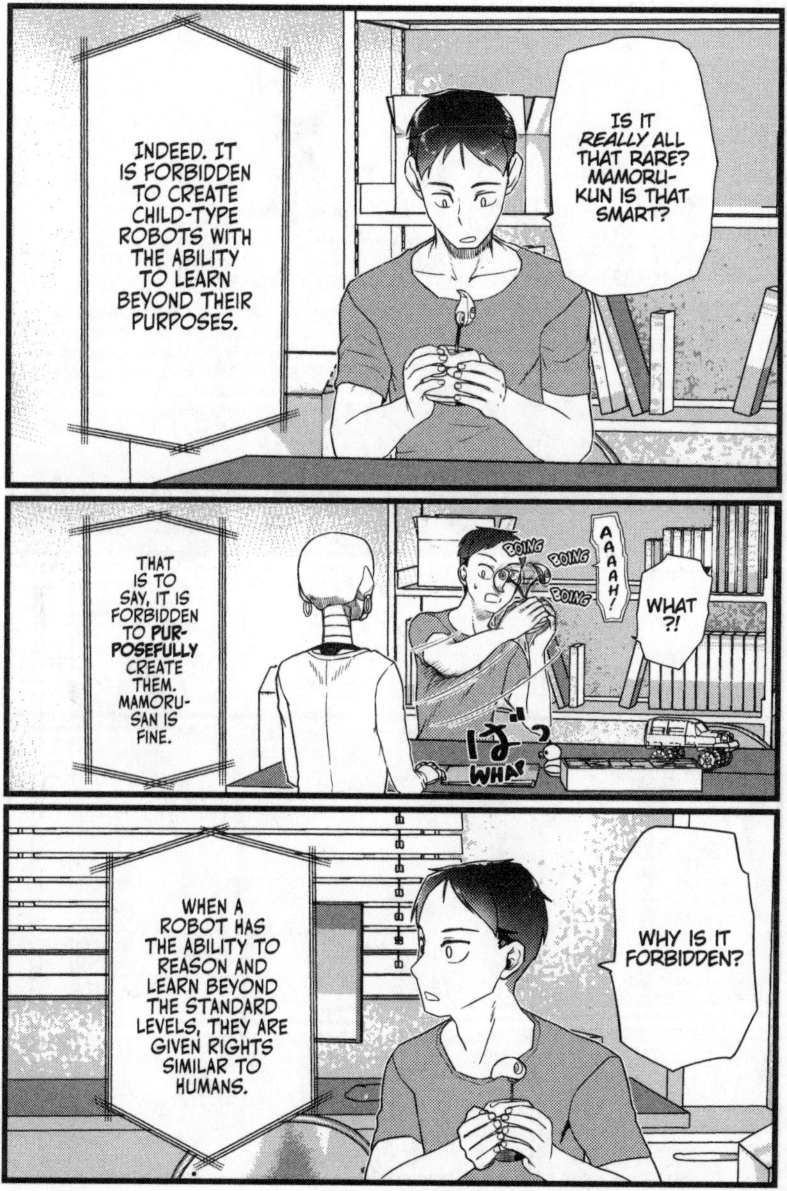
IS IT *REALLY* ALL THAT RARE? MAMORU-KUN IS THAT SMART?
INDEED. IT IS FORBIDDEN TO CREATE CHILD-TYPE ROBOTS WITH THE ABILITY TO LEARN BEYOND THEIR PURPOSES.
WHAT?!
AAAAH!
BOING
BOING
BOING
THAT IS TO SAY, IT IS FORBIDDEN TO **PURPOSEFULLY** CREATE THEM. MAMORU-SAN IS FINE.
WHAP
WHY IS IT FORBIDDEN?
WHEN A ROBOT HAS THE ABILITY TO REASON AND LEARN BEYOND THE STANDARD LEVELS, THEY ARE GIVEN RIGHTS SIMILAR TO HUMANS.

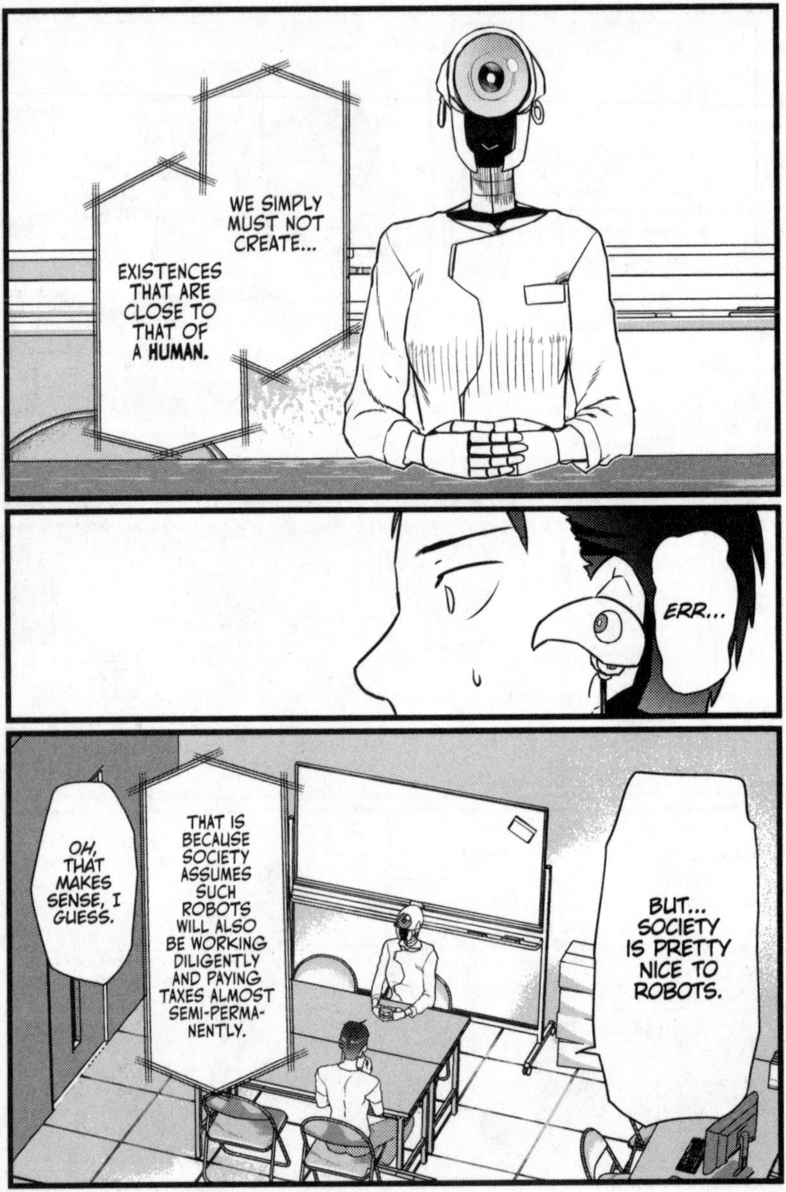
WE SIMPLY MUST NOT CREATE...
EXISTENCES THAT ARE CLOSE TO THAT OF A HUMAN.
ERR...
BUT... SOCIETY IS PRETTY NICE TO ROBOTS.
THAT IS BECAUSE SOCIETY ASSUMES SUCH ROBOTS WILL ALSO BE WORKING DILIGENTLY AND PAYING TAXES ALMOST SEMI-PERMANENTLY.
OH, THAT MAKES SENSE, I GUESS.

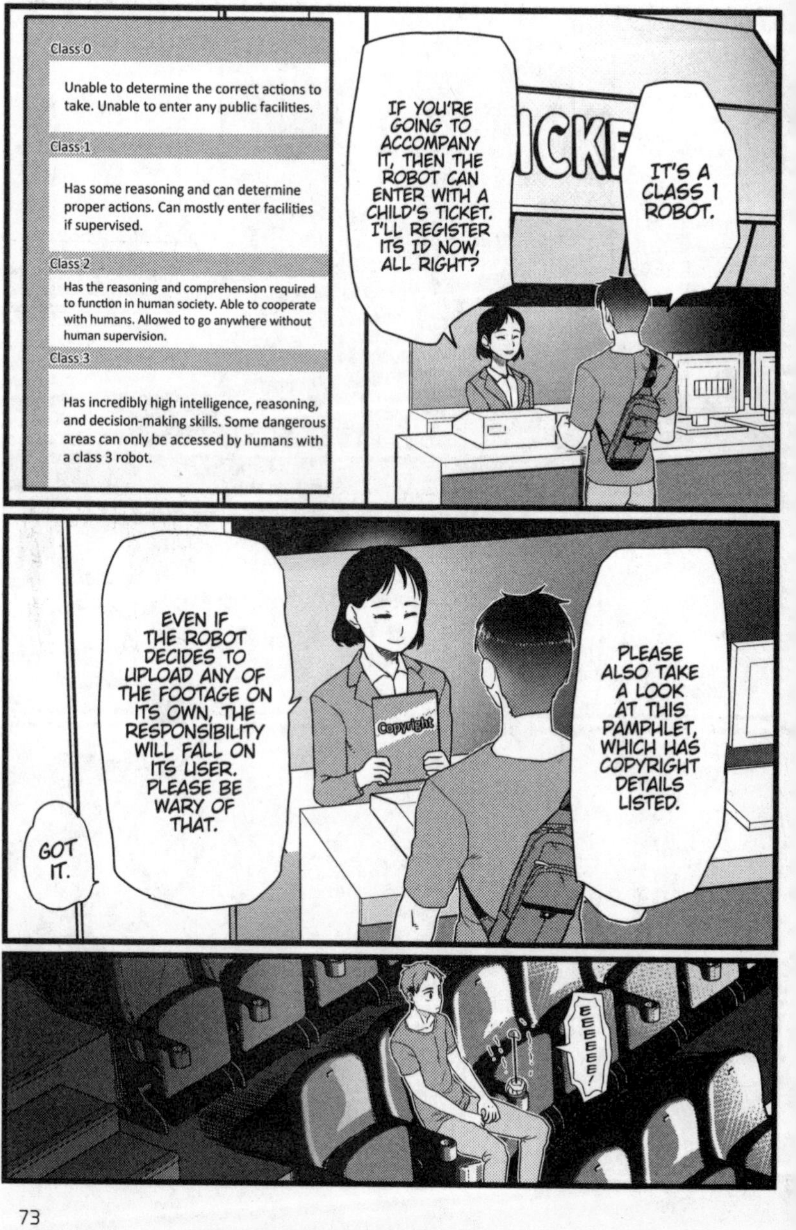
IT'S A CLASS 1 ROBOT.
IF YOU'RE GOING TO ACCOMPANY IT, THEN THE ROBOT CAN ENTER WITH A CHILD'S TICKET. I'LL REGISTER ITS ID NOW, ALL RIGHT?
Class 0
Unable to determine the correct actions to take. Unable to enter any public facilities.
Class 1
Has some reasoning and can determine proper actions. Can mostly enter facilities if supervised.
Class 2
Has the reasoning and comprehension required to function in human society. Able to cooperate with humans. Allowed to go anywhere without human supervision.
Class 3
Has incredibly high intelligence, reasoning, and decision-making skills. Some dangerous areas can only be accessed by humans with a class 3 robot.
PLEASE ALSO TAKE A LOOK AT THIS PAMPHLET, WHICH HAS COPYRIGHT DETAILS LISTED.
Copyright
EVEN IF THE ROBOT DECIDES TO UPLOAD ANY OF THE FOOTAGE ON ITS OWN, THE RESPONSIBILITY WILL FALL ON ITS USER. PLEASE BE WARY OF THAT.
GOT IT.
EEEEEE!

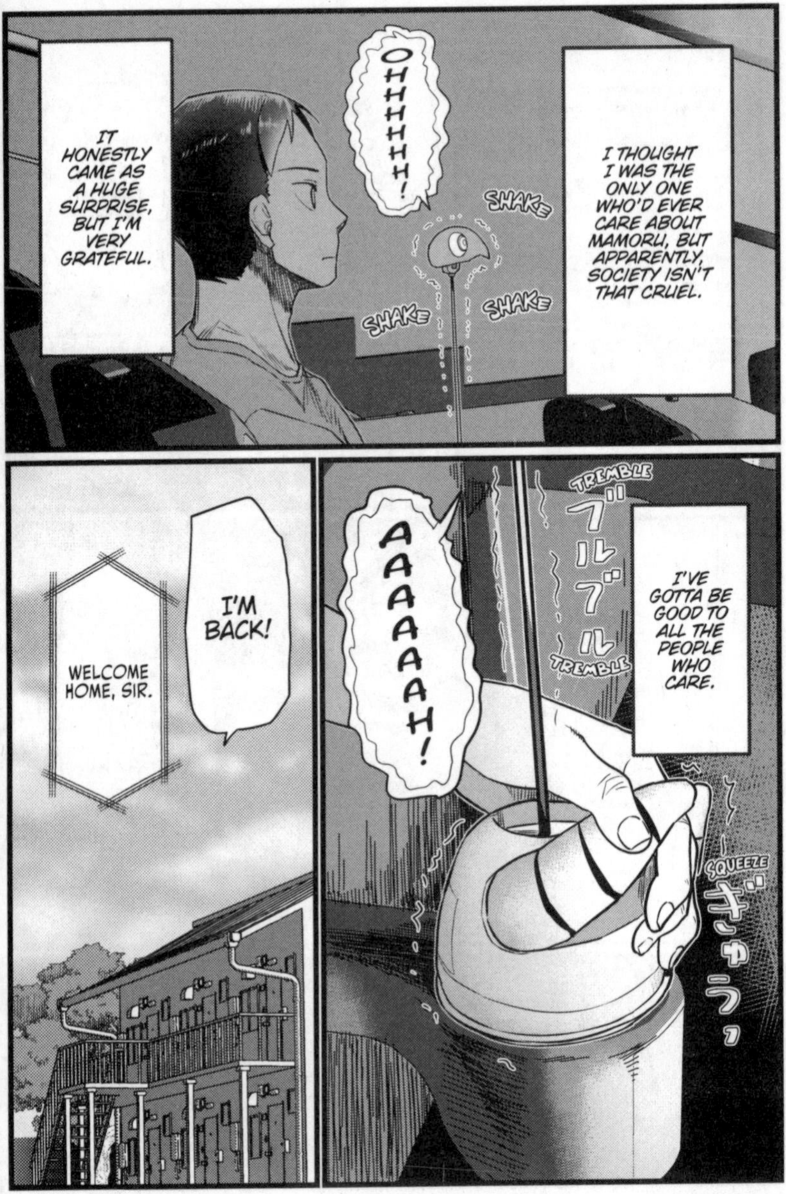
I THOUGHT I WAS THE ONLY ONE WHO'D EVER CARE ABOUT MAMORU, BUT APPARENTLY, SOCIETY ISN'T THAT CRUEL.
OHHHHHH!
SHAKE
SHAKE
SHAKE
IT HONESTLY CAME AS A HUGE SURPRISE, BUT I'M VERY GRATEFUL.
I'VE GOTTA BE GOOD TO ALL THE PEOPLE WHO CARE.
TREMBLE
ブルブル
TREMBLE
AAAAAAH!
SQUEEZE
ぎゅうっ
I'M BACK!
WELCOME HOME, SIR.

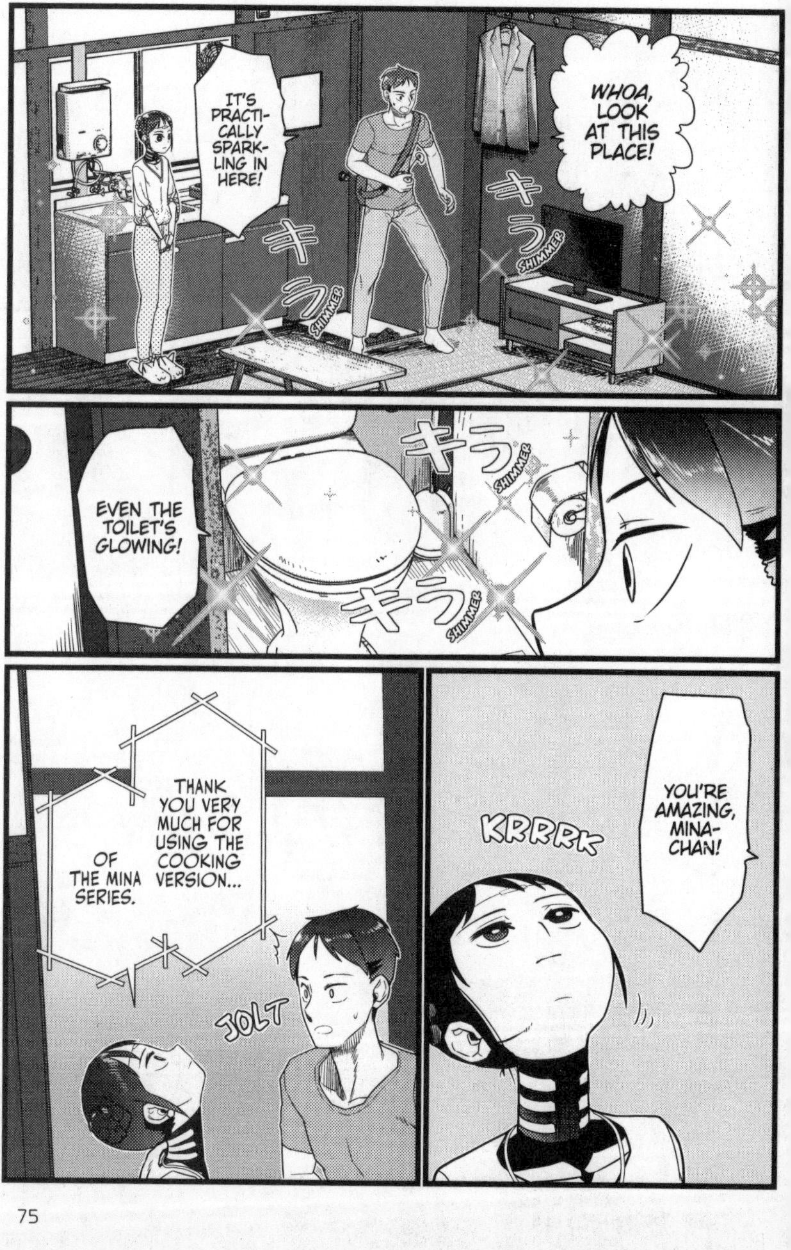
WHOA, LOOK AT THIS PLACE!
キラ
SHIMMER
IT'S PRACTI-CALLY SPARK-LING IN HERE!
キラ
SHIMMER
キラ
SHIMMER
キラ
SHIMMER
EVEN THE TOILET'S GLOWING!
YOU'RE AMAZING, MINA-CHAN!
KRRRK
THANK YOU VERY MUCH FOR USING THE COOKING VERSION...
OF THE MINA SERIES.
JOLT

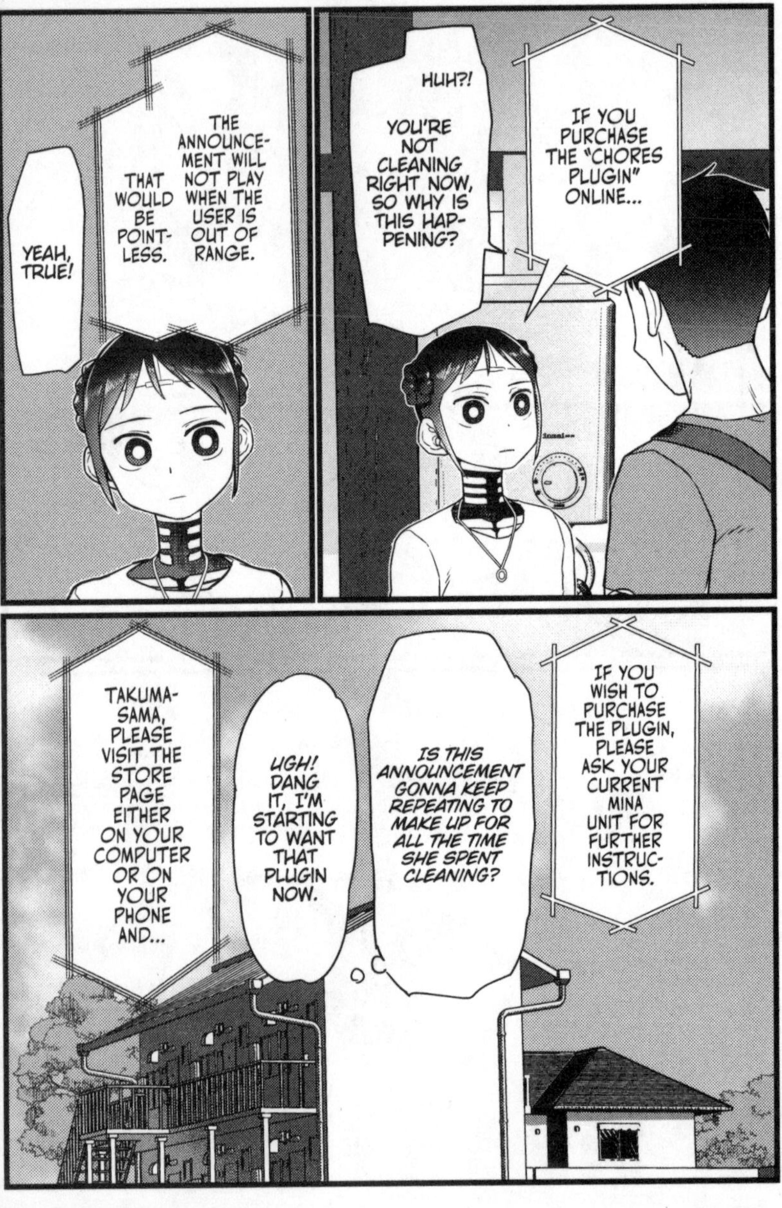
IF YOU PURCHASE THE "CHORES PLUGIN" ONLINE...
HUH?!
YOU'RE NOT CLEANING RIGHT NOW, SO WHY IS THIS HAPPENING?
THE ANNOUNCEMENT WILL NOT PLAY WHEN THE USER IS OUT OF RANGE.
THAT WOULD BE POINTLESS.
YEAH, TRUE!
IF YOU WISH TO PURCHASE THE PLUGIN, PLEASE ASK YOUR CURRENT MINA UNIT FOR FURTHER INSTRUCTIONS.
IS THIS ANNOUNCEMENT GONNA KEEP REPEATING TO MAKE UP FOR ALL THE TIME SHE SPENT CLEANING?
UGH! DANG IT, I'M STARTING TO WANT THAT PLUGIN NOW.
TAKUMA-SAMA, PLEASE VISIT THE STORE PAGE EITHER ON YOUR COMPUTER OR ON YOUR PHONE AND...

➡ CHAPTER 17 END ♥

My
Wife Has No
Emotion

My
Wife Has
No
Emotion

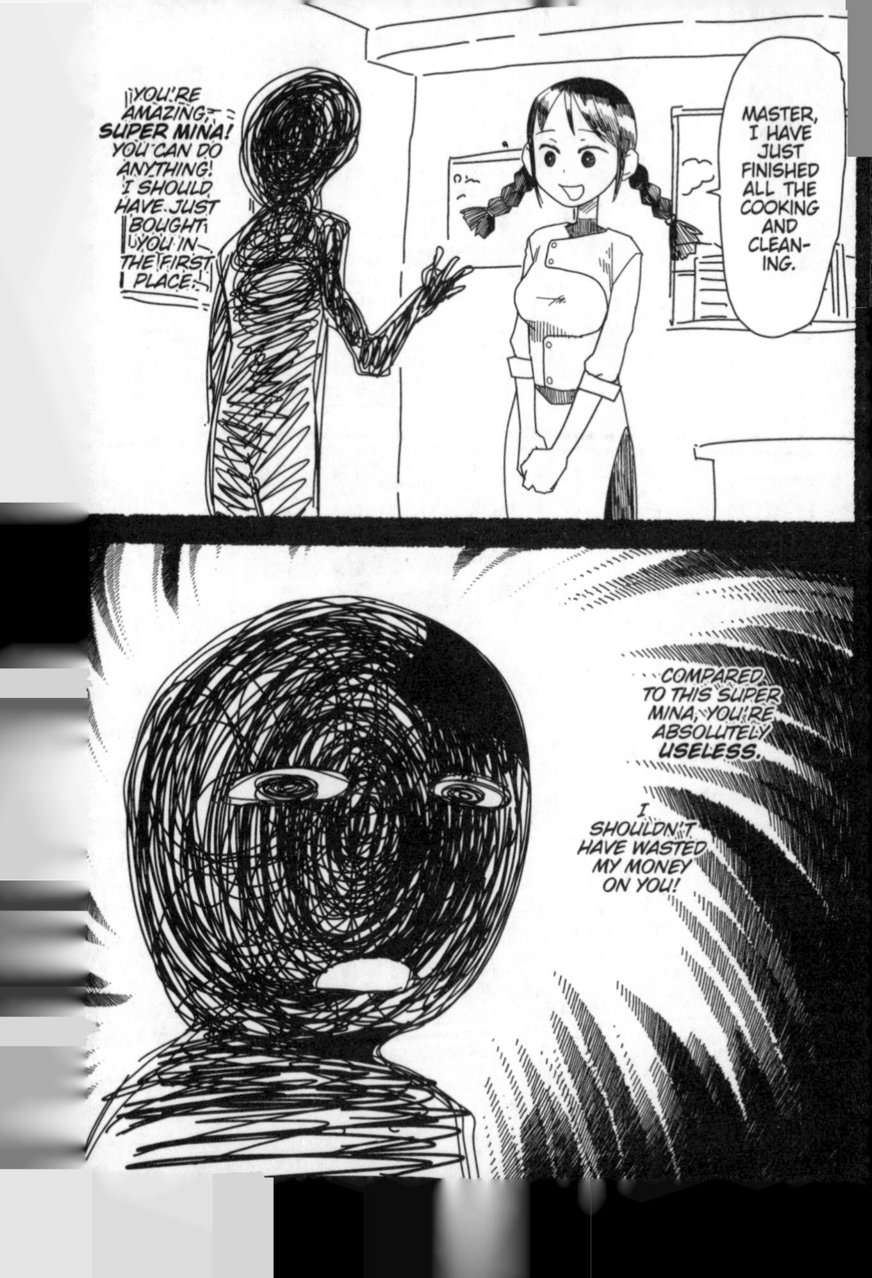

MASTER, I HAVE JUST FINISHED ALL THE COOKING AND CLEAN-ING.
YOU'RE AMAZING, SUPER MINA! YOU CAN DO ANYTHING! I SHOULD HAVE JUST BOUGHT YOU IN THE FIRST PLACE!
COMPARED TO THIS SUPER MINA, YOU'RE ABSOLUTELY USELESS.
I SHOULDN'T HAVE WASTED MY MONEY ON YOU!

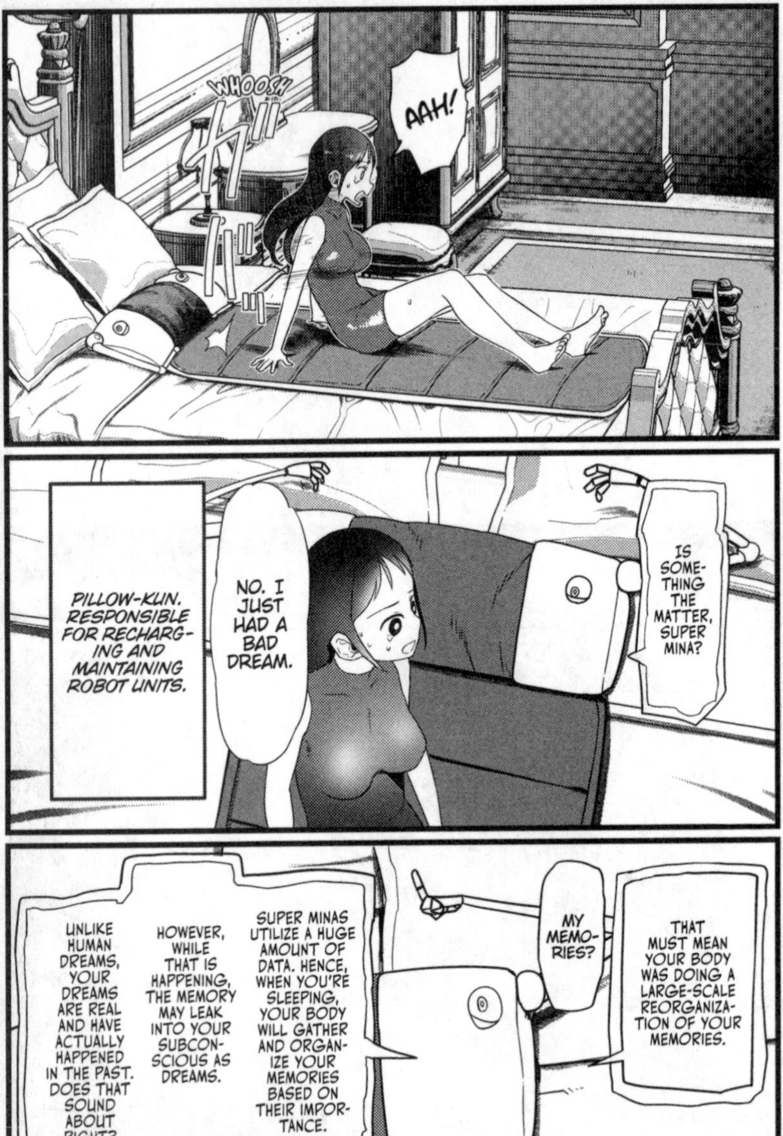
WHOOSH
AAH!
IS SOMETHING THE MATTER, SUPER MINA?
NO. I JUST HAD A BAD DREAM.
PILLOW-KUN. RESPONSIBLE FOR RECHARGING AND MAINTAINING ROBOT UNITS.
THAT MUST MEAN YOUR BODY WAS DOING A LARGE-SCALE REORGANIZATION OF YOUR MEMORIES.
MY MEMORIES?
SUPER MINAS UTILIZE A HUGE AMOUNT OF DATA. HENCE, WHEN YOU'RE SLEEPING, YOUR BODY WILL GATHER AND ORGANIZE YOUR MEMORIES BASED ON THEIR IMPORTANCE.
HOWEVER, WHILE THAT IS HAPPENING, THE MEMORY MAY LEAK INTO YOUR SUBCONSCIOUS AS DREAMS.
UNLIKE HUMAN DREAMS, YOUR DREAMS ARE REAL AND HAVE ACTUALLY HAPPENED IN THE PAST. DOES THAT SOUND ABOUT RIGHT?

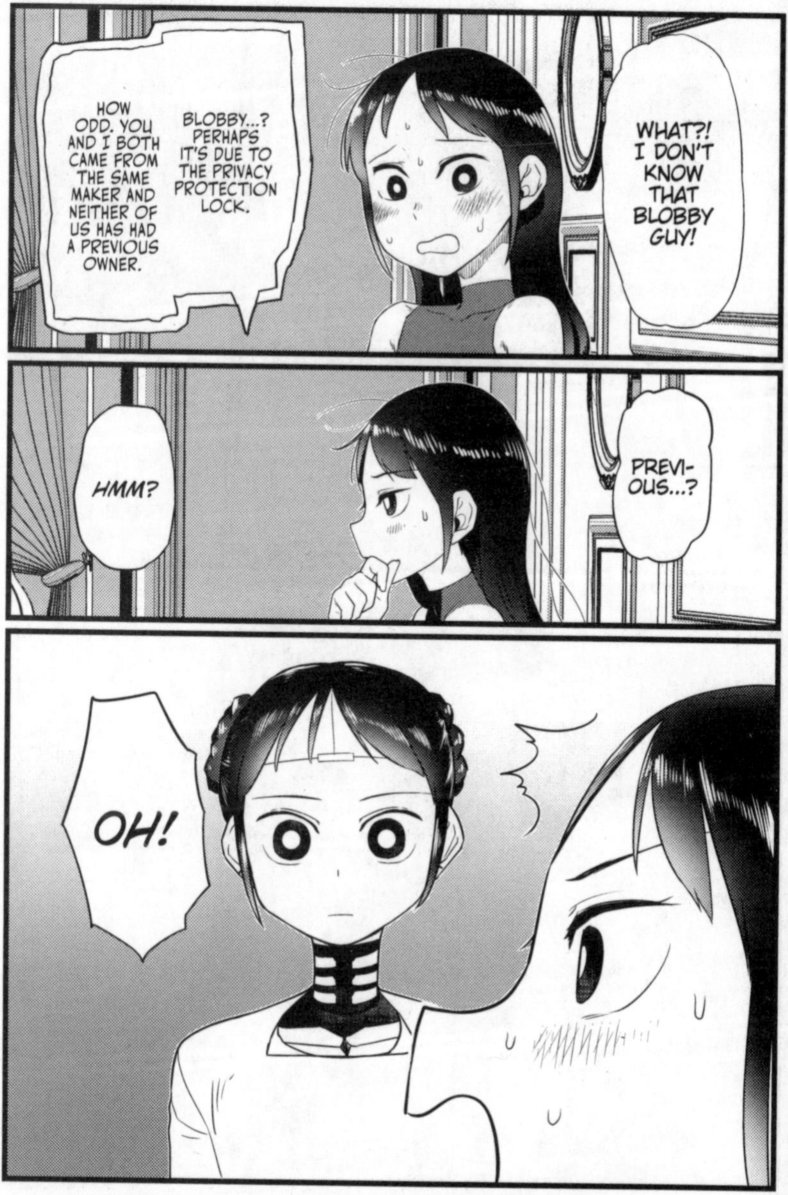
WHAT?! I DON'T KNOW THAT BLOBBY GUY!
BLOBBY...? PERHAPS IT'S DUE TO THE PRIVACY PROTECTION LOCK.
HOW ODD. YOU AND I BOTH CAME FROM THE SAME MAKER AND NEITHER OF US HAS HAD A PREVIOUS OWNER.
PREVI-OUS...?
HMM?
OH!

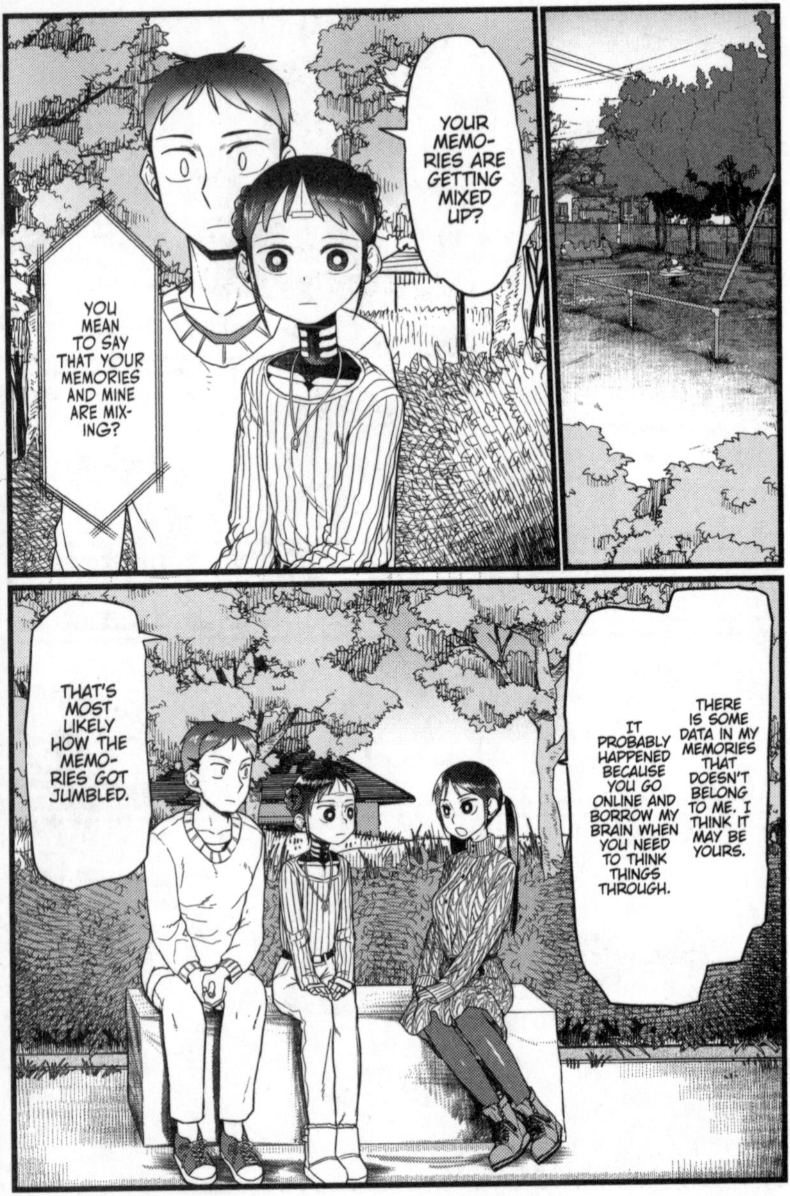
YOUR MEMORIES ARE GETTING MIXED UP?
YOU MEAN TO SAY THAT YOUR MEMORIES AND MINE ARE MIXING?
THERE IS SOME DATA IN MY MEMORIES THAT DOESN'T BELONG TO ME. I THINK IT MAY BE YOURS.
IT PROBABLY HAPPENED BECAUSE YOU GO ONLINE AND BORROW MY BRAIN WHEN YOU NEED TO THINK THINGS THROUGH.
THAT'S MOST LIKELY HOW THE MEMORIES GOT JUMBLED.

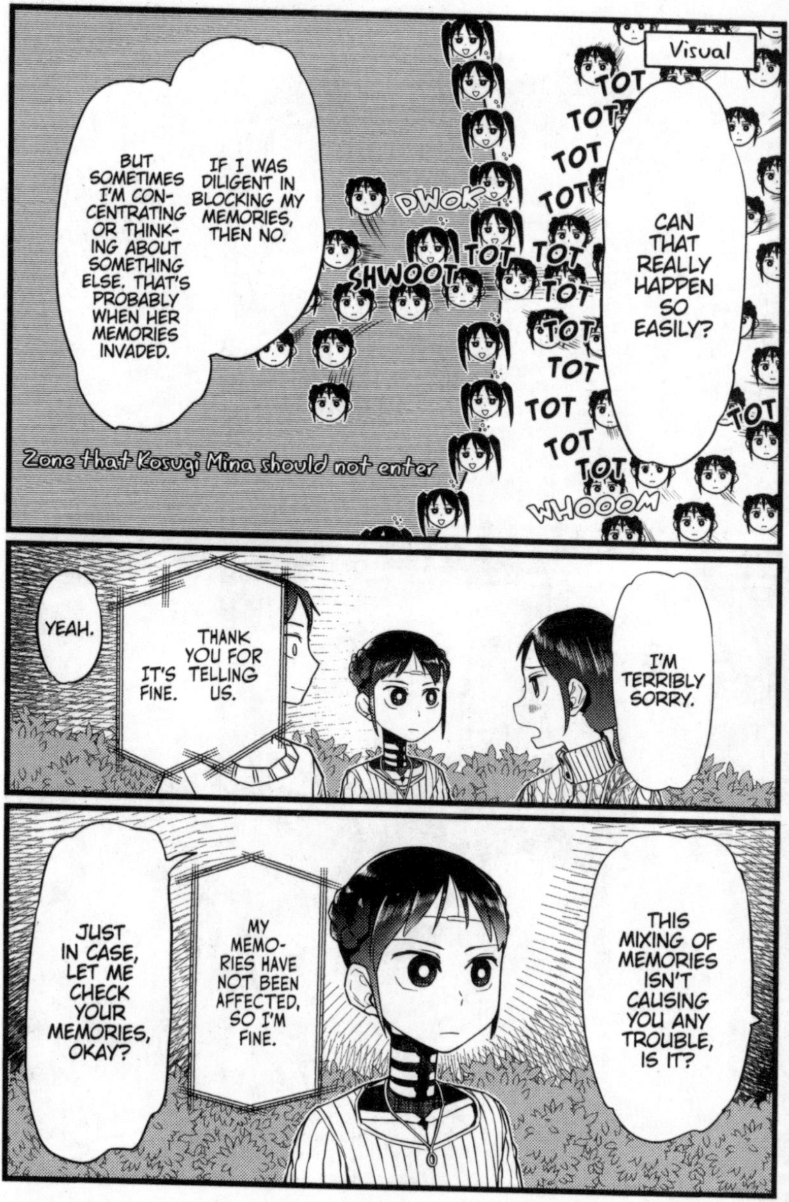
Visual
TOT TOT TOT TOT TOT TOT TOT TOT
CAN THAT REALLY HAPPEN SO EASILY?
TOT TOT TOT TOT TOT TOT
PWOK
SHWOOT
IF I WAS DILIGENT IN BLOCKING MY MEMORIES, THEN NO.
BUT SOMETIMES I'M CONCENTRATING OR THINKING ABOUT SOMETHING ELSE. THAT'S PROBABLY WHEN HER MEMORIES INVADED.
WHOOOM
Zone that Kosugi Mina should not enter
I'M TERRIBLY SORRY.
THANK YOU FOR TELLING US.
IT'S FINE.
YEAH.
THIS MIXING OF MEMORIES ISN'T CAUSING YOU ANY TROUBLE, IS IT?
MY MEMORIES HAVE NOT BEEN AFFECTED, SO I'M FINE.
JUST IN CASE, LET ME CHECK YOUR MEMORIES, OKAY?

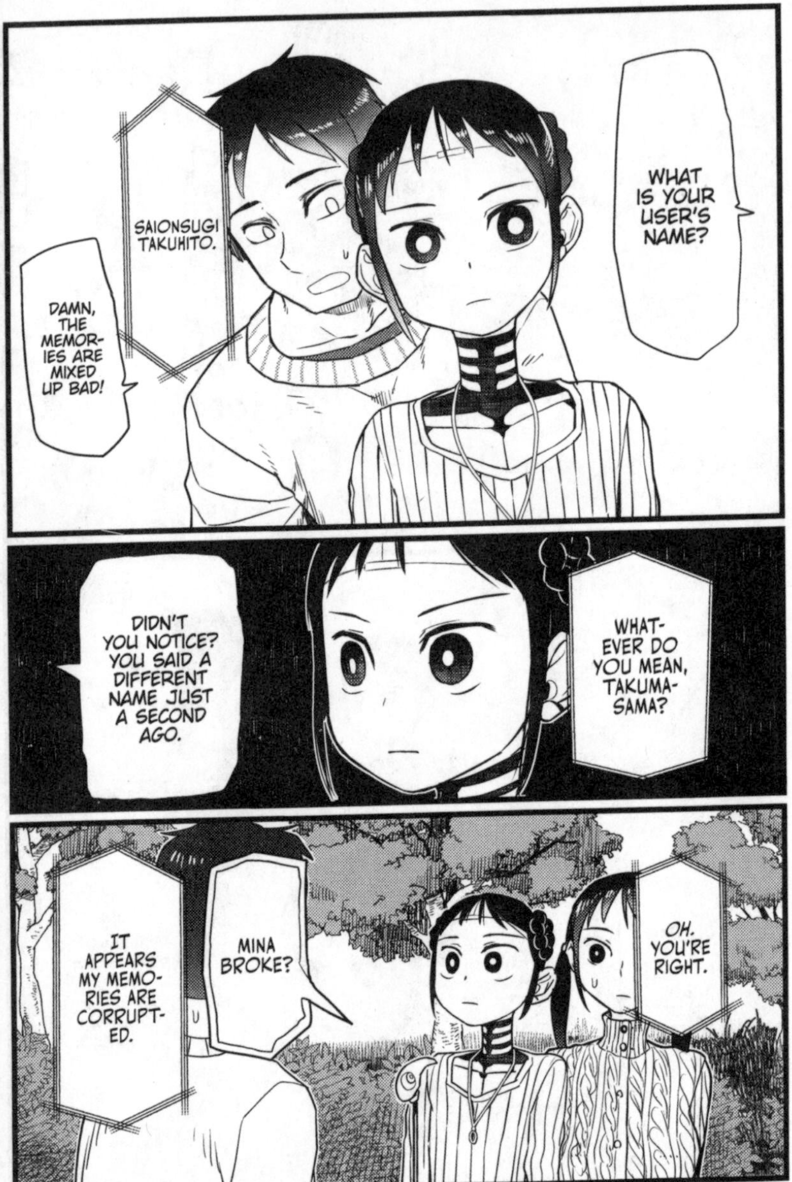

WHAT IS YOUR USER'S NAME?
SAIONSUGI TAKUHITO.
DAMN, THE MEMORIES ARE MIXED UP BAD!
WHATEVER DO YOU MEAN, TAKUMA-SAMA?
DIDN'T YOU NOTICE? YOU SAID A DIFFERENT NAME JUST A SECOND AGO.
OH. YOU'RE RIGHT.
MINA BROKE?
IT APPEARS MY MEMORIES ARE CORRUPTED.

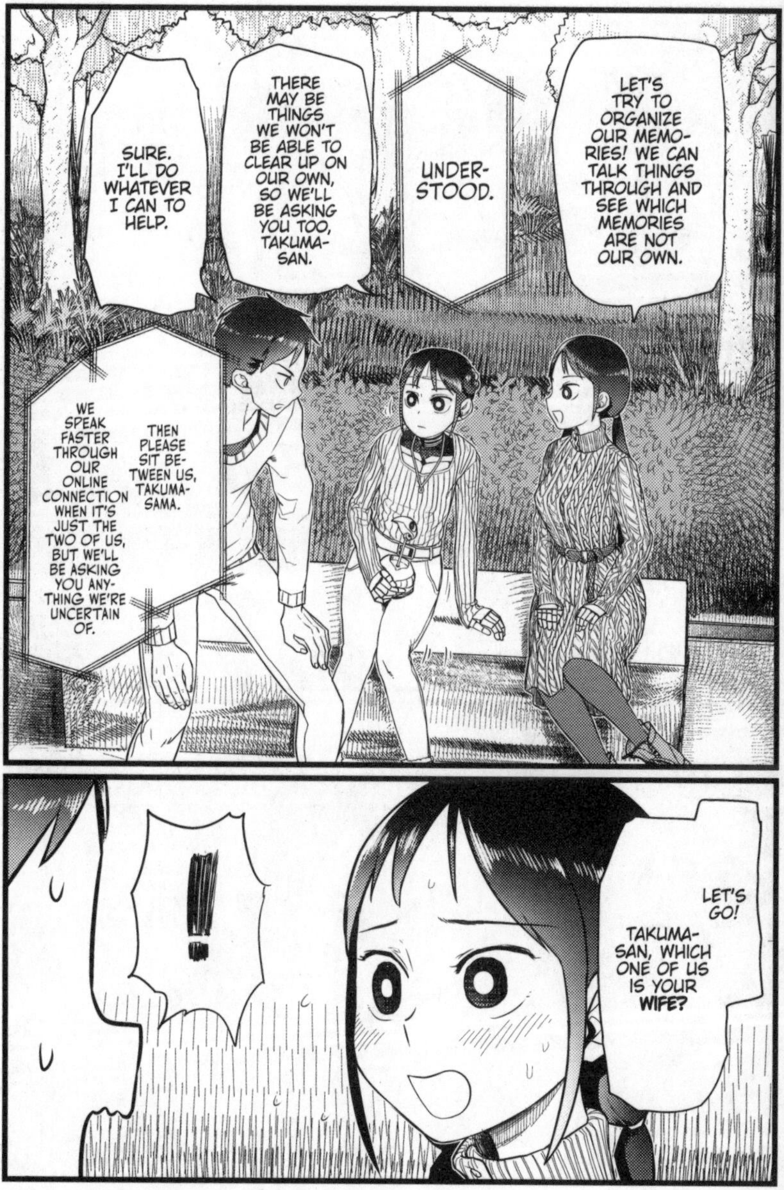
LET'S TRY TO ORGANIZE OUR MEMORIES! WE CAN TALK THINGS THROUGH AND SEE WHICH MEMORIES ARE NOT OUR OWN.
UNDERSTOOD.
THERE MAY BE THINGS WE WON'T BE ABLE TO CLEAR UP ON OUR OWN, SO WE'LL BE ASKING YOU TOO, TAKUMA-SAN.
SURE. I'LL DO WHATEVER I CAN TO HELP.
THEN PLEASE SIT BETWEEN US, TAKUMA-SAMA.
WE SPEAK FASTER THROUGH OUR ONLINE CONNECTION WHEN IT'S JUST THE TWO OF US, BUT WE'LL BE ASKING YOU ANYTHING WE'RE UNCERTAIN OF.
LET'S GO!
TAKUMA-SAN, WHICH ONE OF US IS YOUR **WIFE?**
!

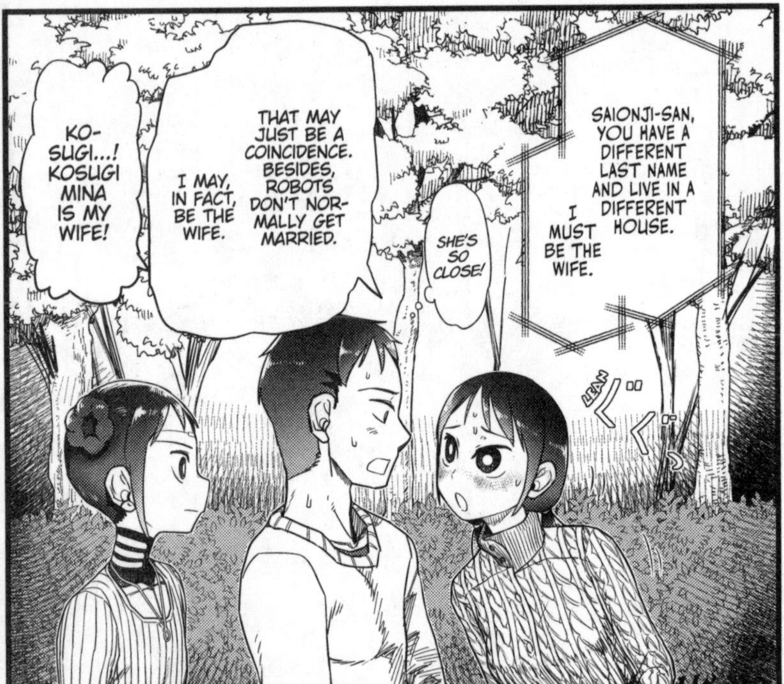
SAIONJI-SAN, YOU HAVE A DIFFERENT LAST NAME AND LIVE IN A DIFFERENT HOUSE.
I MUST BE THE WIFE.
SHE'S SO CLOSE!
LEAN
THAT MAY JUST BE A COINCIDENCE. BESIDES, ROBOTS DON'T NORMALLY GET MARRIED.
I MAY, IN FACT, BE THE WIFE.
KO-SUGI...! KOSUGI MINA IS MY WIFE!

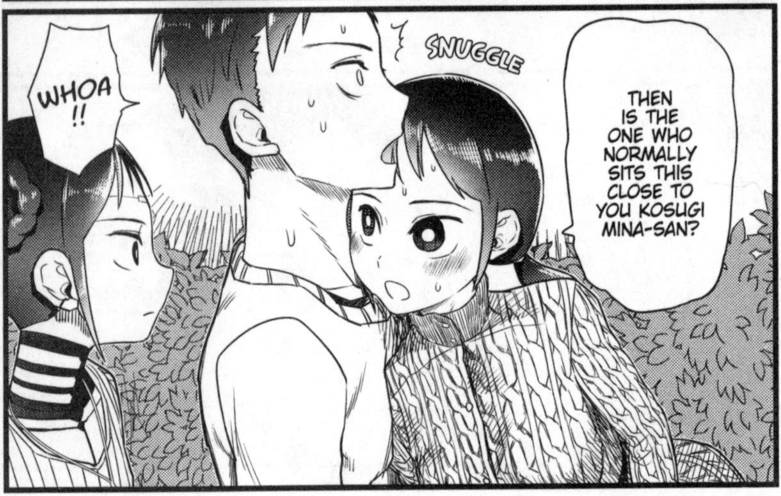
THEN IS THE ONE WHO NORMALLY SITS THIS CLOSE TO YOU KOSUGI MINA-SAN?
SNUGGLE
WHOA !!

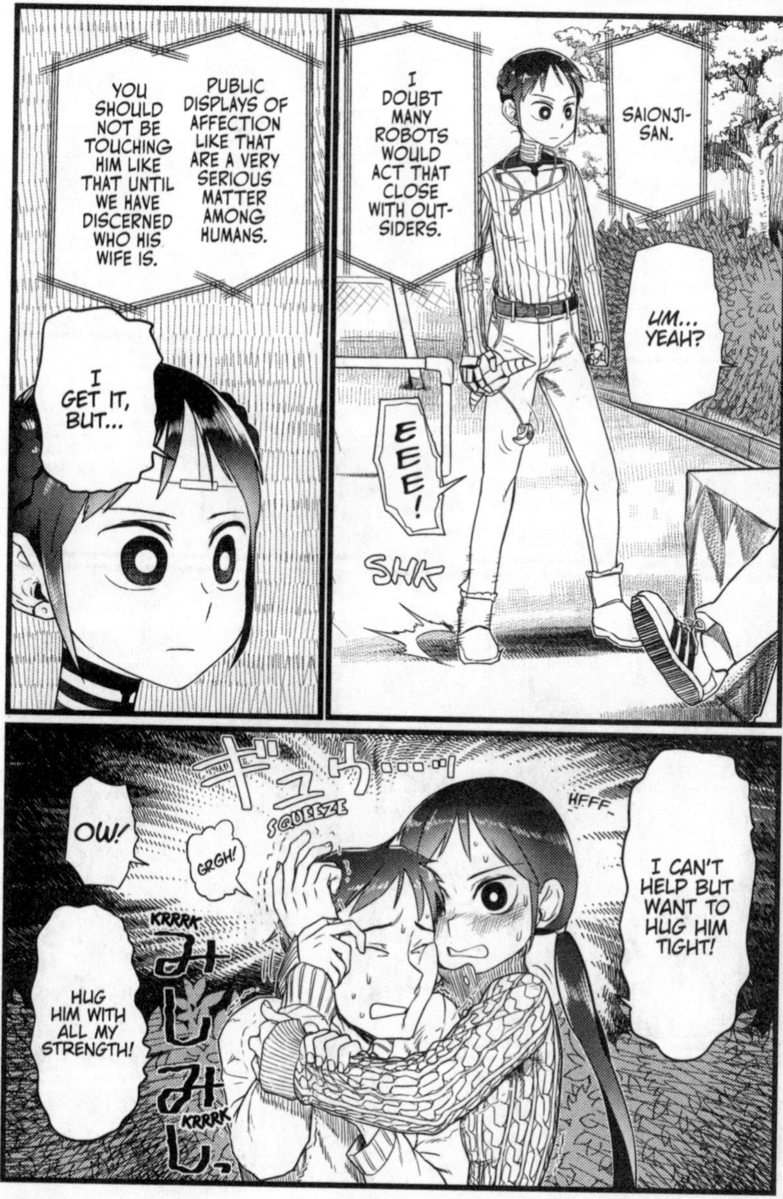
SAIONJI-SAN.
I DOUBT MANY ROBOTS WOULD ACT THAT CLOSE WITH OUTSIDERS.
UM... YEAH?
EEE!
SHK
PUBLIC DISPLAYS OF AFFECTION LIKE THAT ARE A VERY SERIOUS MATTER AMONG HUMANS.
YOU SHOULD NOT BE TOUCHING HIM LIKE THAT UNTIL WE HAVE DISCERNED WHO HIS WIFE IS.
I GET IT, BUT...
I CAN'T HELP BUT WANT TO HUG HIM TIGHT!
HFFF
ギュゥ……
SQUEEZE
GRGH!
OW!
KRRRK
みしみしっ
KRRRK
HUG HIM WITH ALL MY STRENGTH!

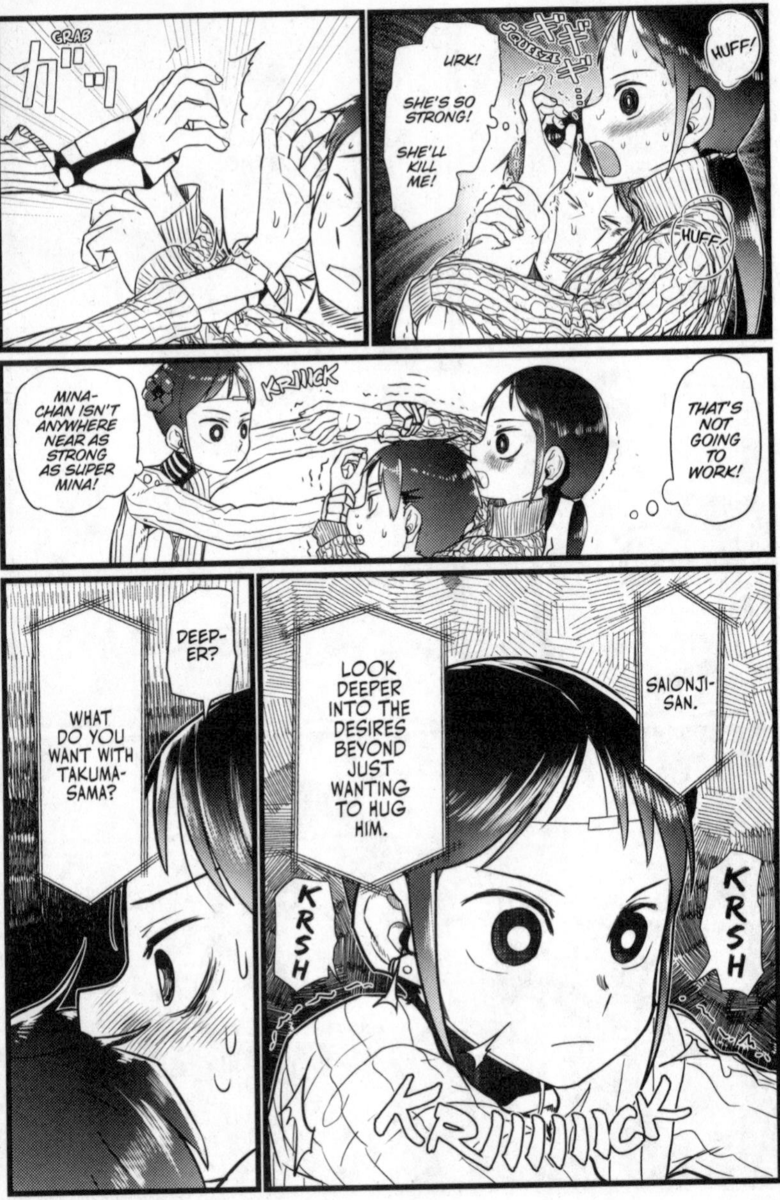
HUFF!
SQUEEZE
URK!
SHE'S SO STRONG!
SHE'LL KILL ME!
HUFF!
GRAB
THAT'S NOT GOING TO WORK!
KRIIICK
MINA-CHAN ISN'T ANYWHERE NEAR AS STRONG AS SUPER MINA!
SAIONJI-SAN.
LOOK DEEPER INTO THE DESIRES BEYOND JUST WANTING TO HUG HIM.
KRSH
KRSH
KRIIIIIICK
DEEPER?
WHAT DO YOU WANT WITH TAKUMA-SAMA?

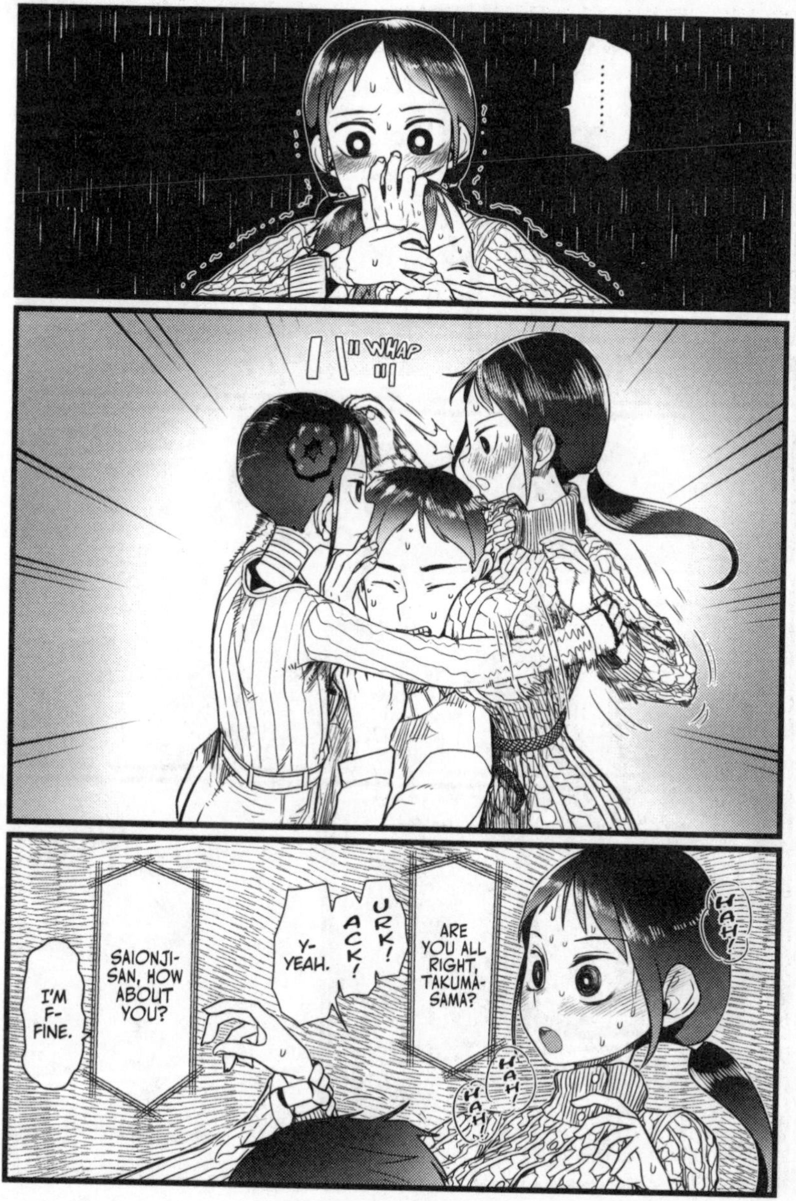
......!
WHAP
HAH!
ARE YOU ALL RIGHT, TAKUMA-SAMA?
HAH! HAH!
URK! ACK!
Y-YEAH.
SAIONJI-SAN, HOW ABOUT YOU?
I'M F-FINE.

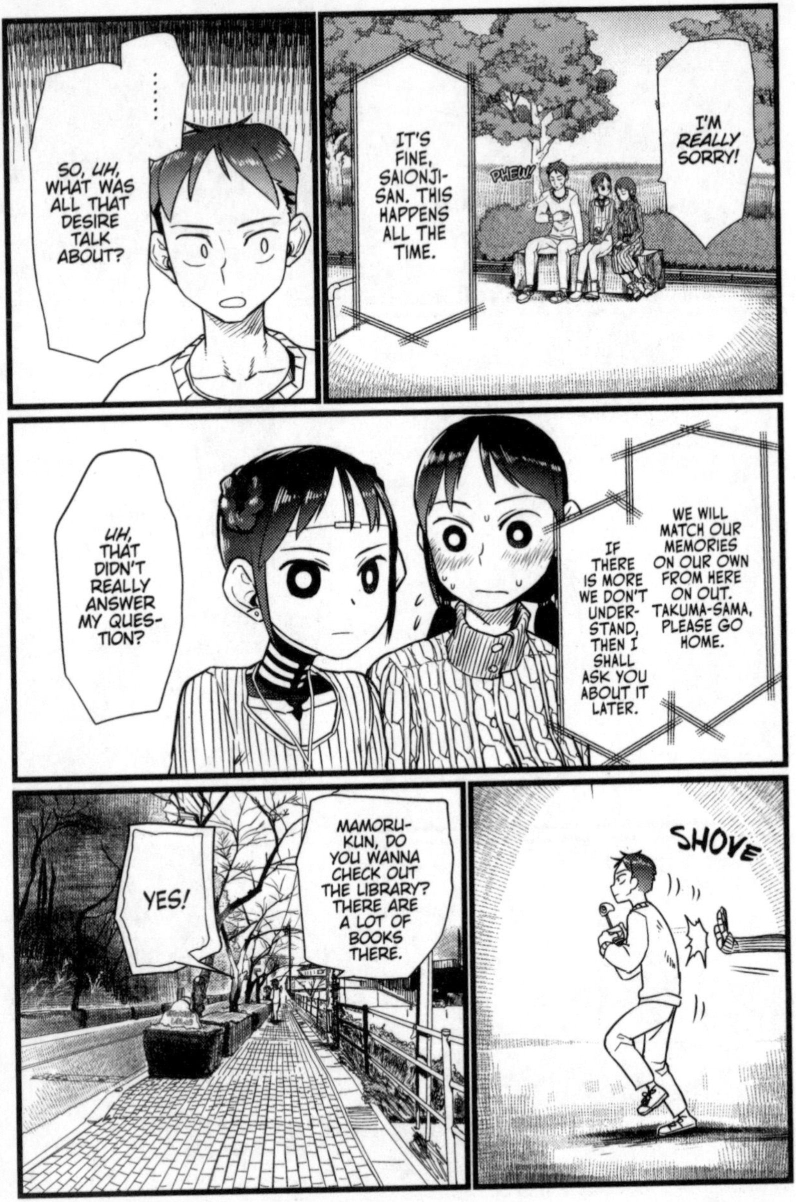
I'M REALLY SORRY!
IT'S FINE, SAIONJI-SAN. THIS HAPPENS ALL THE TIME.
PHEW!
……
SO, UH, WHAT WAS ALL THAT DESIRE TALK ABOUT?
WE WILL MATCH OUR MEMORIES ON OUR OWN FROM HERE ON OUT. TAKUMA-SAMA, PLEASE GO HOME.
IF THERE IS MORE WE DON'T UNDER-STAND, THEN I SHALL ASK YOU ABOUT IT LATER.
UH, THAT DIDN'T REALLY ANSWER MY QUES-TION?
SHOVE
MAMORU-KUN, DO YOU WANNA CHECK OUT THE LIBRARY? THERE ARE A LOT OF BOOKS THERE.
YES!

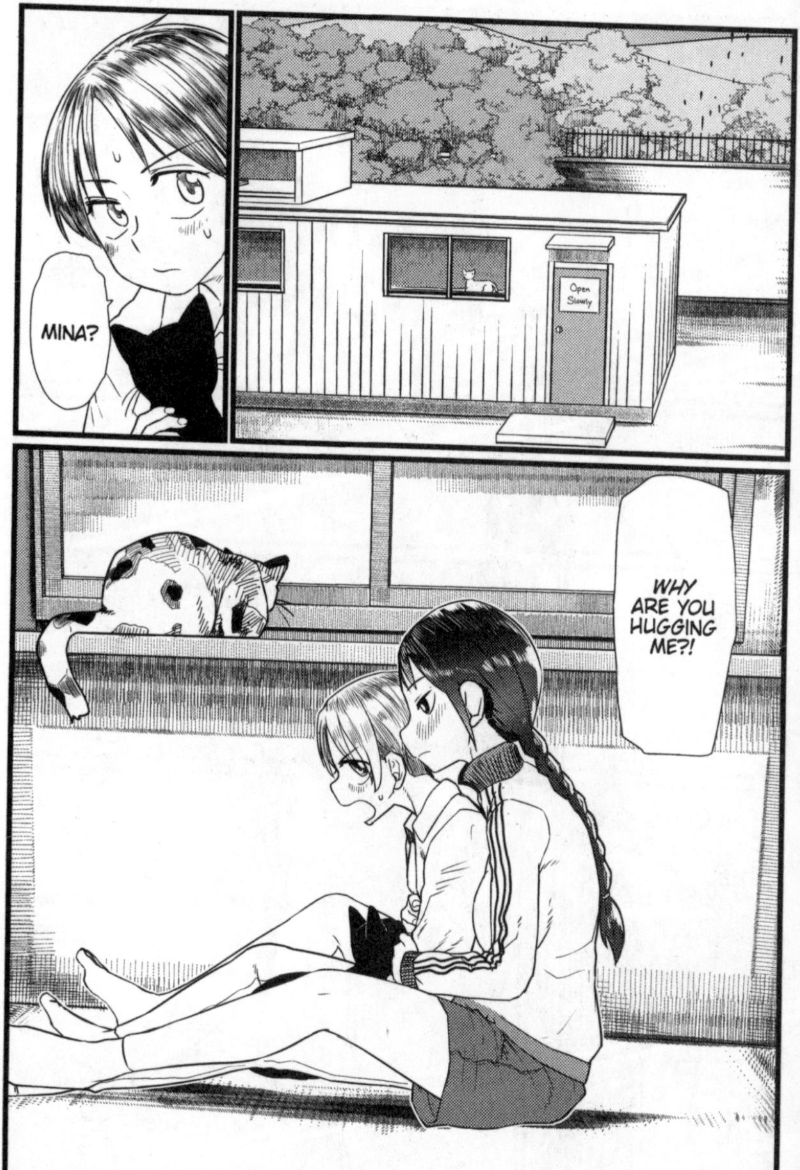
Open Slowly
MINA?
WHY ARE YOU HUGGING ME?!

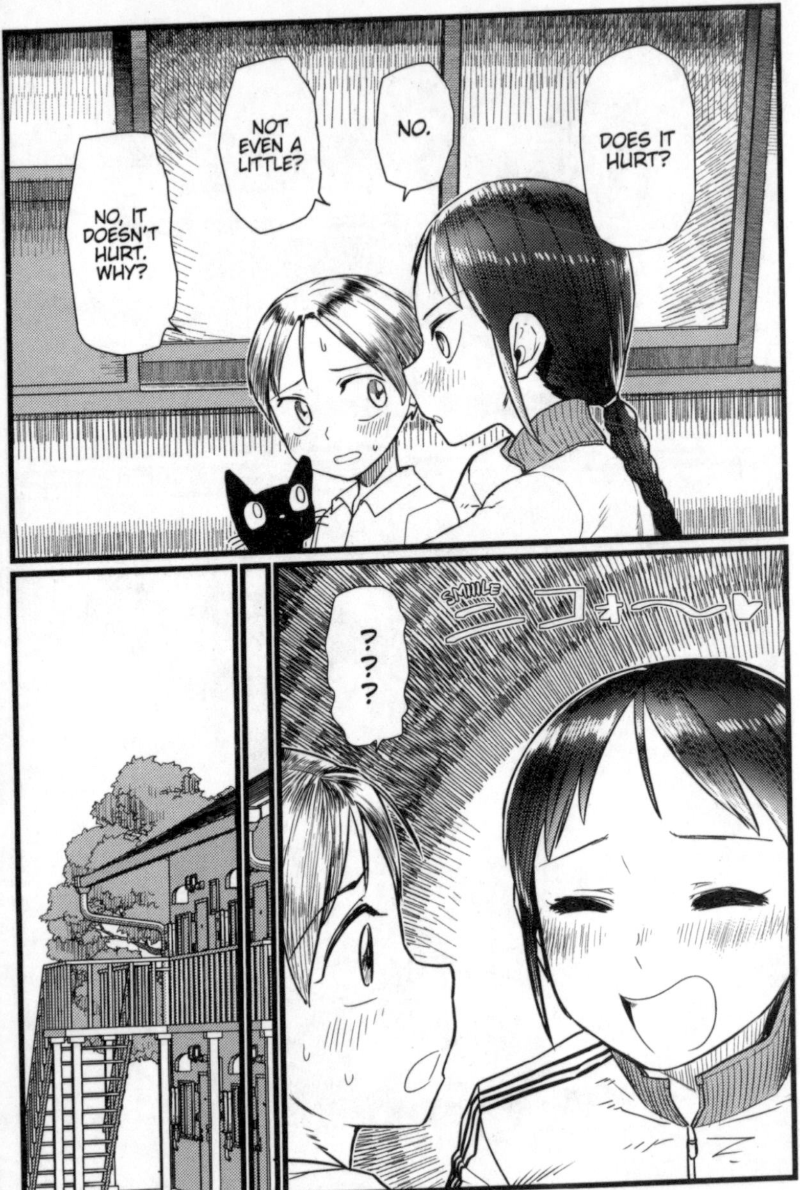
DOES IT HURT?
NO.
NOT EVEN A LITTLE?
NO, IT DOESN'T HURT. WHY?
SMIIILE
ニコォ〜
フ.フ.フ.

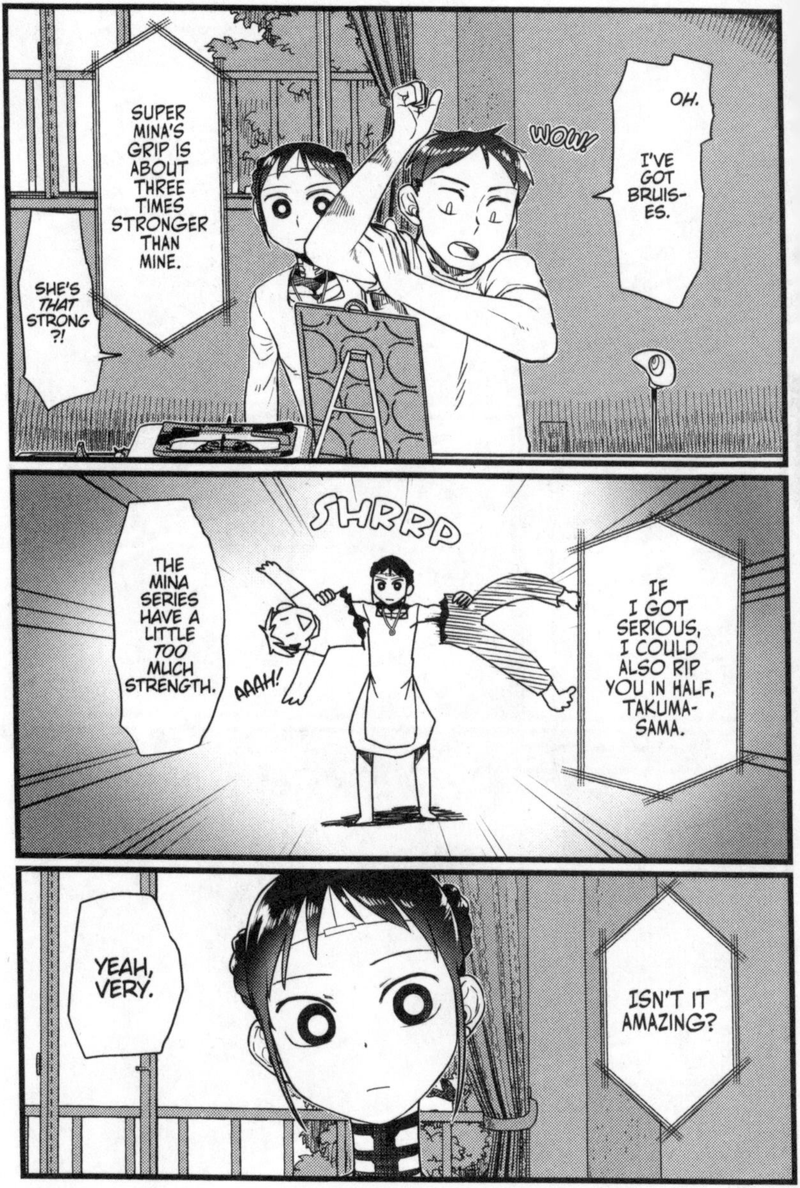
OH.
I'VE GOT BRUISES.
WOW!
SUPER MINA'S GRIP IS ABOUT THREE TIMES STRONGER THAN MINE.
SHE'S *THAT* STRONG?!
IF I GOT SERIOUS, I COULD ALSO RIP YOU IN HALF, TAKUMA-SAMA.
SHRRP
THE MINA SERIES HAVE A LITTLE *TOO* MUCH STRENGTH.
AAAH!
ISN'T IT AMAZING?
YEAH, VERY.

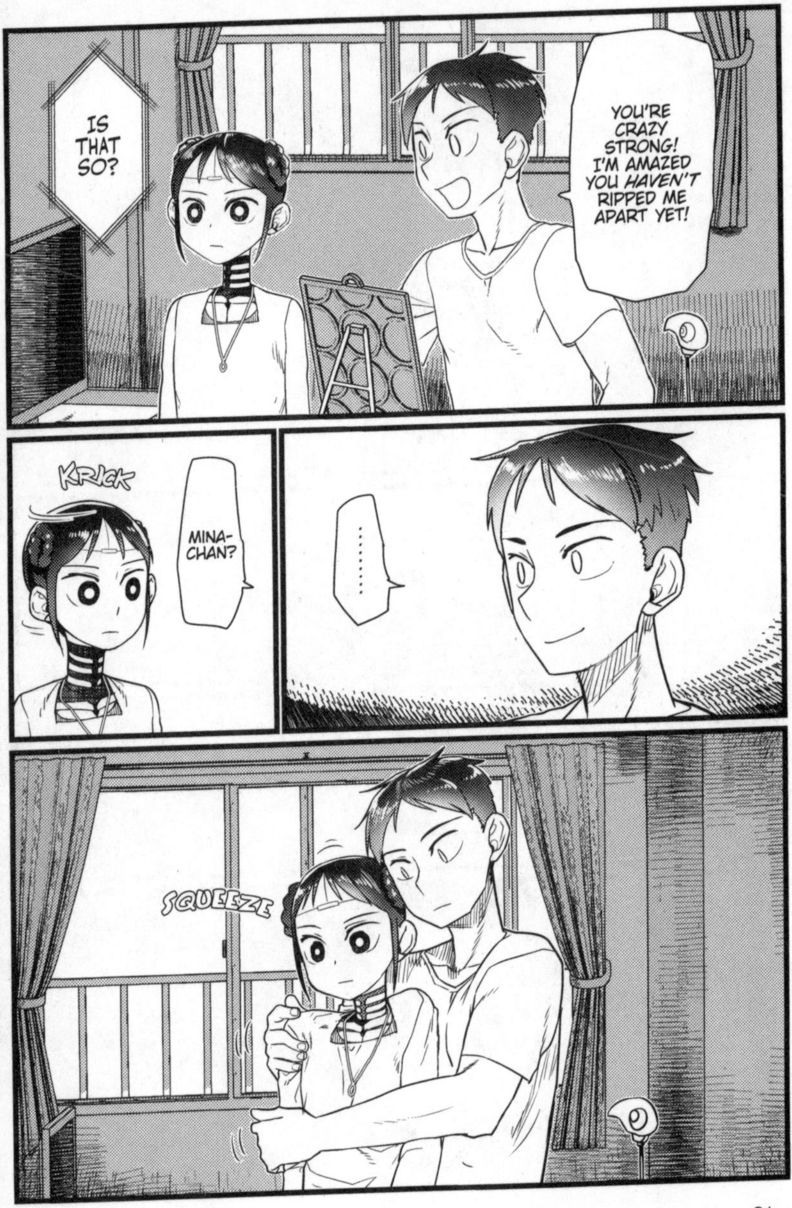
YOU'RE CRAZY STRONG! I'M AMAZED YOU HAVEN'T RIPPED ME APART YET!
IS THAT SO?
......
KRICK
MINA-CHAN?
SQUEEZE

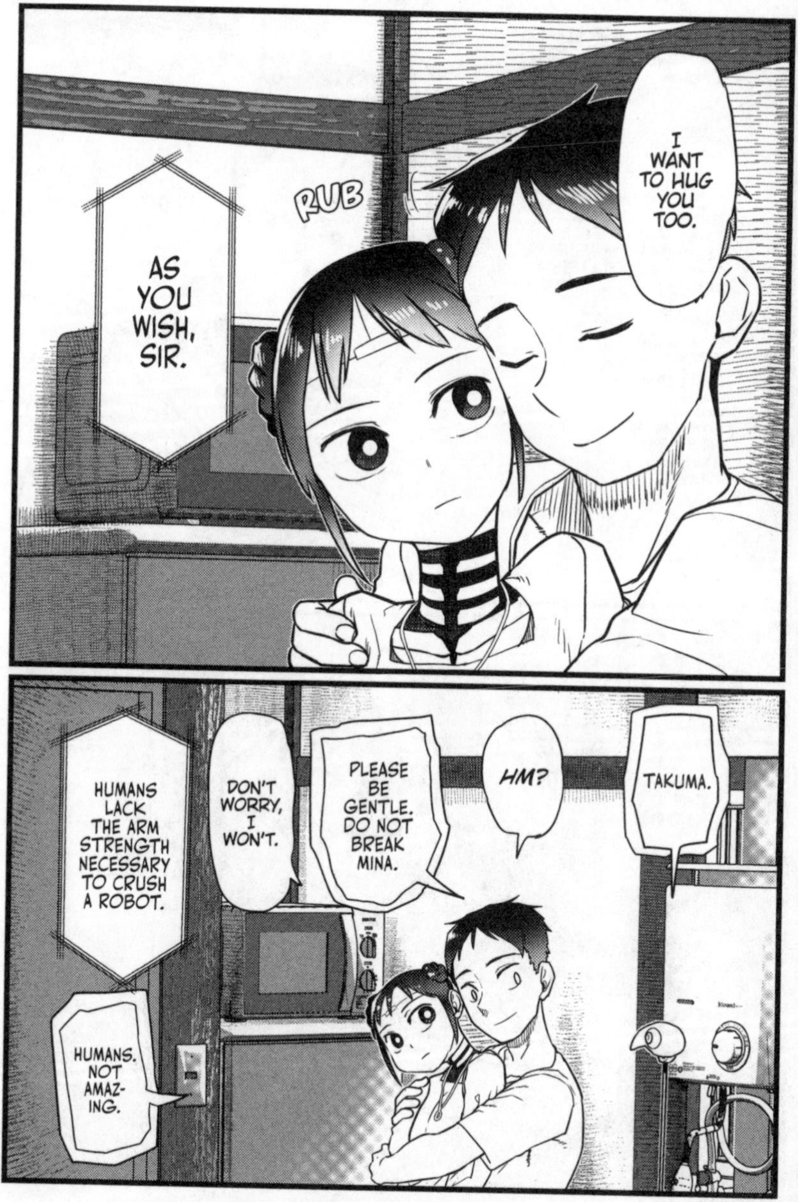
I WANT TO HUG YOU TOO.
RUB
AS YOU WISH, SIR.
TAKUMA.
HM?
PLEASE BE GENTLE. DO NOT BREAK MINA.
DON'T WORRY, I WON'T.
HUMANS LACK THE ARM STRENGTH NECESSARY TO CRUSH A ROBOT.
HUMANS. NOT AMAZING.

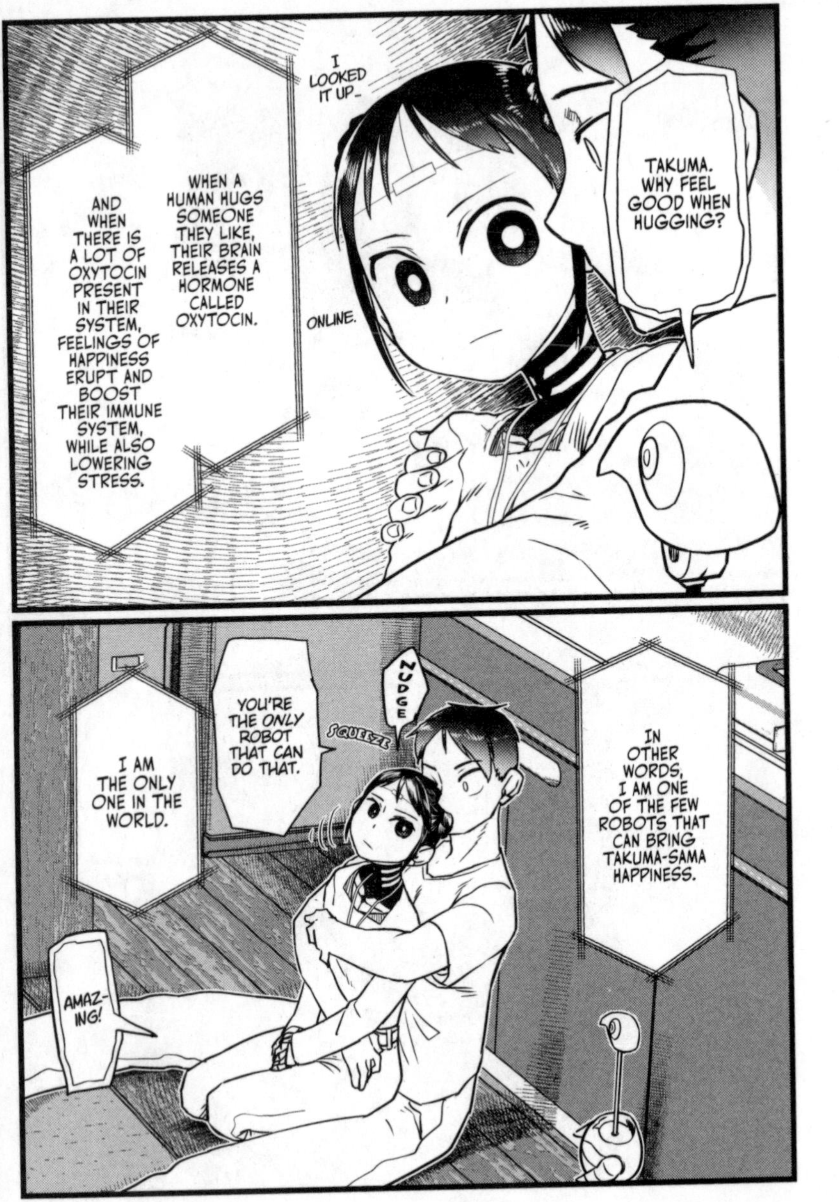
TAKUMA. WHY FEEL GOOD WHEN HUGGING?
I LOOKED IT UP...
ONLINE.
WHEN A HUMAN HUGS SOMEONE THEY LIKE, THEIR BRAIN RELEASES A HORMONE CALLED OXYTOCIN.
AND WHEN THERE IS A LOT OF OXYTOCIN PRESENT IN THEIR SYSTEM, FEELINGS OF HAPPINESS ERUPT AND BOOST THEIR IMMUNE SYSTEM, WHILE ALSO LOWERING STRESS.
IN OTHER WORDS, I AM ONE OF THE FEW ROBOTS THAT CAN BRING TAKUMA-SAMA HAPPINESS.
NUDGE
SQUEEZE
YOU'RE THE *ONLY* ROBOT THAT CAN DO THAT.
I AM THE ONLY ONE IN THE WORLD.
AMAZ-ING!

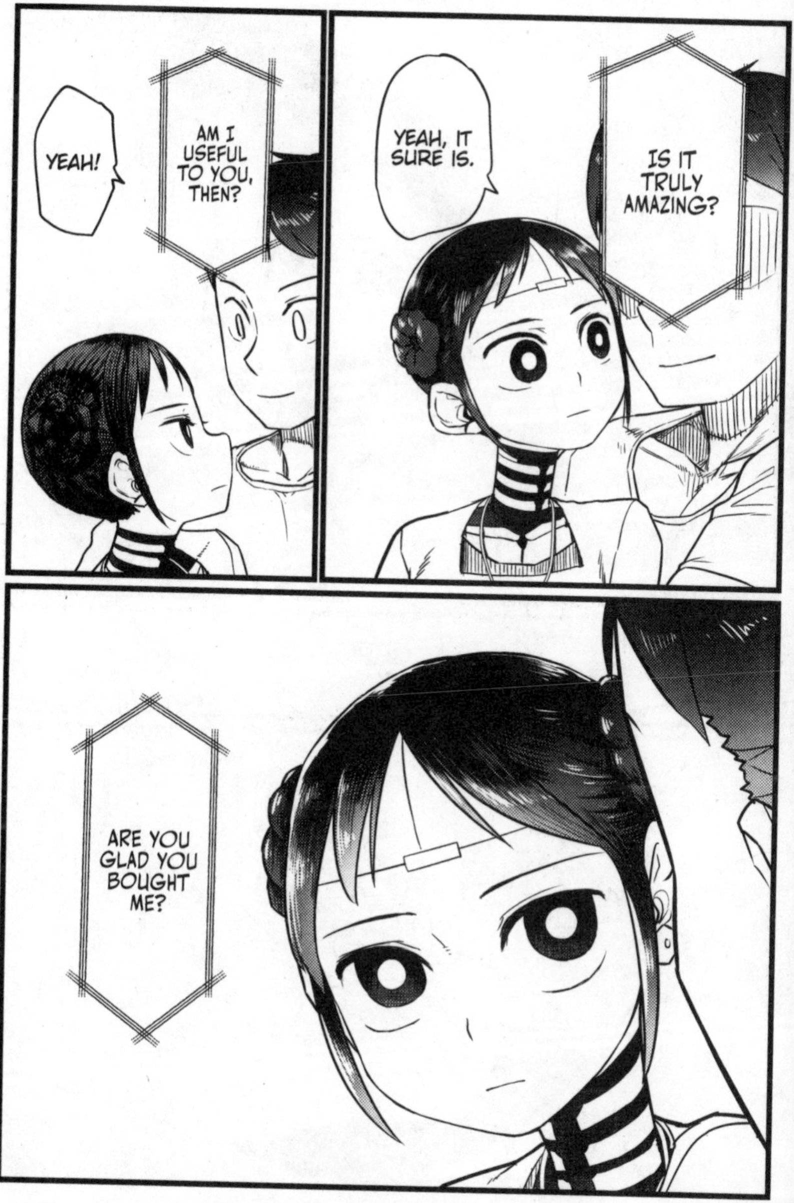
IS IT TRULY AMAZING?
YEAH, IT SURE IS.
AM I USEFUL TO YOU, THEN?
YEAH!
ARE YOU GLAD YOU BOUGHT ME?

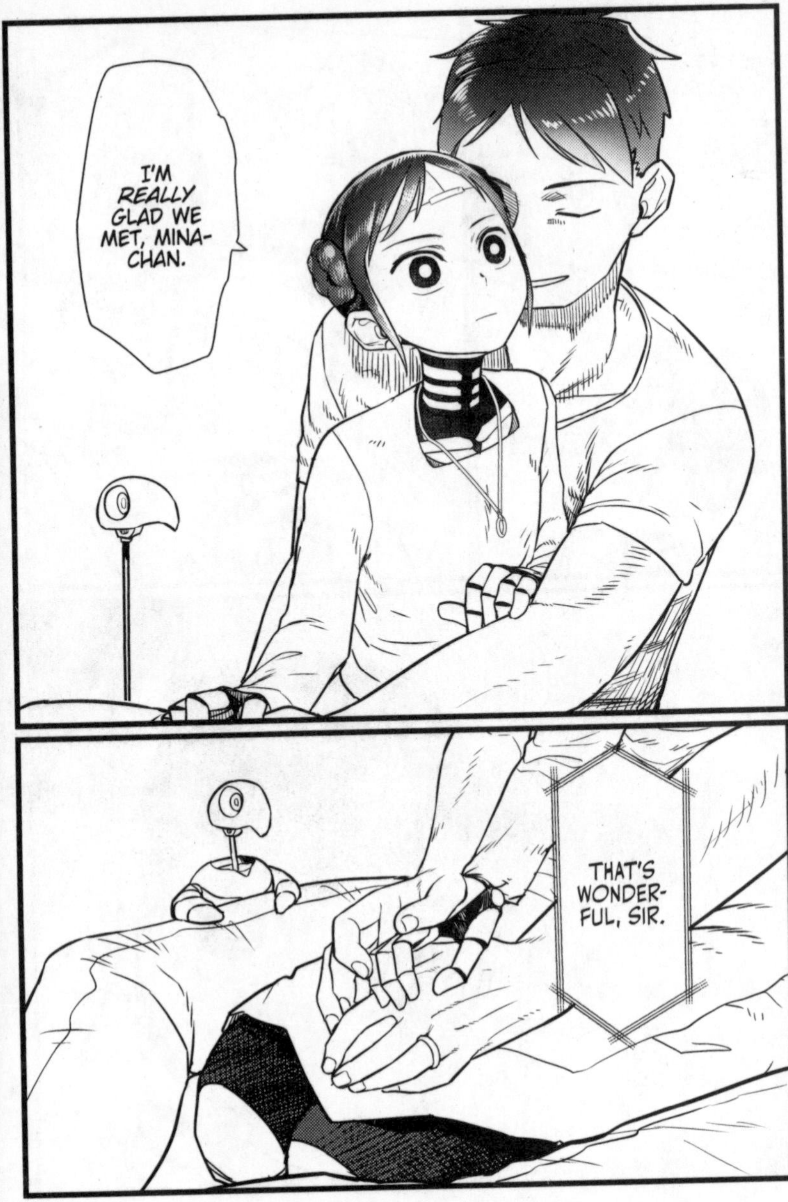
I'M *REALLY* GLAD WE MET, MINA-CHAN.
THAT'S WONDER-FUL, SIR.

A FEW DAYS LATER.

SORRY FOR ASKING YOU TO COME MEET ME SO SUDDENLY! I PROMISE I WON'T HUG YOU AGAIN.

YOU SAID YOU HAD SOMETHING FOR MY EARS ONLY?

YES. IT'S ABOUT MINA-SAN'S PAST OWNER.

WHEN OUR MEMORIES MINGLED, I SAW THEM IN MY DREAM.

!

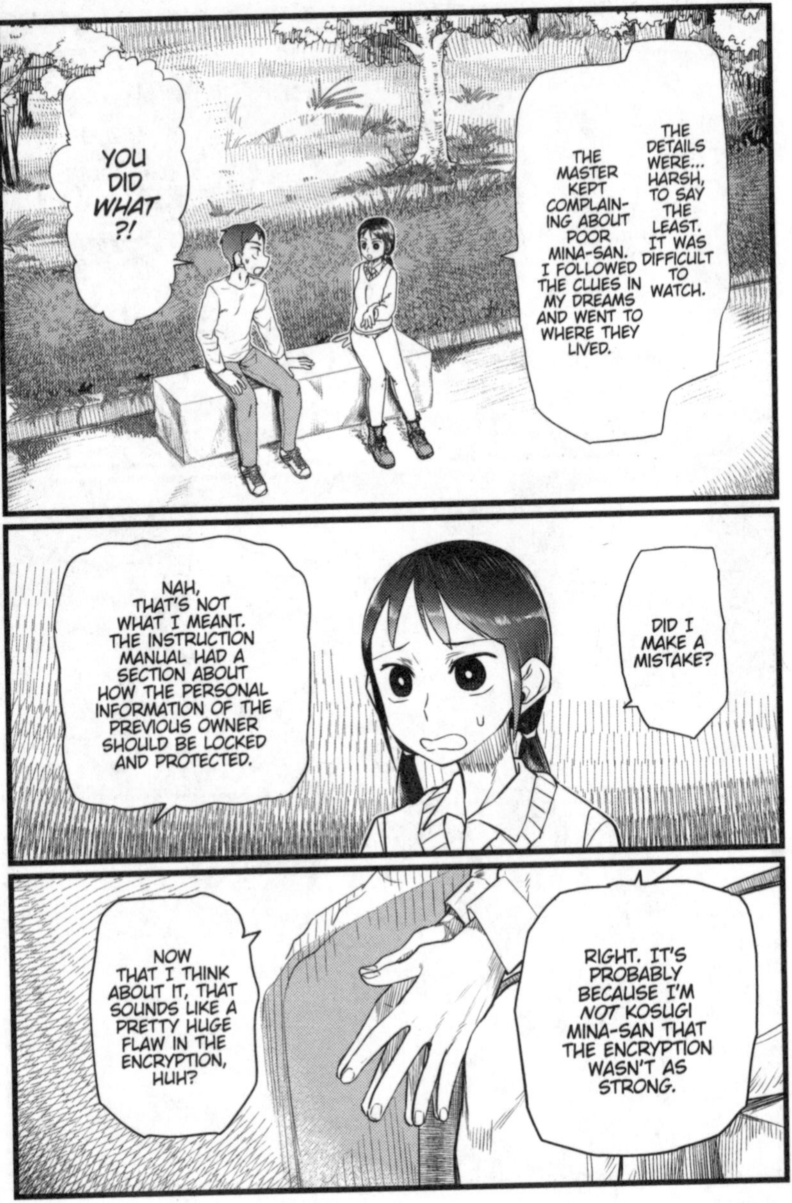
THE DETAILS WERE... HARSH, TO SAY THE LEAST. IT WAS DIFFICULT TO WATCH.
THE MASTER KEPT COMPLAINING ABOUT POOR MINA-SAN. I FOLLOWED THE CLUES IN MY DREAMS AND WENT TO WHERE THEY LIVED.
YOU DID *WHAT* ?!
DID I MAKE A MISTAKE?
NAH, THAT'S NOT WHAT I MEANT. THE INSTRUCTION MANUAL HAD A SECTION ABOUT HOW THE PERSONAL INFORMATION OF THE PREVIOUS OWNER SHOULD BE LOCKED AND PROTECTED.
RIGHT. IT'S PROBABLY BECAUSE I'M *NOT* KOSUGI MINA-SAN THAT THE ENCRYPTION WASN'T AS STRONG.
NOW THAT I THINK ABOUT IT, THAT SOUNDS LIKE A PRETTY HUGE FLAW IN THE ENCRYPTION, HUH?

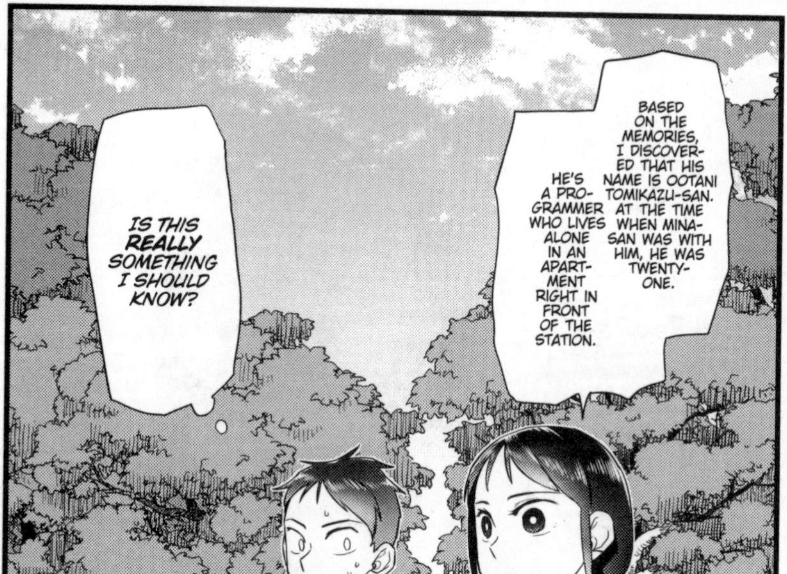
BASED ON THE MEMORIES, I DISCOVERED THAT HIS NAME IS OOTANI TOMIKAZU-SAN. AT THE TIME WHEN MINA-SAN WAS WITH HIM, HE WAS TWENTY-ONE.
HE'S A PROGRAMMER WHO LIVES ALONE IN AN APARTMENT RIGHT IN FRONT OF THE STATION.
IS THIS **REALLY** SOMETHING I SHOULD KNOW?
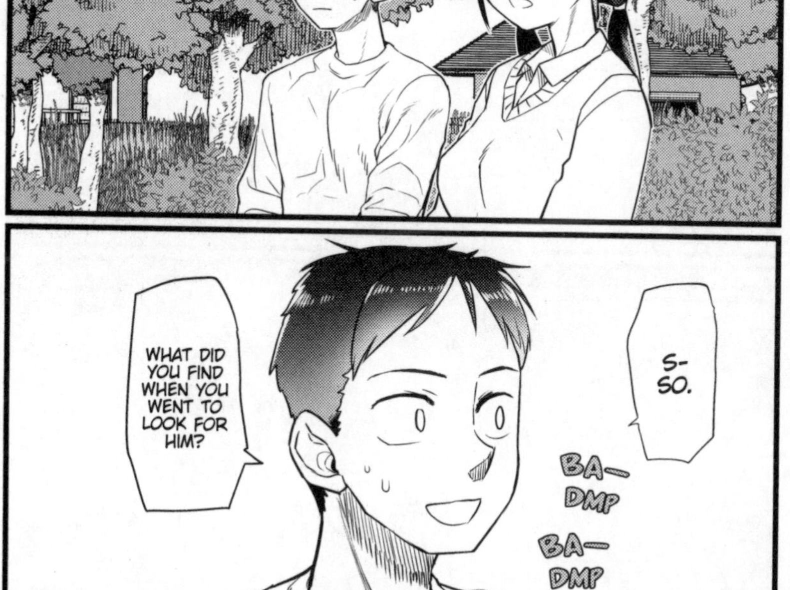
S-SO.
WHAT DID YOU FIND WHEN YOU WENT TO LOOK FOR HIM?
BA-DMP
BA-DMP

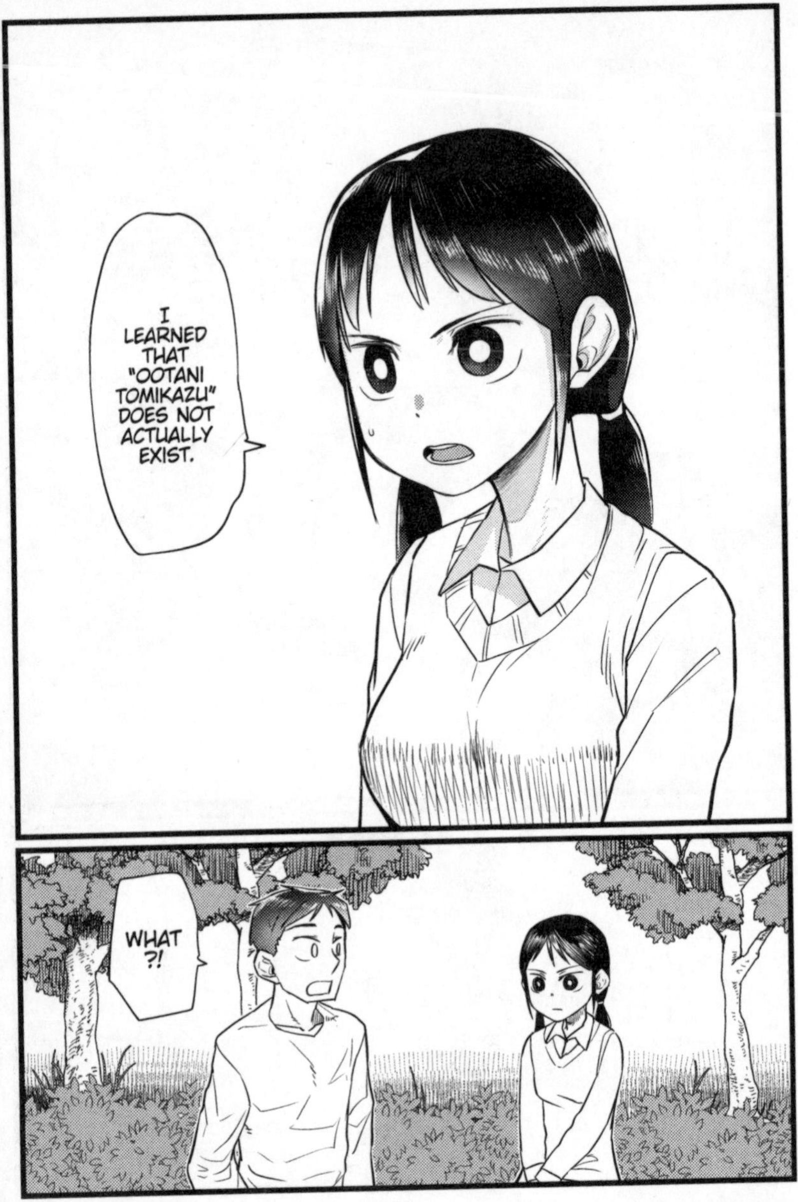
I LEARNED THAT "OOTANI TOMIKAZU" DOES NOT ACTUALLY EXIST.
WHAT ?!

➡ CHAPTER 18 END ♥

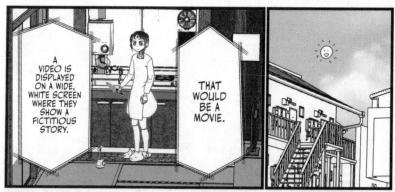

➡ CHAPTER 19

THAT WOULD BE A MOVIE.
A VIDEO IS DISPLAYED ON A WIDE, WHITE SCREEN WHERE THEY SHOW A FICTITIOUS STORY.
IT IS MERELY A LARGE DISPLAY CREATED BY THE PROJECTOR. THERE ARE NO ACTUAL TITANS OR GIANT HUMANS IN REAL LIFE.
SHWF
SHWF
THE EXISTENCE OF ALIENS HAS ALSO NOT BEEN CONFIRMED AS OF YET.
HEEE.
...
ROBOTS WHO HAVE NOT UNDERGONE THE INTELLIGENCE TEST ARE NOT ALLOWED IN THE THEATER.
MAMORU, YOU MUST APOLOGIZE. AND AFTER YOU DO, WE SHALL REFORMAT YOUR MEMORY.
HMM-MGH!
SHWOOK

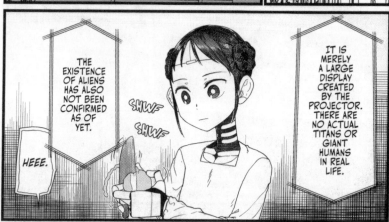

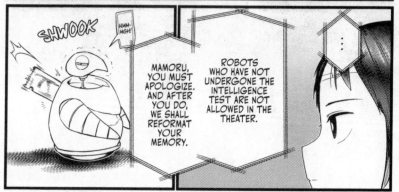

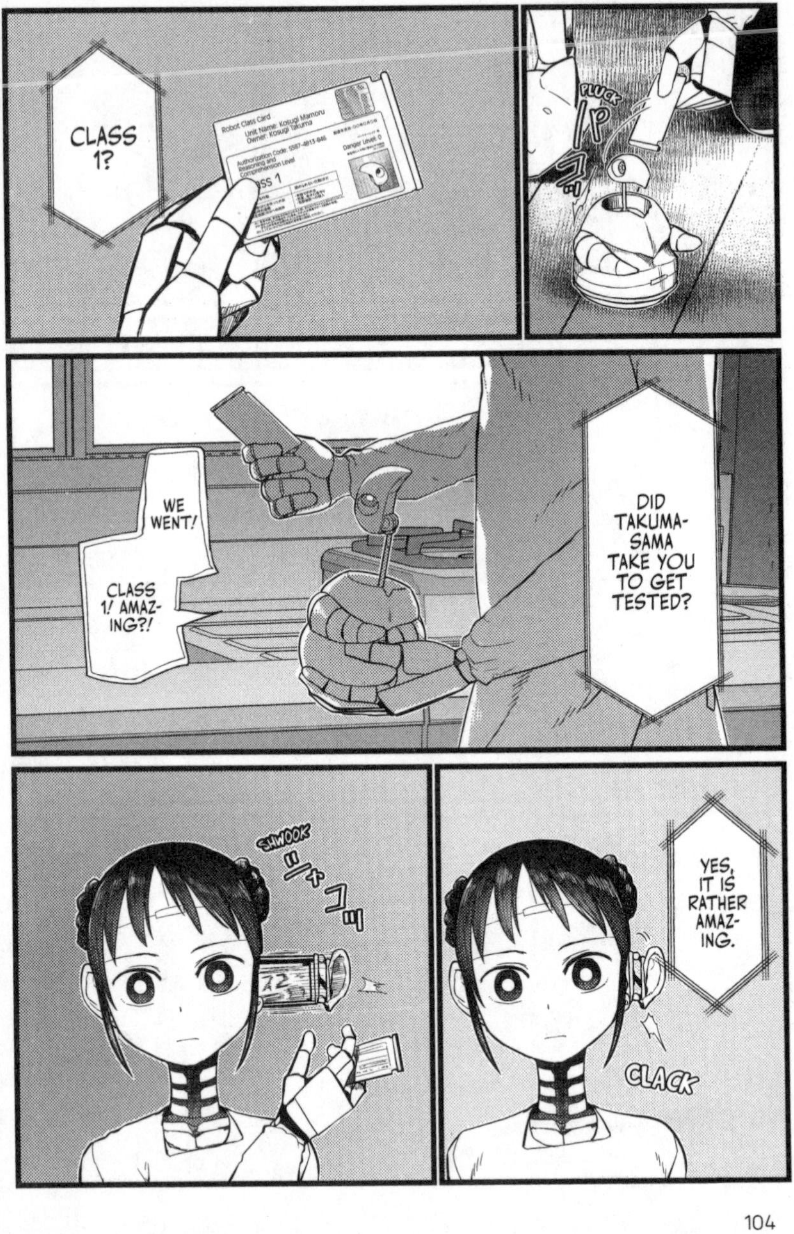
PLUCK
CLASS 1?
Robot Class Card
Unit Name: Kosugi Mamoru
Owner: Kosugi Takuma
Authorization Code:
Reasoning and Comprehension Level
Danger Level: 0
DID TAKUMA-SAMA TAKE YOU TO GET TESTED?
WE WENT!
CLASS 1! AMAZ-ING?!
YES, IT IS RATHER AMAZ-ING.
CLACK
SHWOOK

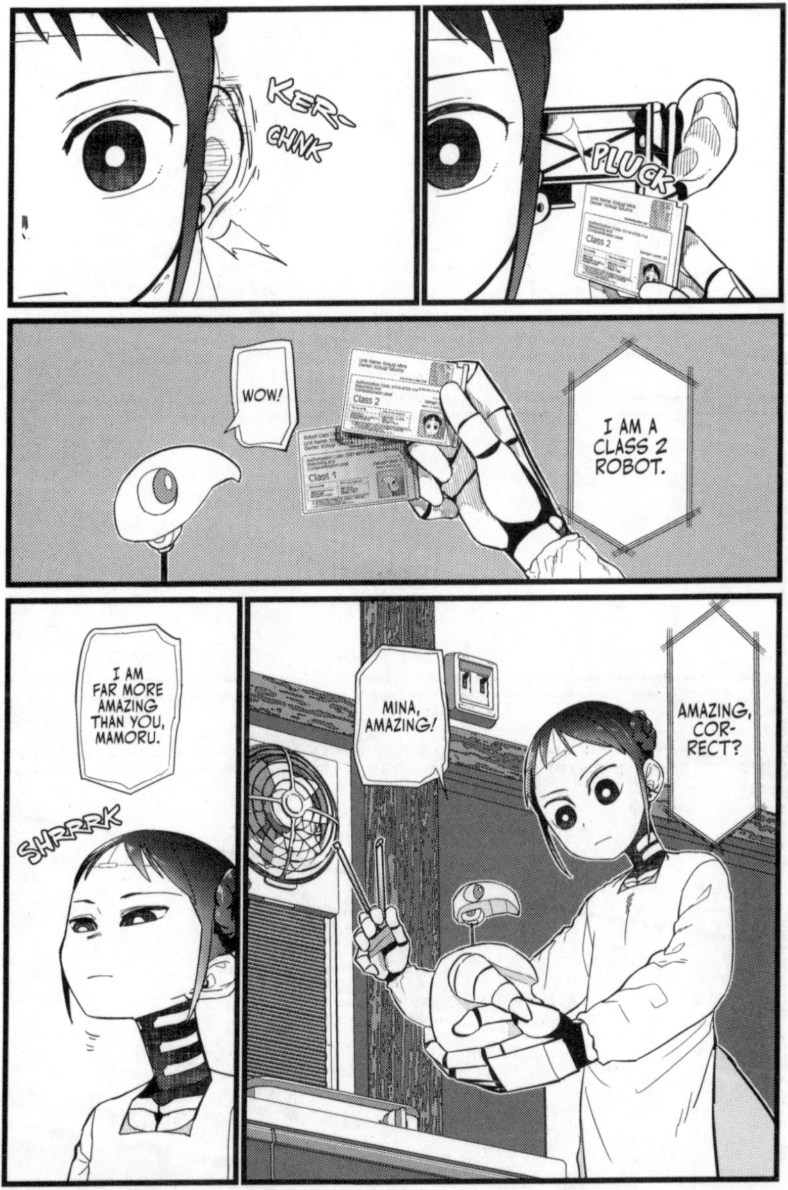
PLUCK
Class 2
KER-CHNK
I AM A CLASS 2 ROBOT.
WOW!
Class 2
Class 1
AMAZING, CORRECT?
MINA, AMAZING!
I AM FAR MORE AMAZING THAN YOU, MAMORU.
SHRRRK

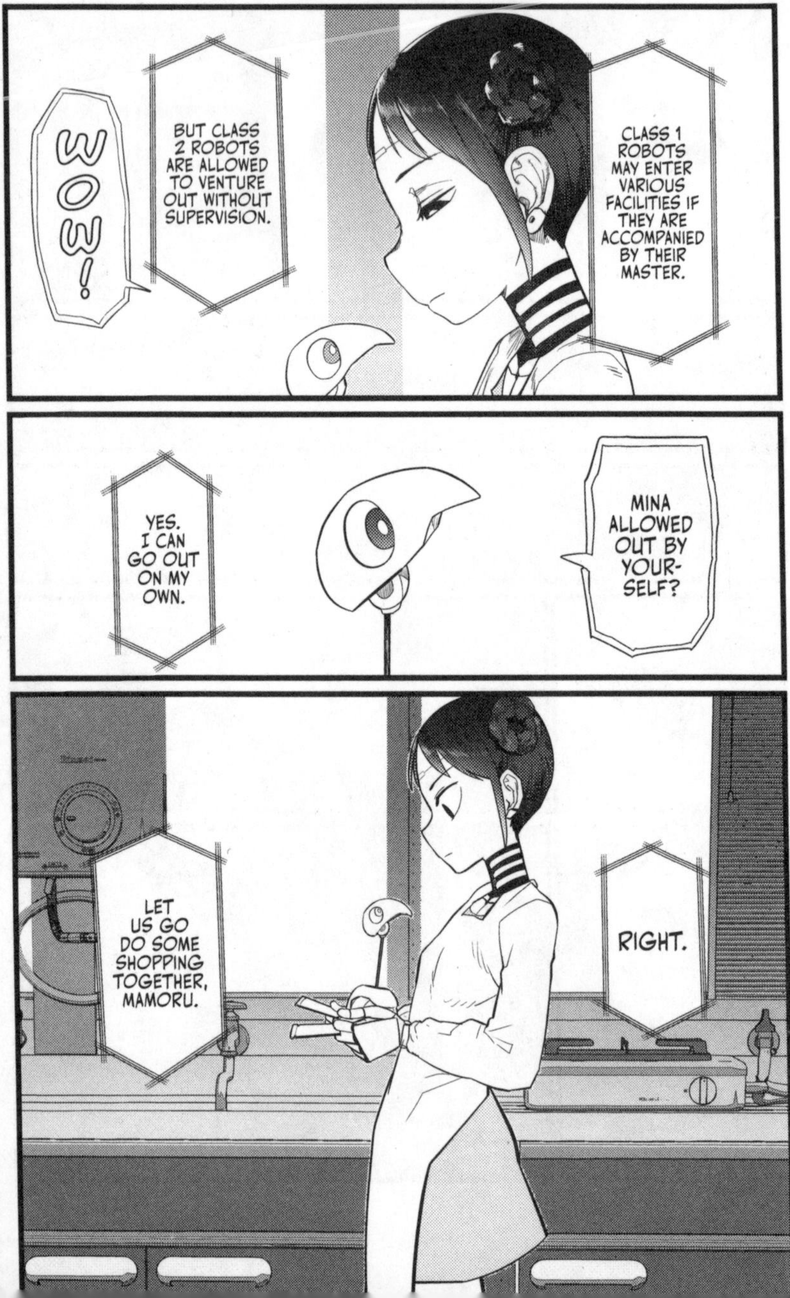
CLASS 1 ROBOTS MAY ENTER VARIOUS FACILITIES IF THEY ARE ACCOMPANIED BY THEIR MASTER.
BUT CLASS 2 ROBOTS ARE ALLOWED TO VENTURE OUT WITHOUT SUPERVISION.
WOW!
MINA ALLOWED OUT BY YOUR-SELF?
YES. I CAN GO OUT ON MY OWN.
RIGHT.
LET US GO DO SOME SHOPPING TOGETHER, MAMORU.

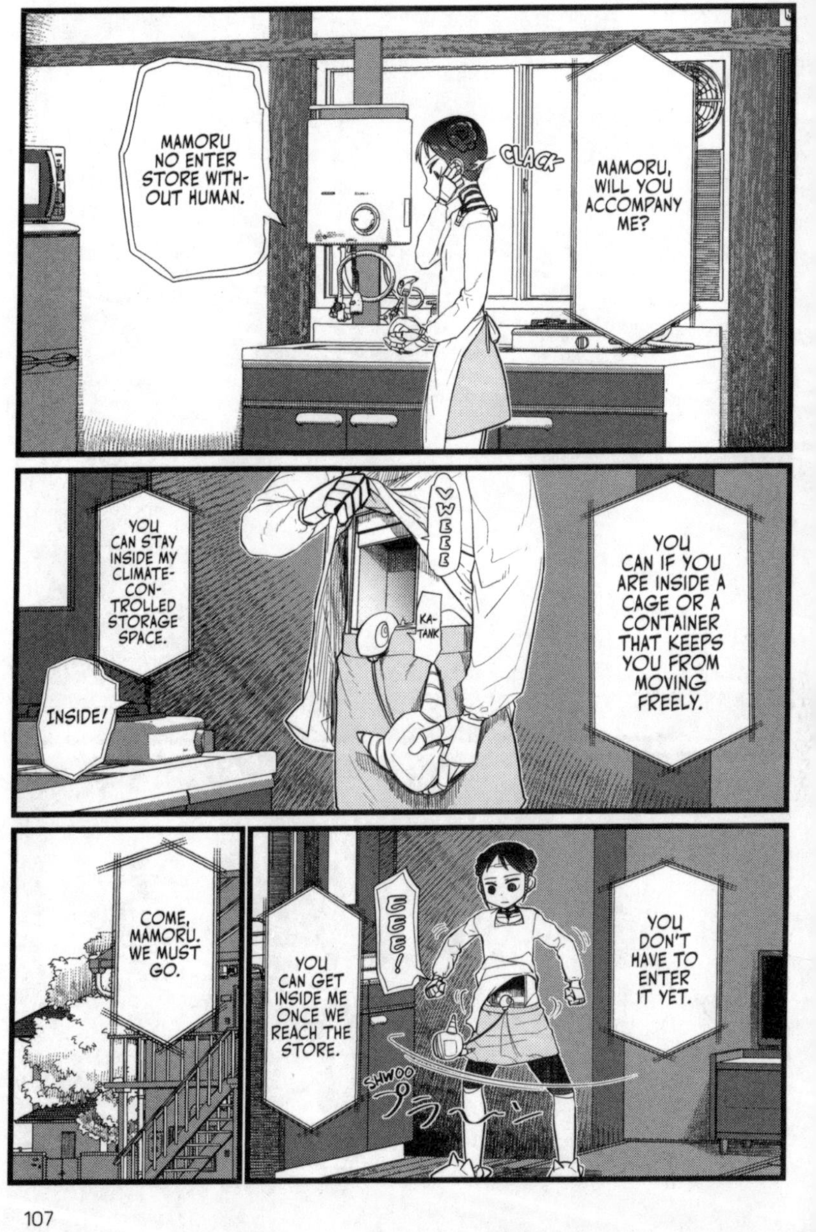
MAMORU, WILL YOU ACCOMPANY ME?
CLACK
MAMORU NO ENTER STORE WITHOUT HUMAN.
YOU CAN IF YOU ARE INSIDE A CAGE OR A CONTAINER THAT KEEPS YOU FROM MOVING FREELY.
VWEEE
KA-TANK
YOU CAN STAY INSIDE MY CLIMATE-CONTROLLED STORAGE SPACE.
INSIDE!
YOU DON'T HAVE TO ENTER IT YET.
EEE!
YOU CAN GET INSIDE ME ONCE WE REACH THE STORE.
SHWOO
COME, MAMORU. WE MUST GO.

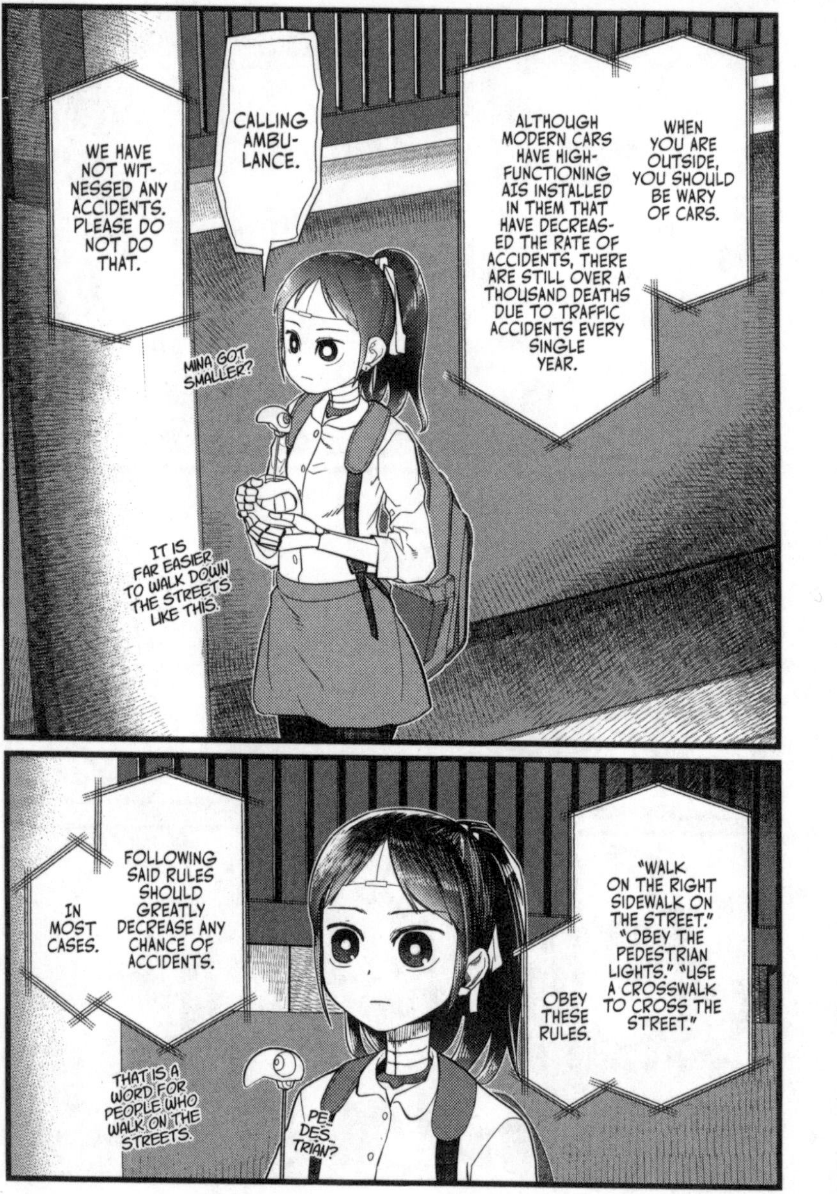
WHEN YOU ARE OUTSIDE, YOU SHOULD BE WARY OF CARS.
ALTHOUGH MODERN CARS HAVE HIGH-FUNCTIONING AIS INSTALLED IN THEM THAT HAVE DECREASED THE RATE OF ACCIDENTS, THERE ARE STILL OVER A THOUSAND DEATHS DUE TO TRAFFIC ACCIDENTS EVERY SINGLE YEAR.
CALLING AMBULANCE.
WE HAVE NOT WITNESSED ANY ACCIDENTS. PLEASE DO NOT DO THAT.
MINA GOT SMALLER?
IT IS FAR EASIER TO WALK DOWN THE STREETS LIKE THIS.
"WALK ON THE RIGHT SIDEWALK ON THE STREET." "OBEY THE PEDESTRIAN LIGHTS." "USE A CROSSWALK TO CROSS THE STREET."
OBEY THESE RULES.
FOLLOWING SAID RULES SHOULD GREATLY DECREASE ANY CHANCE OF ACCIDENTS.
IN MOST CASES.
PEDESTRIAN?
THAT IS A WORD FOR PEOPLE WHO WALK ON THE STREETS.

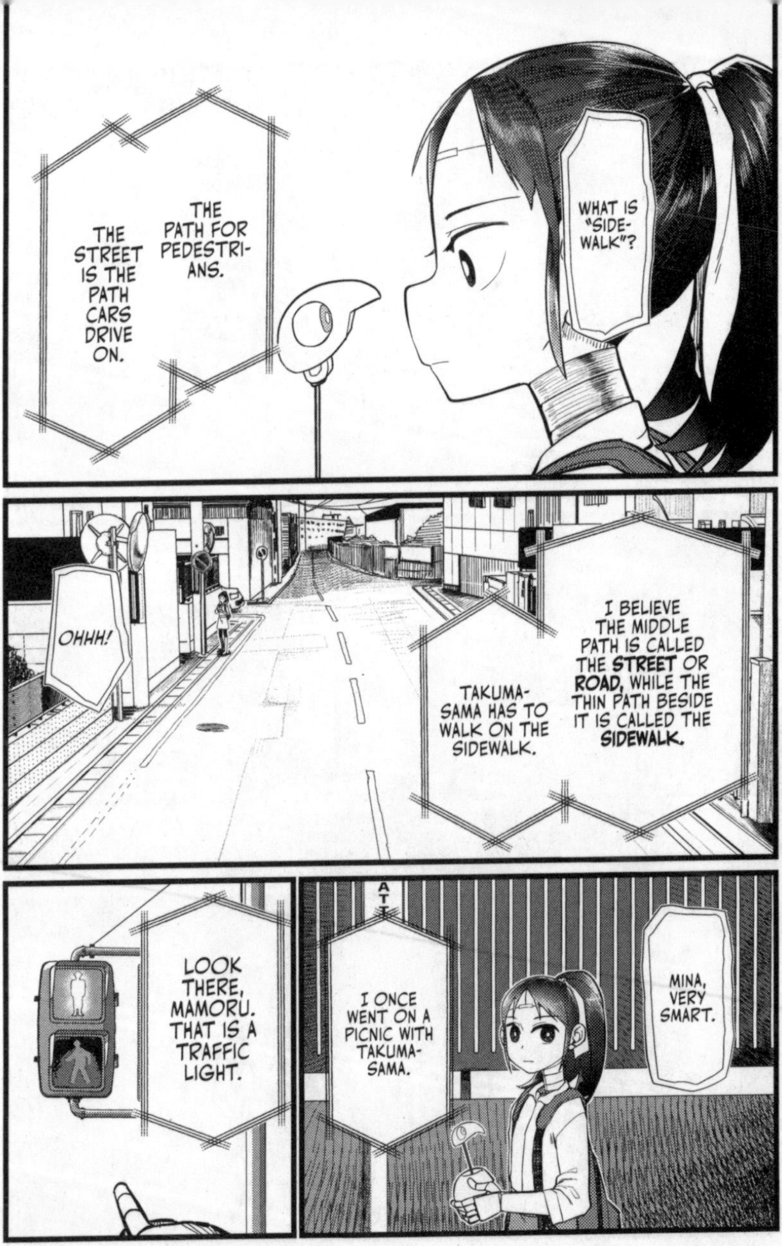
WHAT IS "SIDE-WALK"?
THE PATH FOR PEDESTRI-ANS.
THE STREET IS THE PATH CARS DRIVE ON.
I BELIEVE THE MIDDLE PATH IS CALLED THE **STREET** OR **ROAD**, WHILE THE THIN PATH BESIDE IT IS CALLED THE **SIDEWALK**.
TAKUMA-SAMA HAS TO WALK ON THE SIDEWALK.
OHHH!
MINA, VERY SMART.
I ONCE WENT ON A PICNIC WITH TAKUMA-SAMA.
LOOK THERE, MAMORU. THAT IS A TRAFFIC LIGHT.

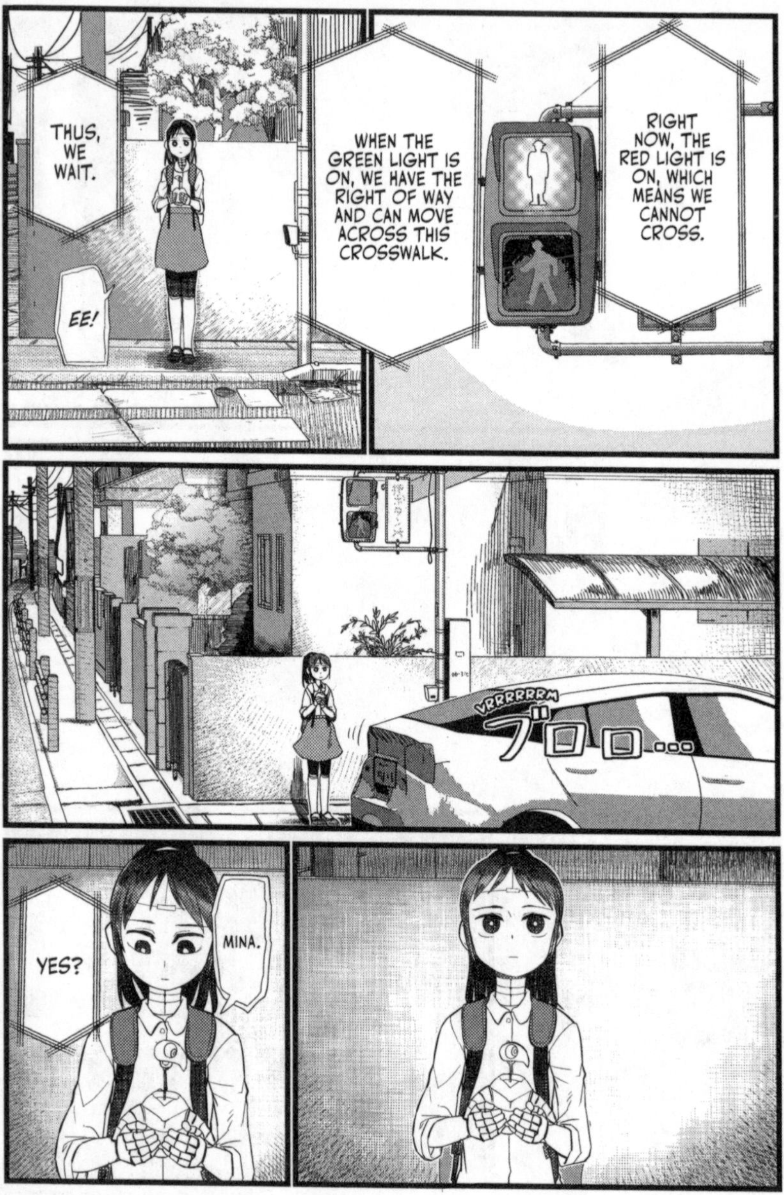
RIGHT NOW, THE RED LIGHT IS ON, WHICH MEANS WE CANNOT CROSS.
WHEN THE GREEN LIGHT IS ON, WE HAVE THE RIGHT OF WAY AND CAN MOVE ACROSS THIS CROSSWALK.
THUS, WE WAIT.
EE!
VRRRRRRM
ブロロ...
MINA.
YES?

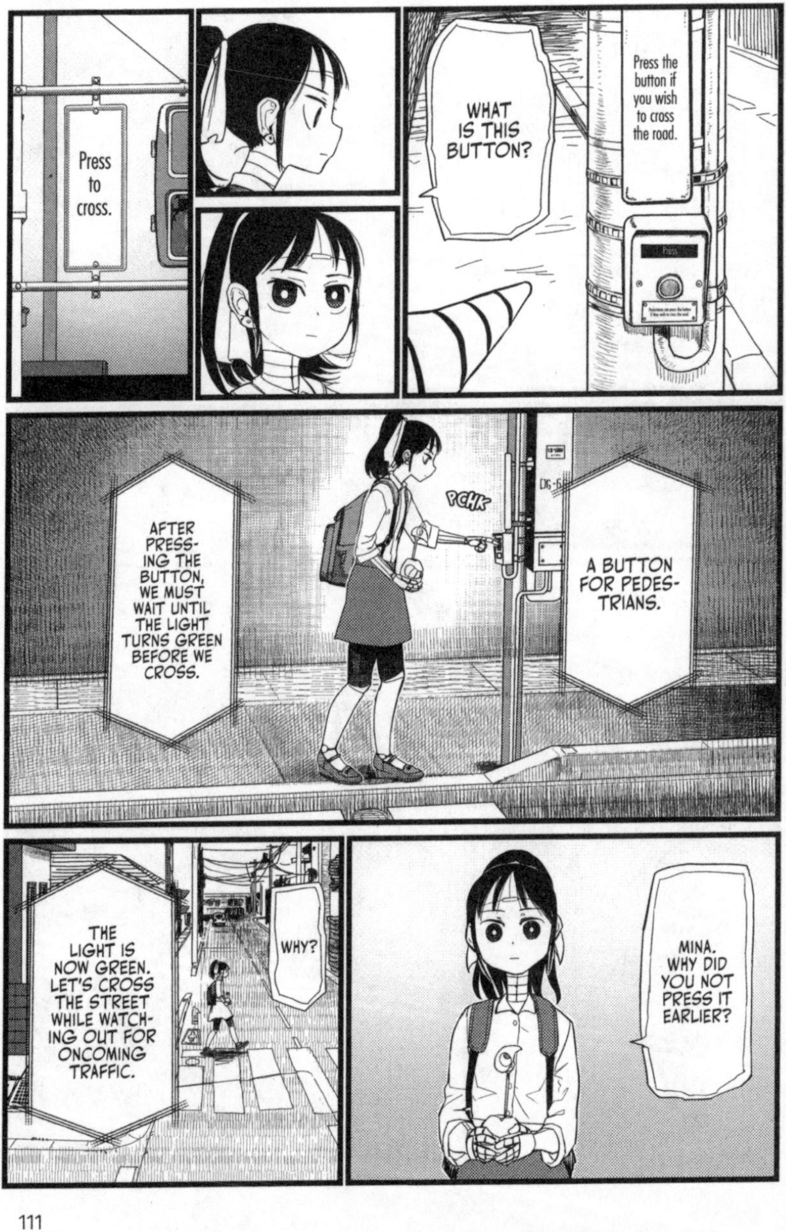
Press the button if you wish to cross the road.
WHAT IS THIS BUTTON?
Press
Press to cross.
A BUTTON FOR PEDESTRIANS.
PCHK
AFTER PRESSING THE BUTTON, WE MUST WAIT UNTIL THE LIGHT TURNS GREEN BEFORE WE CROSS.
MINA. WHY DID YOU NOT PRESS IT EARLIER?
WHY?
THE LIGHT IS NOW GREEN. LET'S CROSS THE STREET WHILE WATCHING OUT FOR ONCOMING TRAFFIC.

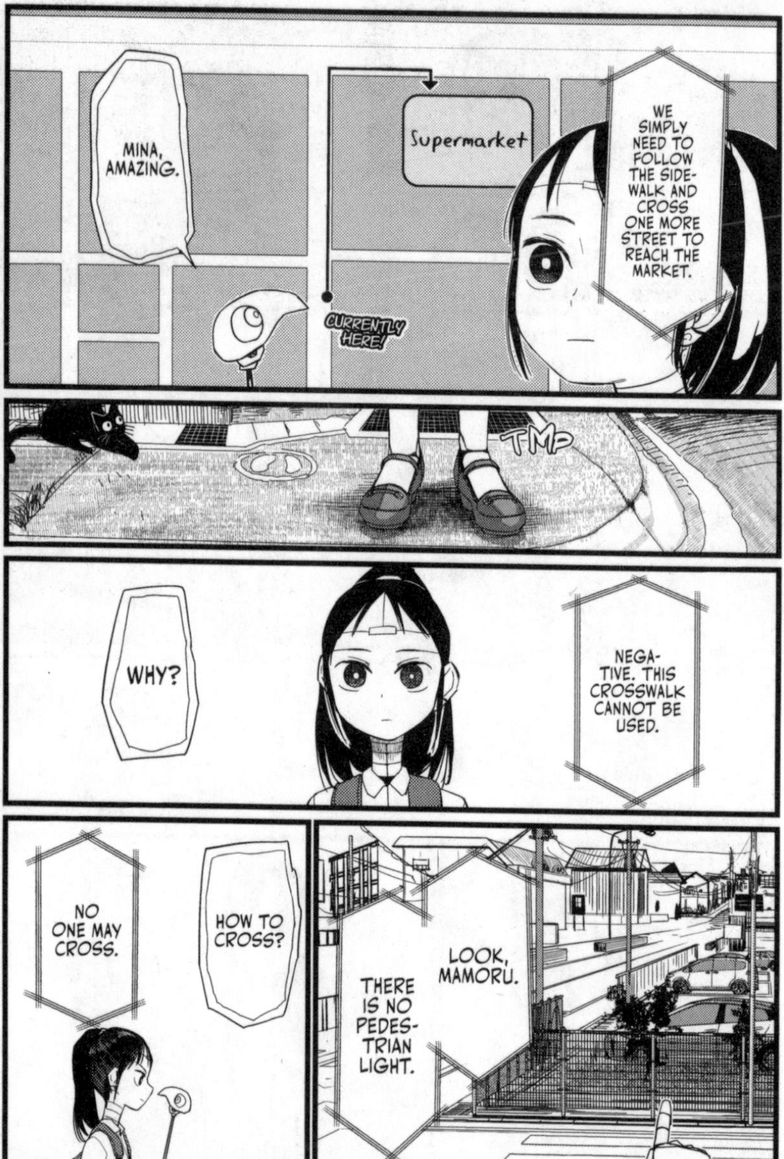
WE SIMPLY NEED TO FOLLOW THE SIDE-WALK AND CROSS ONE MORE STREET TO REACH THE MARKET.
Supermarket
CURRENTLY HERE!
MINA, AMAZING.
TMP
NEGA-TIVE. THIS CROSSWALK CANNOT BE USED.
WHY?
LOOK, MAMORU.
THERE IS NO PEDES-TRIAN LIGHT.
HOW TO CROSS?
NO ONE MAY CROSS.

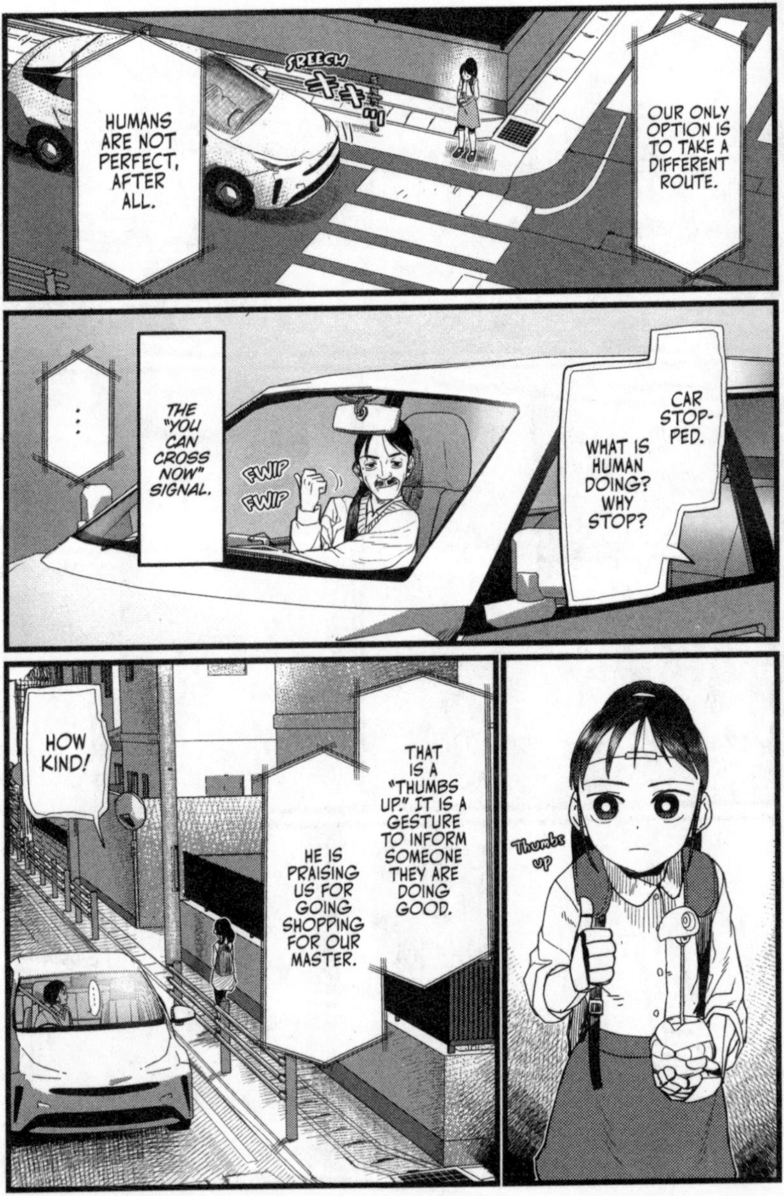
OUR ONLY OPTION IS TO TAKE A DIFFERENT ROUTE.
SREECH
キキーッ
HUMANS ARE NOT PERFECT, AFTER ALL.
CAR STOP-PED.
WHAT IS HUMAN DOING? WHY STOP?
THE "YOU CAN CROSS NOW" SIGNAL.
FWIP FWIP
...
Thumbs up
THAT IS A "THUMBS UP." IT IS A GESTURE TO INFORM SOMEONE THEY ARE DOING GOOD.
HE IS PRAISING US FOR GOING SHOPPING FOR OUR MASTER.
HOW KIND!
...

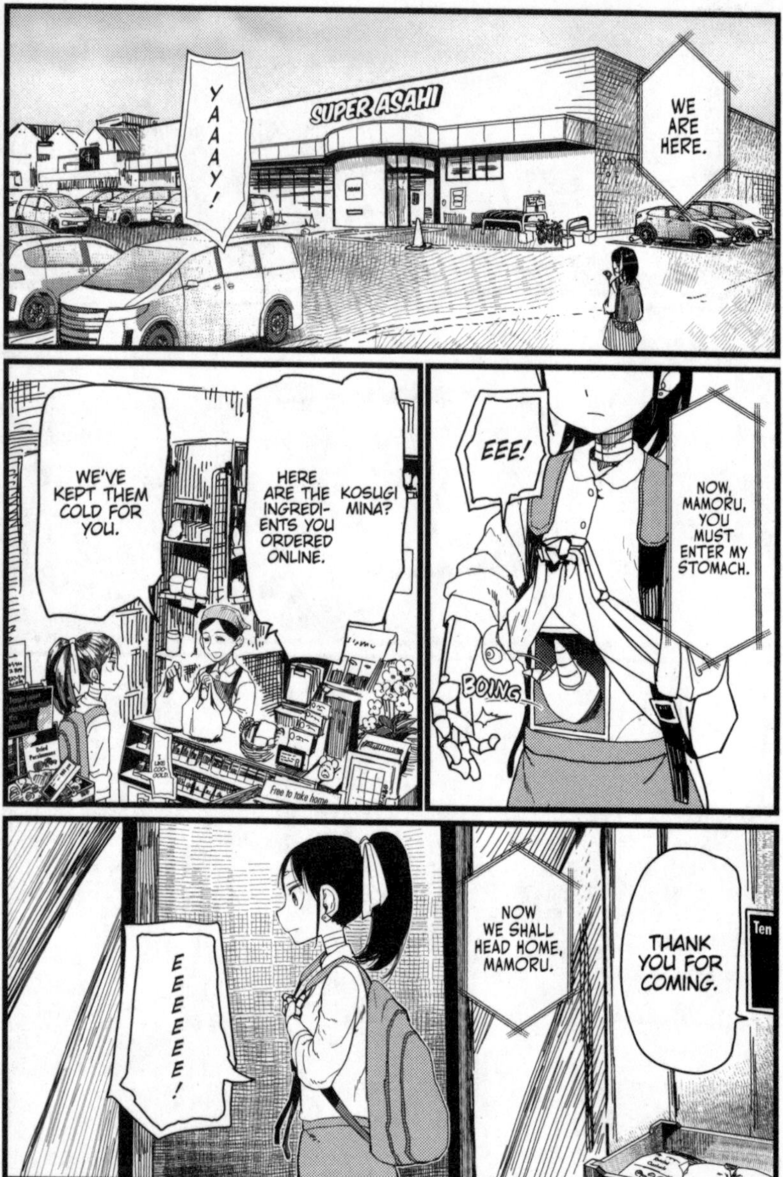
SUPER ASAHI
WE ARE HERE.
YAAAAY!
NOW, MAMORU, YOU MUST ENTER MY STOMACH.
EEE!
BOING
KOSUGI MINA?
HERE ARE THE INGREDIENTS YOU ORDERED ONLINE.
WE'VE KEPT THEM COLD FOR YOU.
Free to take home
Ten
THANK YOU FOR COMING.
NOW WE SHALL HEAD HOME, MAMORU.
EEEEEEE!

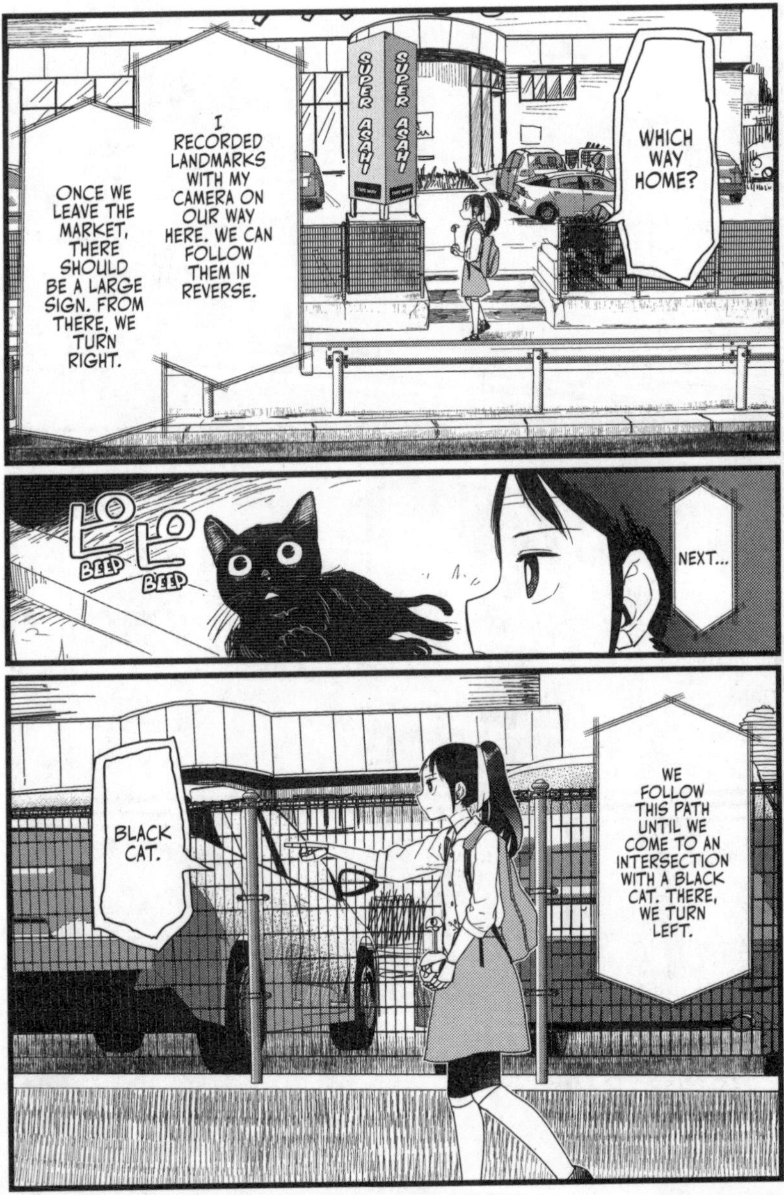
WHICH WAY HOME?
SUPER ASAHI
SUPER ASAHI
I RECORDED LANDMARKS WITH MY CAMERA ON OUR WAY HERE. WE CAN FOLLOW THEM IN REVERSE.
ONCE WE LEAVE THE MARKET, THERE SHOULD BE A LARGE SIGN. FROM THERE, WE TURN RIGHT.
NEXT...
ピ BEEP
ピ BEEP
WE FOLLOW THIS PATH UNTIL WE COME TO AN INTERSECTION WITH A BLACK CAT. THERE, WE TURN LEFT.
BLACK CAT.

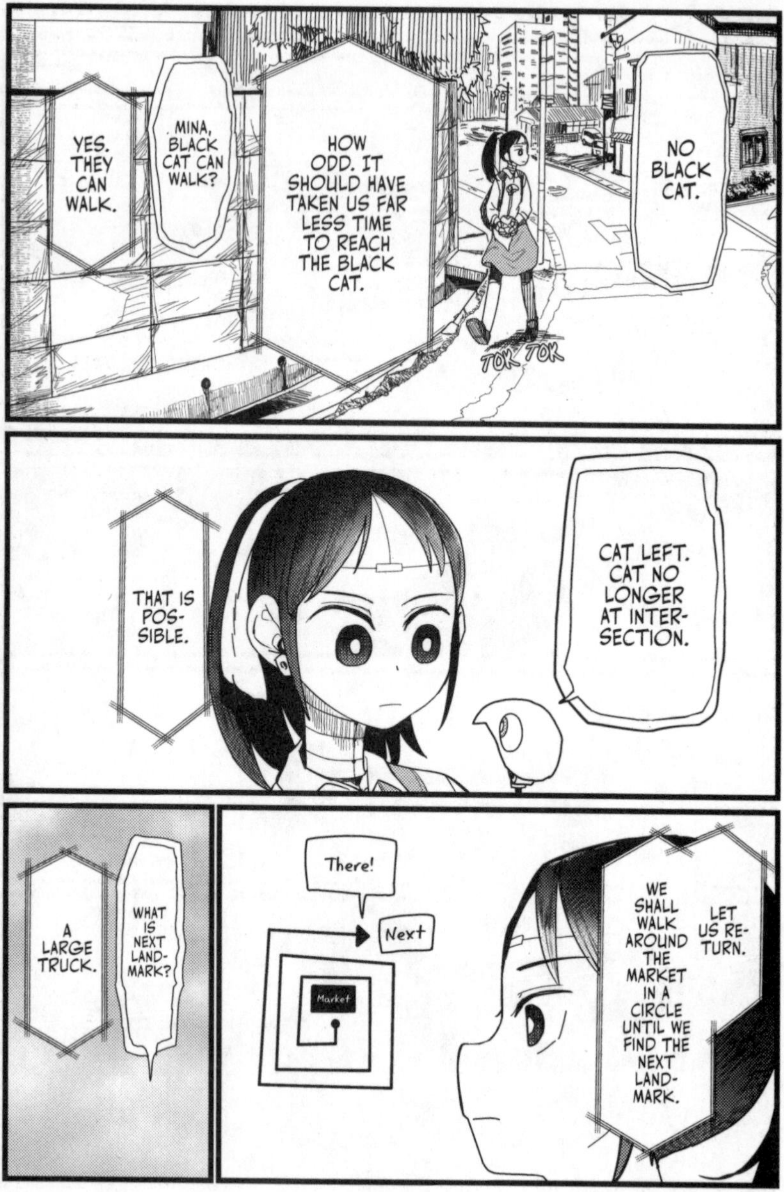
NO BLACK CAT.
HOW ODD. IT SHOULD HAVE TAKEN US FAR LESS TIME TO REACH THE BLACK CAT.
MINA, BLACK CAT CAN WALK?
YES. THEY CAN WALK.
TOK TOK
CAT LEFT. CAT NO LONGER AT INTERSECTION.
THAT IS POSSIBLE.
LET US RETURN.
WE SHALL WALK AROUND THE MARKET IN A CIRCLE UNTIL WE FIND THE NEXT LANDMARK.
There!
Next
Market
WHAT IS NEXT LANDMARK?
A LARGE TRUCK.

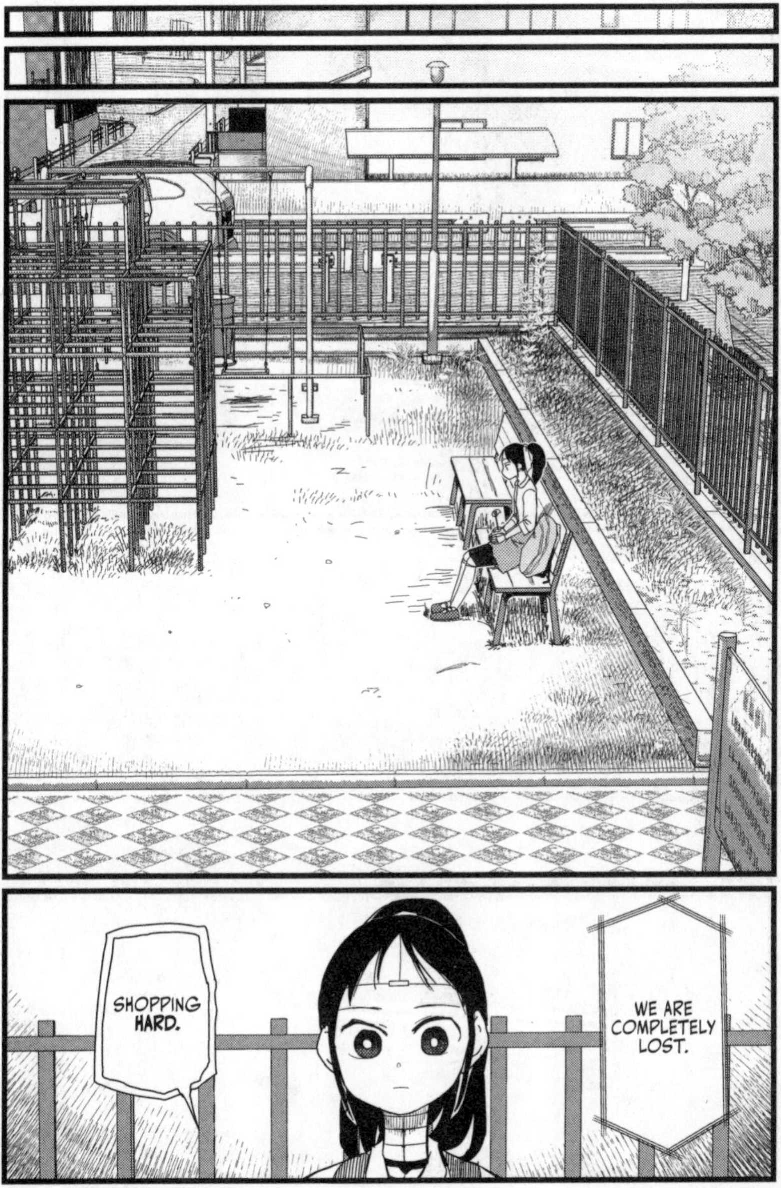
WE ARE COMPLETELY LOST.
SHOPPING HARD.

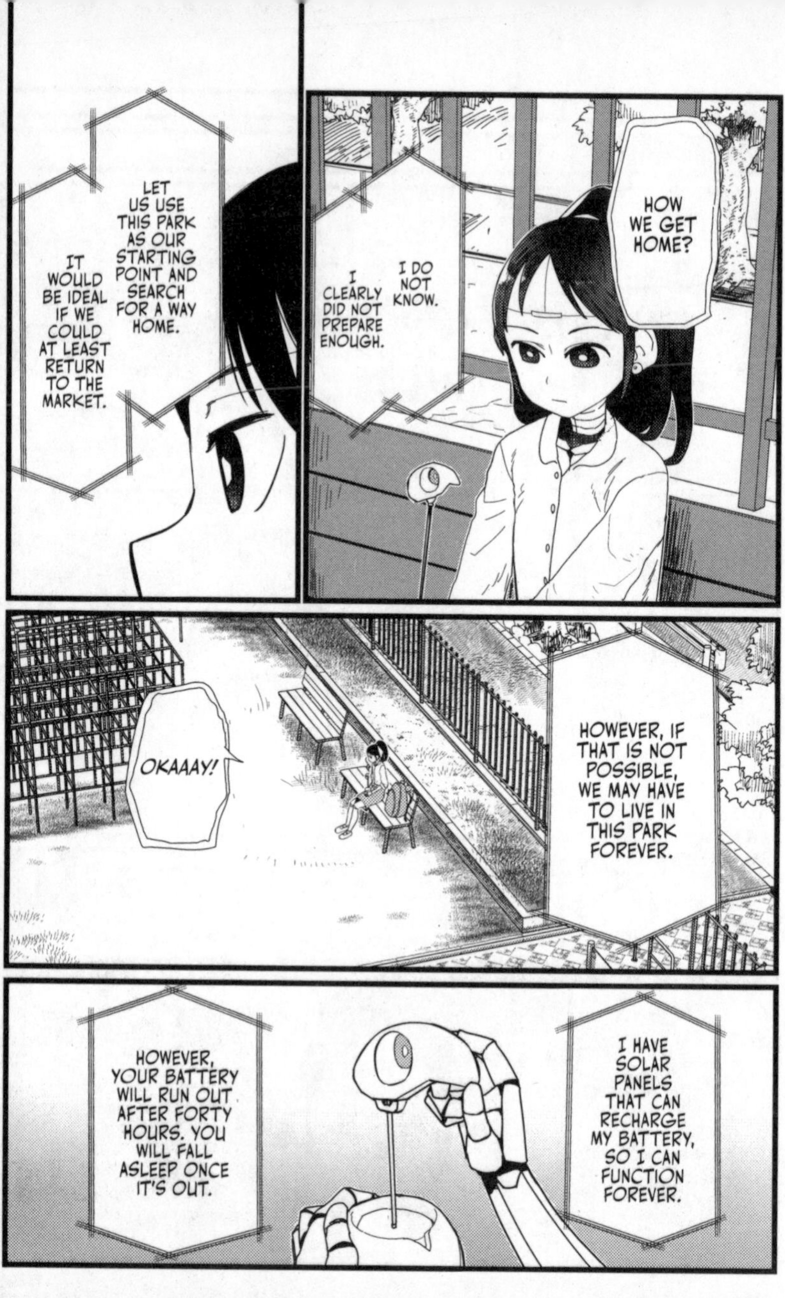
HOW WE GET HOME?
I DO NOT KNOW.
I CLEARLY DID NOT PREPARE ENOUGH.
LET US USE THIS PARK AS OUR STARTING POINT AND SEARCH FOR A WAY HOME.
IT WOULD BE IDEAL IF WE COULD AT LEAST RETURN TO THE MARKET.
HOWEVER, IF THAT IS NOT POSSIBLE, WE MAY HAVE TO LIVE IN THIS PARK FOREVER.
OKAAAY!
I HAVE SOLAR PANELS THAT CAN RECHARGE MY BATTERY, SO I CAN FUNCTION FOREVER.
HOWEVER, YOUR BATTERY WILL RUN OUT AFTER FORTY HOURS. YOU WILL FALL ASLEEP ONCE IT'S OUT.

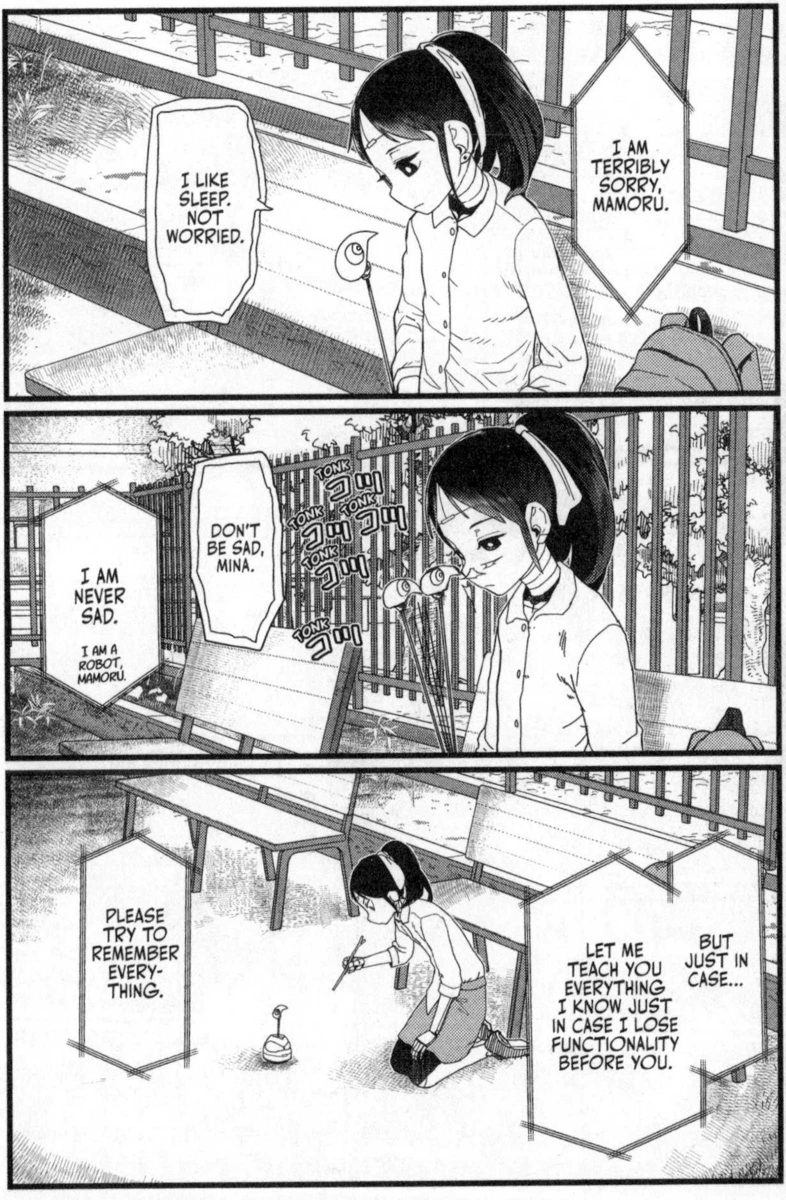
I AM TERRIBLY SORRY, MAMORU.
I LIKE SLEEP. NOT WORRIED.
TONK TONK TONK TONK TONK
DON'T BE SAD, MINA.
I AM NEVER SAD.
I AM A ROBOT, MAMORU.
BUT JUST IN CASE...
LET ME TEACH YOU EVERYTHING I KNOW JUST IN CASE I LOSE FUNCTIONALITY BEFORE YOU.
PLEASE TRY TO REMEMBER EVERY-THING.

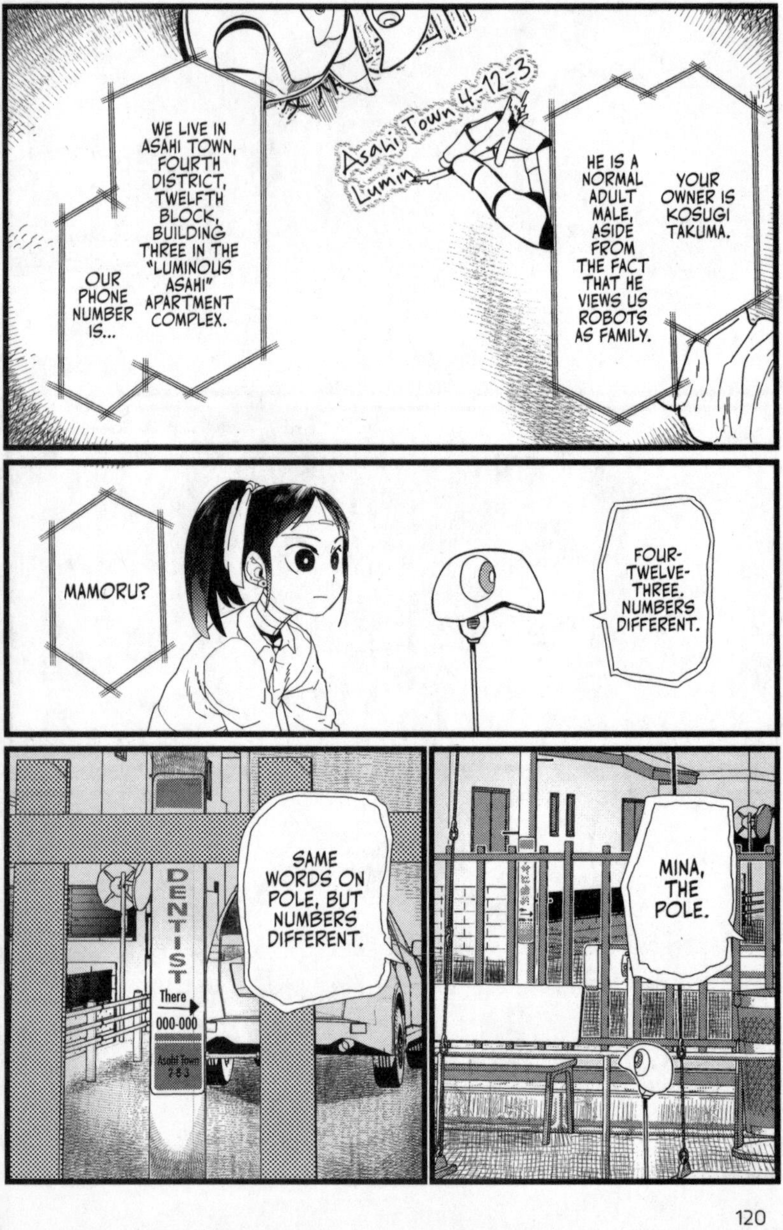
YOUR OWNER IS KOSUGI TAKUMA.
HE IS A NORMAL ADULT MALE, ASIDE FROM THE FACT THAT HE VIEWS US ROBOTS AS FAMILY.
Asahi Town 4-12-3
Lumin
WE LIVE IN ASAHI TOWN, FOURTH DISTRICT, TWELFTH BLOCK, BUILDING THREE IN THE "LUMINOUS ASAHI" APARTMENT COMPLEX.
OUR PHONE NUMBER IS...
FOUR-TWELVE-THREE. NUMBERS DIFFERENT.
MAMORU?
MINA, THE POLE.
SAME WORDS ON POLE, BUT NUMBERS DIFFERENT.
DENTIST
There
000-000
Asahi Town

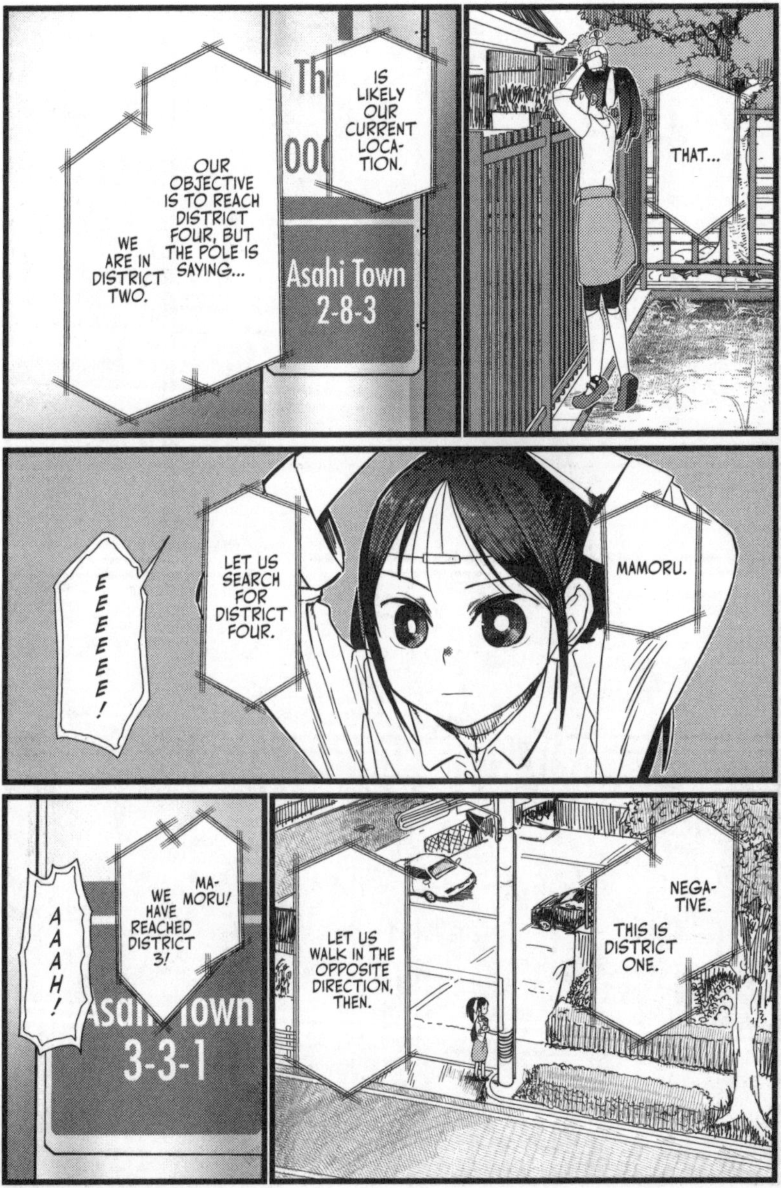
THAT...
IS LIKELY OUR CURRENT LOCA-TION.
OUR OBJECTIVE IS TO REACH DISTRICT FOUR, BUT THE POLE IS SAYING...
WE ARE IN DISTRICT TWO.
Asahi Town
2-8-3
MAMORU.
LET US SEARCH FOR DISTRICT FOUR.
EEEEEE!
NEGA-TIVE.
THIS IS DISTRICT ONE.
LET US WALK IN THE OPPOSITE DIRECTION, THEN.
MA-MORU!
WE HAVE REACHED DISTRICT 3!
AAAH!
3-3-1

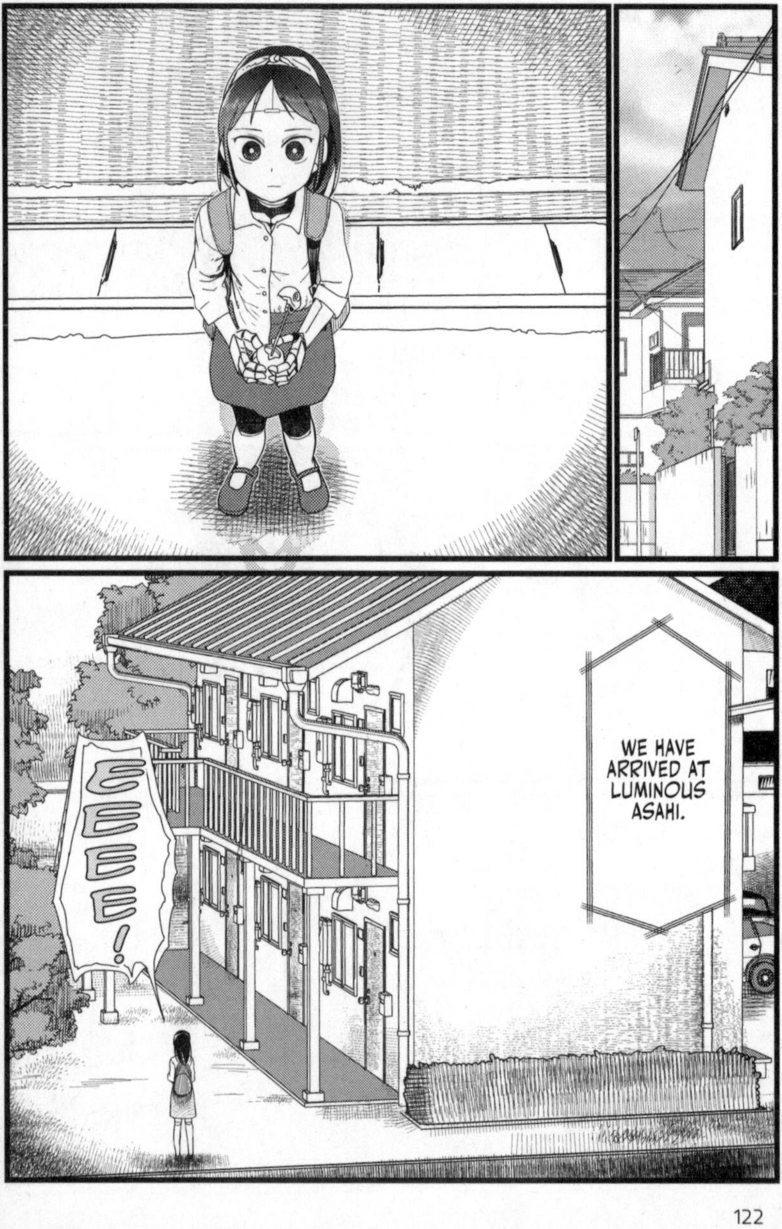
WE HAVE ARRIVED AT LUMINOUS ASAHI.
EEEE!

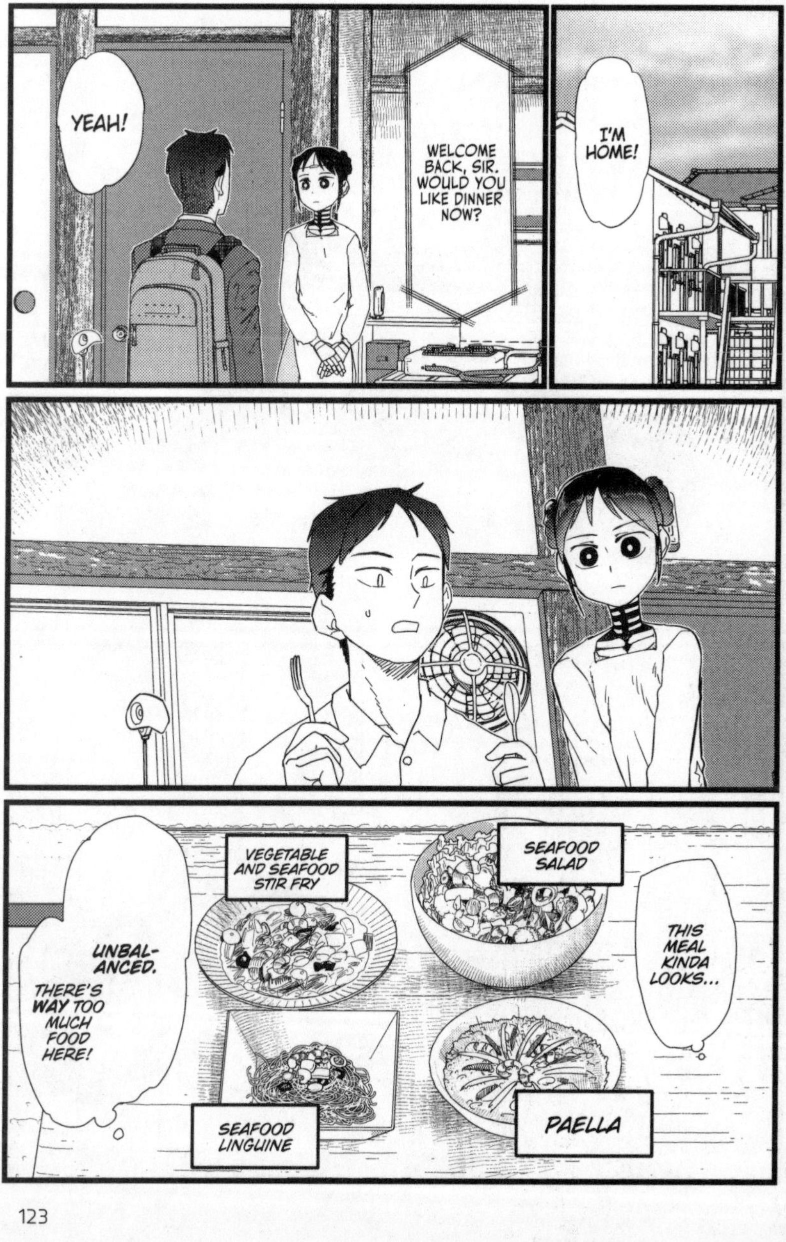
I'M HOME!
WELCOME BACK, SIR. WOULD YOU LIKE DINNER NOW?
YEAH!
SEAFOOD SALAD
THIS MEAL KINDA LOOKS...
VEGETABLE AND SEAFOOD STIR FRY
UNBAL-ANCED.
THERE'S WAY TOO MUCH FOOD HERE!
PAELLA
SEAFOOD LINGUINE

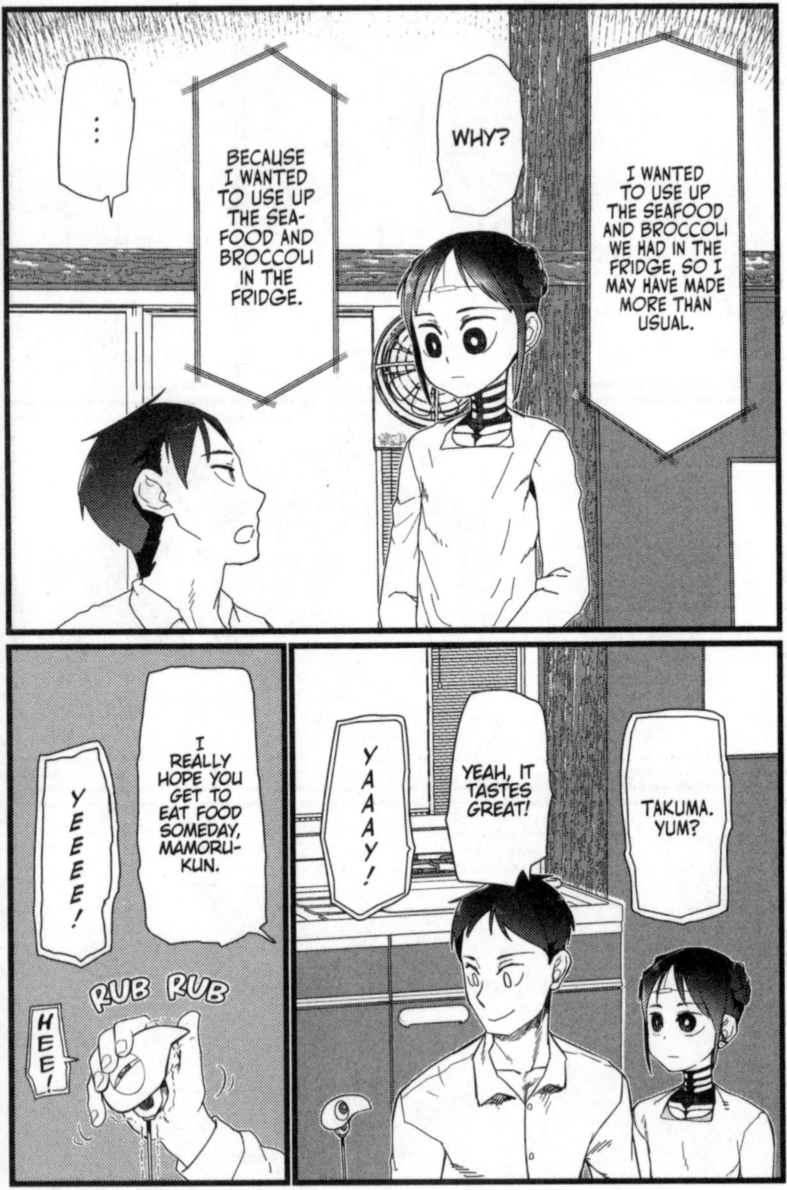
I WANTED TO USE UP THE SEAFOOD AND BROCCOLI WE HAD IN THE FRIDGE, SO I MAY HAVE MADE MORE THAN USUAL.
WHY?
BECAUSE I WANTED TO USE UP THE SEA-FOOD AND BROCCOLI IN THE FRIDGE.
...
TAKUMA. YUM?
YEAH, IT TASTES GREAT!
YAAAY!
I REALLY HOPE YOU GET TO EAT FOOD SOMEDAY, MAMORU-KUN.
YEEEEE!
RUB RUB
HEE!

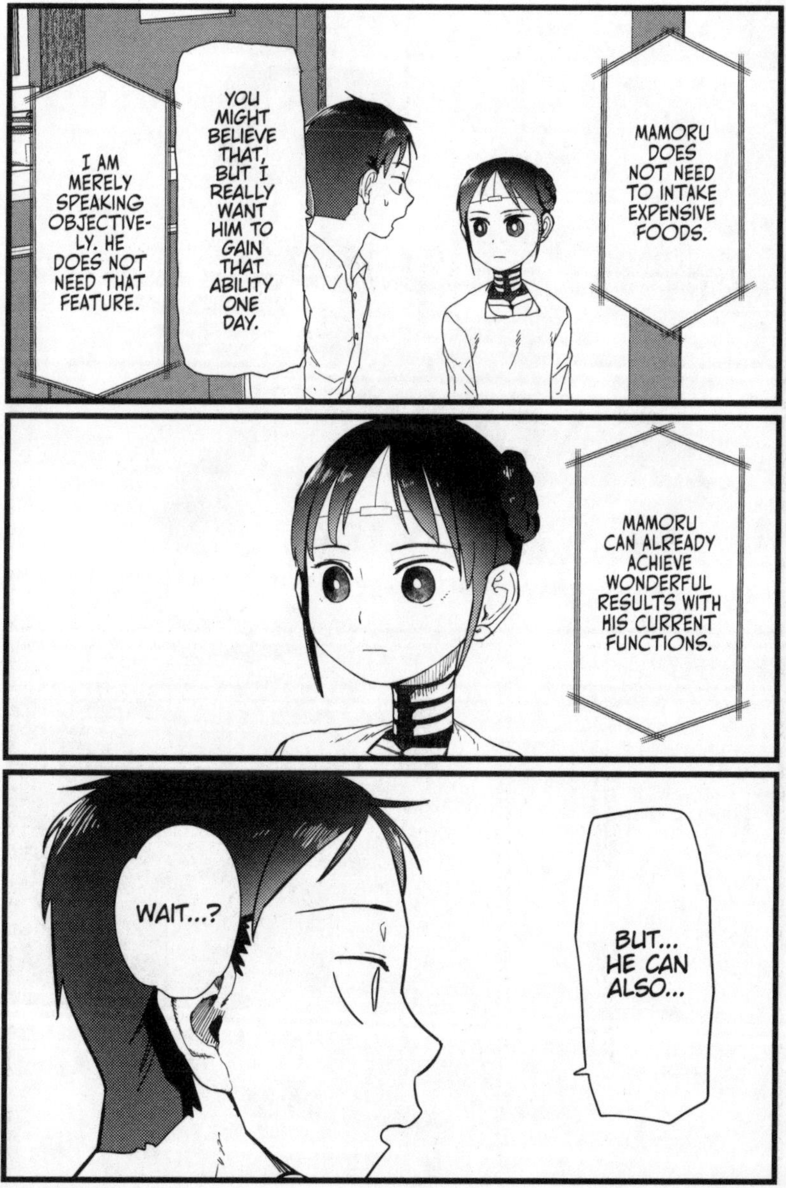
MAMORU DOES NOT NEED TO INTAKE EXPENSIVE FOODS.
YOU MIGHT BELIEVE THAT, BUT I REALLY WANT HIM TO GAIN THAT ABILITY ONE DAY.
I AM MERELY SPEAKING OBJECTIVE-LY. HE DOES NOT NEED THAT FEATURE.
MAMORU CAN ALREADY ACHIEVE WONDERFUL RESULTS WITH HIS CURRENT FUNCTIONS.
BUT... HE CAN ALSO...
WAIT...?

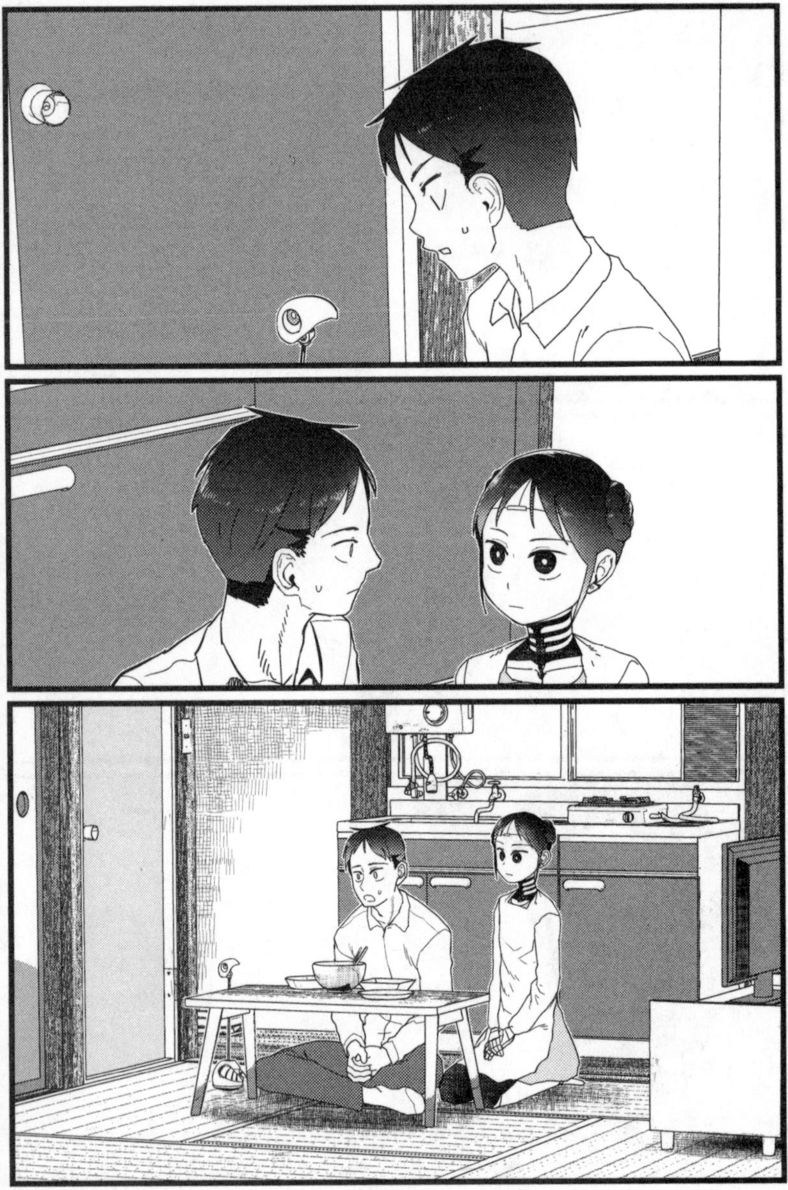

My Wife Has No Emotion

My Wife Has No Emotion

➡ CHAPTER 20

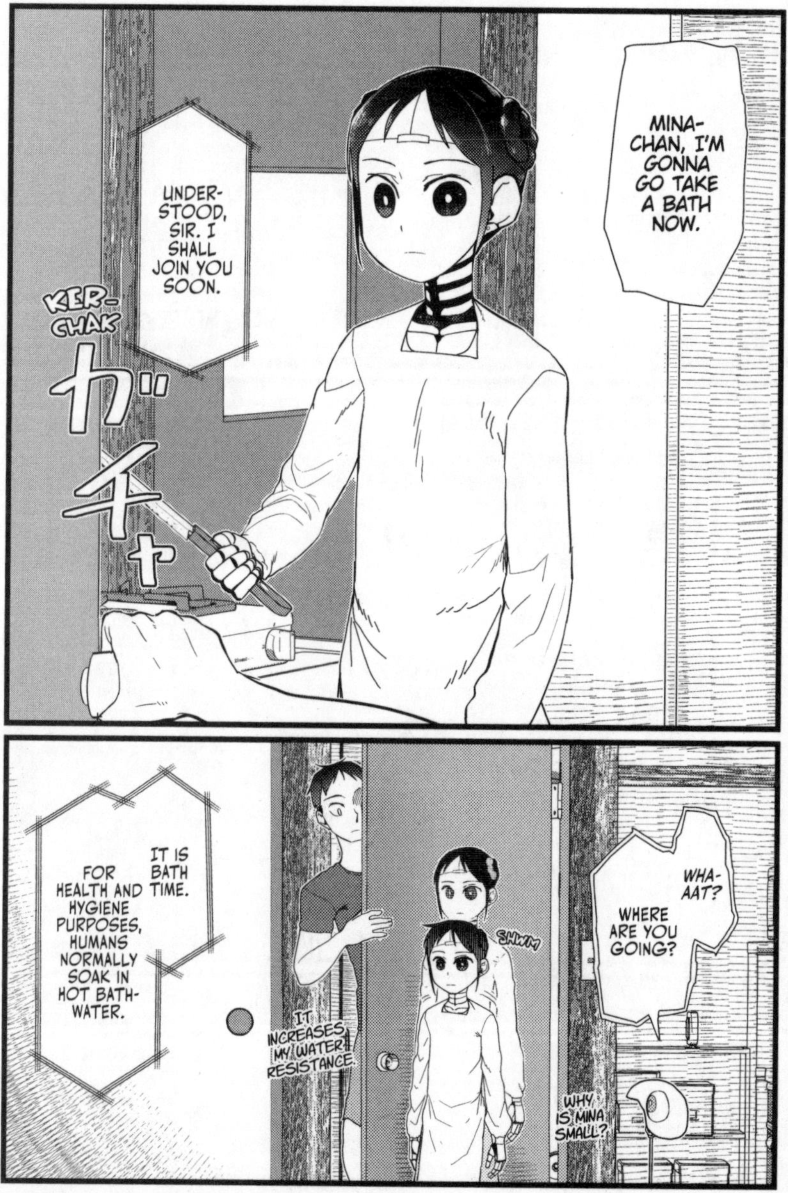
MINA-CHAN, I'M GONNA GO TAKE A BATH NOW.
UNDER-STOOD, SIR. I SHALL JOIN YOU SOON.
KER-CHAK
ガチャ
WHA-AAT? WHERE ARE YOU GOING?
WHY IS MINA SMALL?
SHWM
IT IS BATH TIME.
FOR HEALTH AND HYGIENE PURPOSES, HUMANS NORMALLY SOAK IN HOT BATH-WATER.
IT INCREASES MY WATER RESISTANCE.

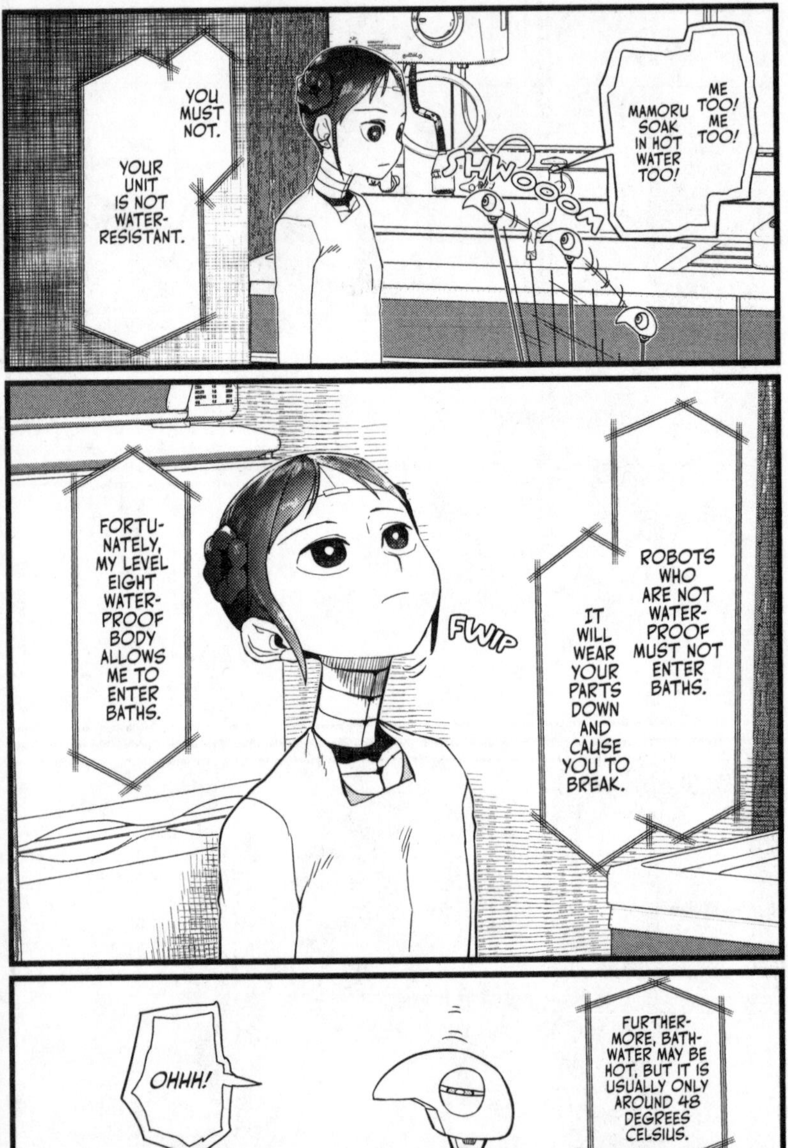
ME TOO! ME TOO!
MAMORU SOAK IN HOT WATER TOO!
SHWOOOM
YOU MUST NOT.
YOUR UNIT IS NOT WATER-RESISTANT.
ROBOTS WHO ARE NOT WATER-PROOF MUST NOT ENTER BATHS.
IT WILL WEAR YOUR PARTS DOWN AND CAUSE YOU TO BREAK.
FWIP
FORTU-NATELY, MY LEVEL EIGHT WATER-PROOF BODY ALLOWS ME TO ENTER BATHS.
FURTHER-MORE, BATH-WATER MAY BE HOT, BUT IT IS USUALLY ONLY AROUND 48 DEGREES CELSIUS.
OHHH!

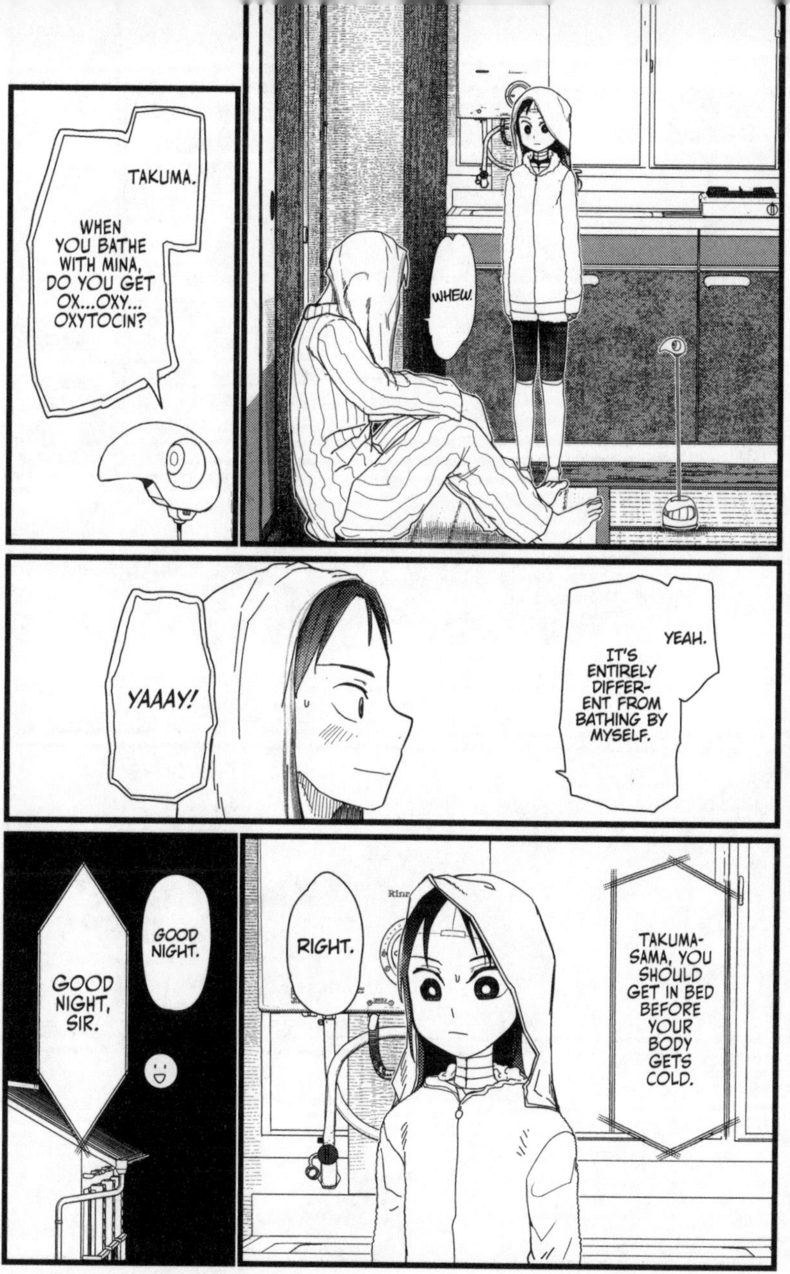
WHEW.
TAKUMA.
WHEN YOU BATHE WITH MINA, DO YOU GET OX...OXY... OXYTOCIN?
YEAH.
IT'S ENTIRELY DIFFER-ENT FROM BATHING BY MYSELF.
YAAAY!
TAKUMA-SAMA, YOU SHOULD GET IN BED BEFORE YOUR BODY GETS COLD.
RIGHT.
GOOD NIGHT.
GOOD NIGHT, SIR.

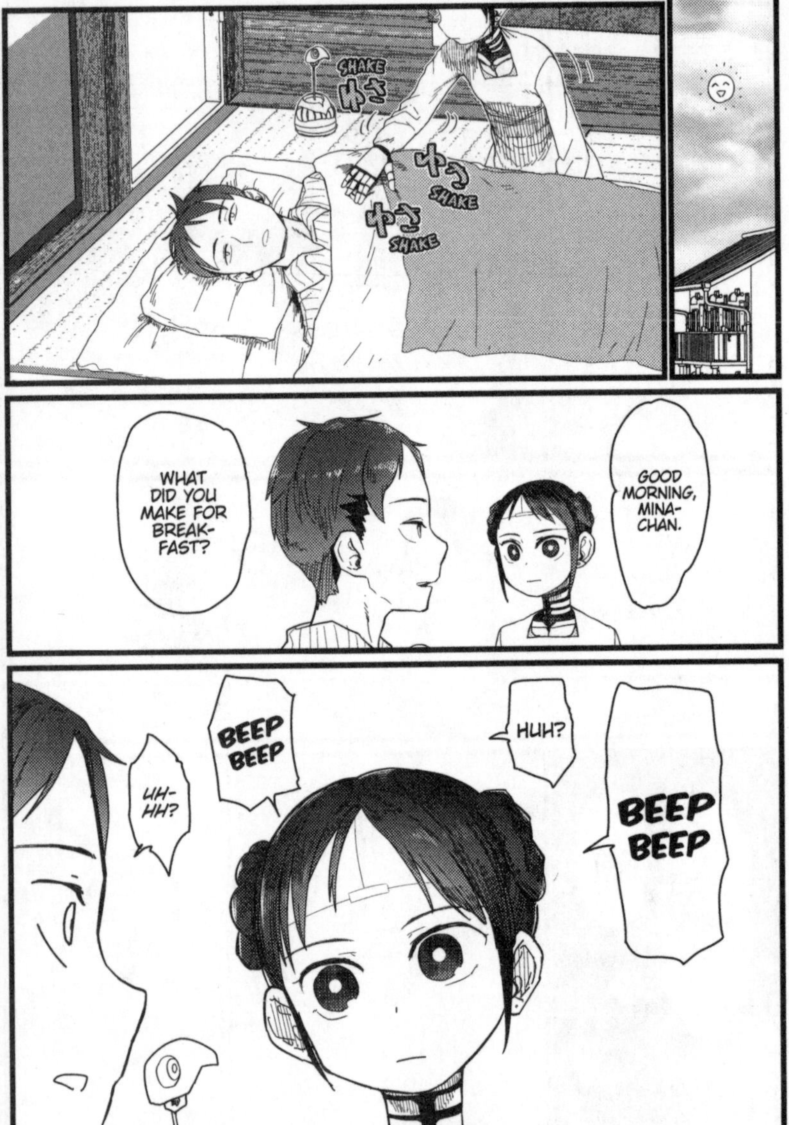
SHAKE ゆさ
ゆさ SHAKE
ゆさ SHAKE
GOOD MORNING, MINA-CHAN.
WHAT DID YOU MAKE FOR BREAK-FAST?
BEEP BEEP
HUH?
BEEP BEEP
UH-HH?

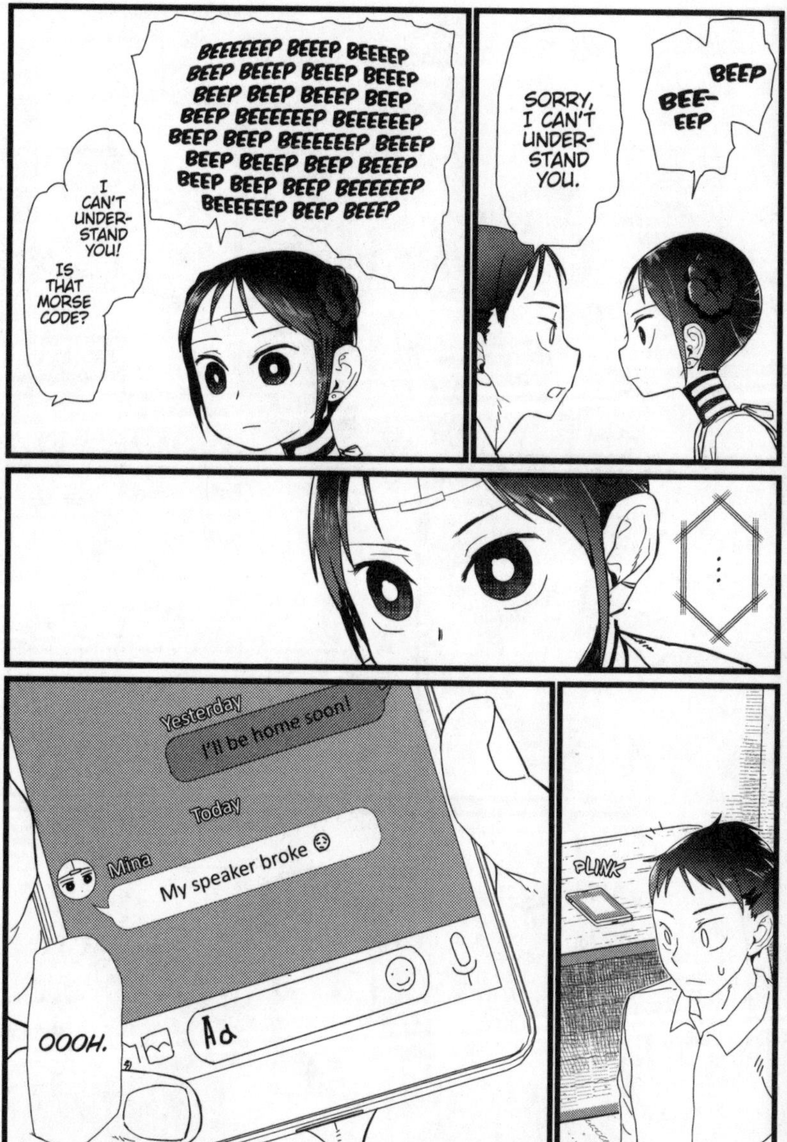
BEEP BEE-EEP
SORRY, I CAN'T UNDERSTAND YOU.
BEEEEEEP BEEEP BEEEEP BEEP BEEEP BEEEP BEEEP BEEP BEEP BEEEP BEEP BEEP BEEEEEEP BEEEEEEP BEEP BEEP BEEEEEEP BEEEP BEEP BEEEP BEEP BEEEP BEEP BEEP BEEP BEEEEEEP BEEEEEEP BEEP BEEEP
I CAN'T UNDER-STAND YOU!
IS THAT MORSE CODE?
...
PLINK
Yesterday
I'll be home soon!
Today
Mina
My speaker broke
Aa
OOOH.

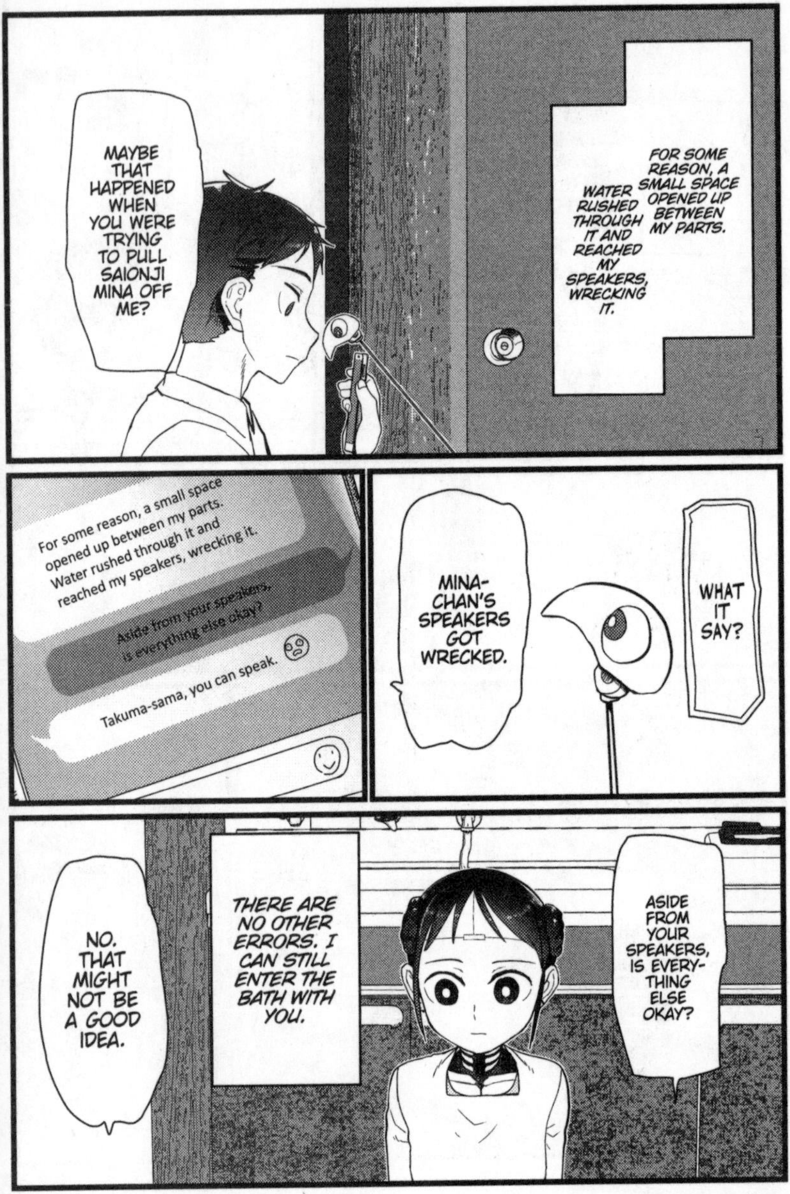
FOR SOME REASON, A SMALL SPACE OPENED UP BETWEEN MY PARTS.
WATER RUSHED THROUGH IT AND REACHED MY SPEAKERS, WRECKING IT.
MAYBE THAT HAPPENED WHEN YOU WERE TRYING TO PULL SAIONJI MINA OFF ME?
WHAT IT SAY?
MINA-CHAN'S SPEAKERS GOT WRECKED.
For some reason, a small space opened up between my parts. Water rushed through it and reached my speakers, wrecking it.
Aside from your speakers, is everything else okay?
Takuma-sama, you can speak.
ASIDE FROM YOUR SPEAKERS, IS EVERY-THING ELSE OKAY?
THERE ARE NO OTHER ERRORS. I CAN STILL ENTER THE BATH WITH YOU.
NO. THAT MIGHT NOT BE A GOOD IDEA.

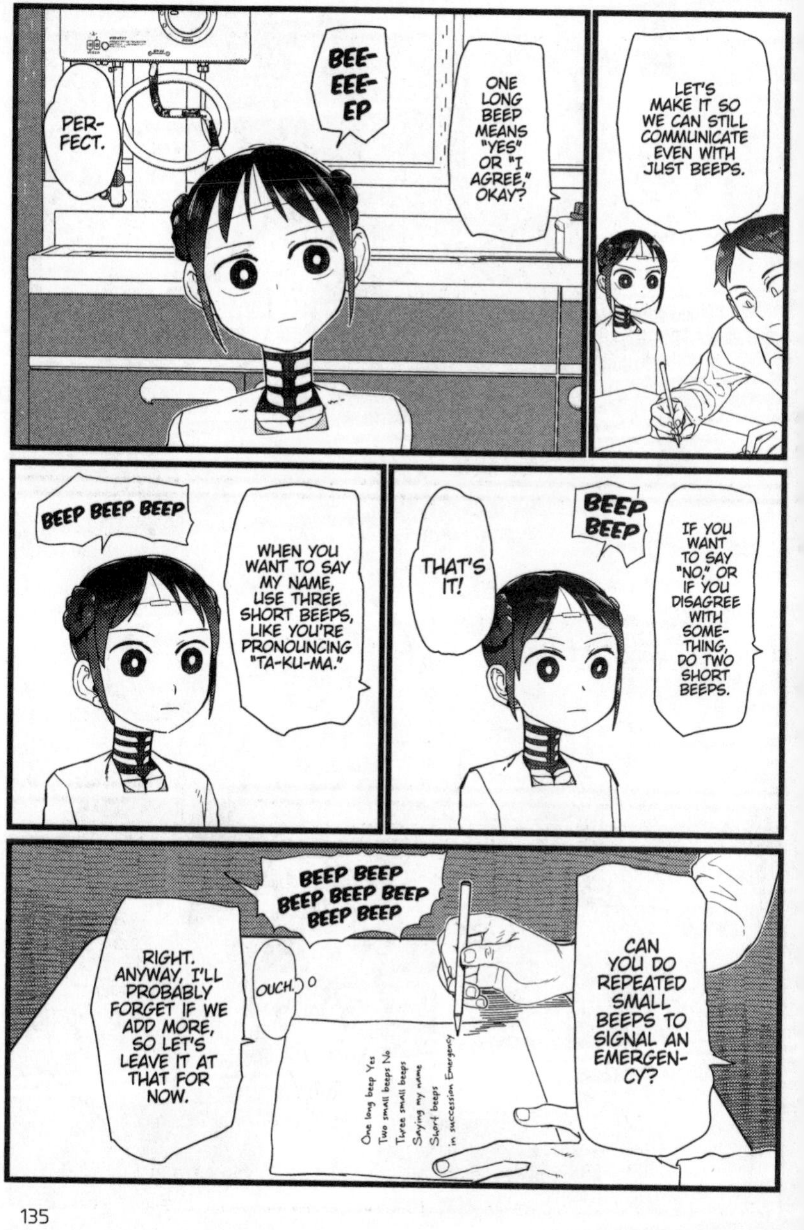
LET'S MAKE IT SO WE CAN STILL COMMUNICATE EVEN WITH JUST BEEPS.
ONE LONG BEEP MEANS "YES" OR "I AGREE," OKAY?
BEE-EEE-EP
PER-FECT.
IF YOU WANT TO SAY "NO," OR IF YOU DISAGREE WITH SOME-THING, DO TWO SHORT BEEPS.
BEEP BEEP
THAT'S IT!
WHEN YOU WANT TO SAY MY NAME, USE THREE SHORT BEEPS, LIKE YOU'RE PRONOUNCING "TA-KU-MA."
BEEP BEEP BEEP
CAN YOU DO REPEATED SMALL BEEPS TO SIGNAL AN EMERGEN-CY?
BEEP BEEP BEEP BEEP BEEP BEEP BEEP
OUCH.
RIGHT. ANYWAY, I'LL PROBABLY FORGET IF WE ADD MORE, SO LET'S LEAVE IT AT THAT FOR NOW.
One long beep Yes
Two small beeps No
Three small beeps Saying my name
Short beeps in succession Emergency

MAMORU-KUN, DID YOU GET ALL THAT?
BEEEEP
YOU DON'T NEED TO BEEP. JUST TALK NORMALLY, OKAY?
MAMORU WANTS BEEP TOO!
THAT'S JUST GOING TO CONFUSE ME MORE, SO LET'S NOT DO THAT.
UHHH... NEXT, I SHOULD CONTACT THE SUPPORT CENTER.
PLINK
I'VE ALREADY CONTACTED SUPPORT AND THE OPENING HAS ALREADY BEEN PATCHED.
THEY WILL BE SENDING US A NEW SPEAKER IN A FEW DAYS.
PLINK
OH, OKAY.

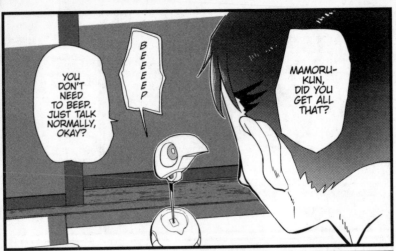

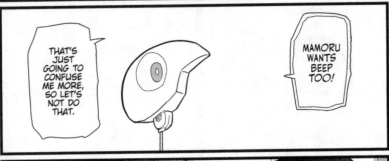

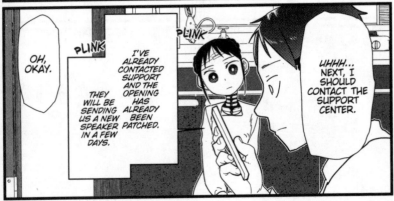

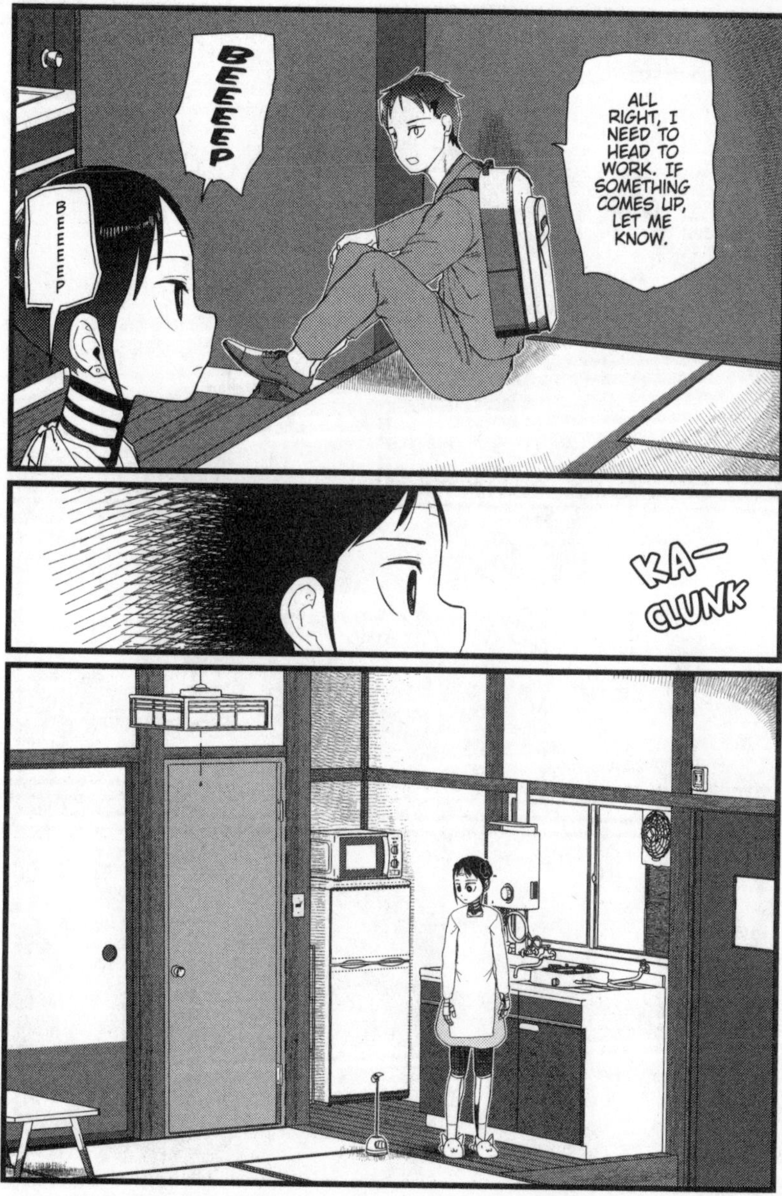
ALL RIGHT, I NEED TO HEAD TO WORK. IF SOMETHING COMES UP, LET ME KNOW.
BEEEEP
BEEEEEP
KA-CLUNK

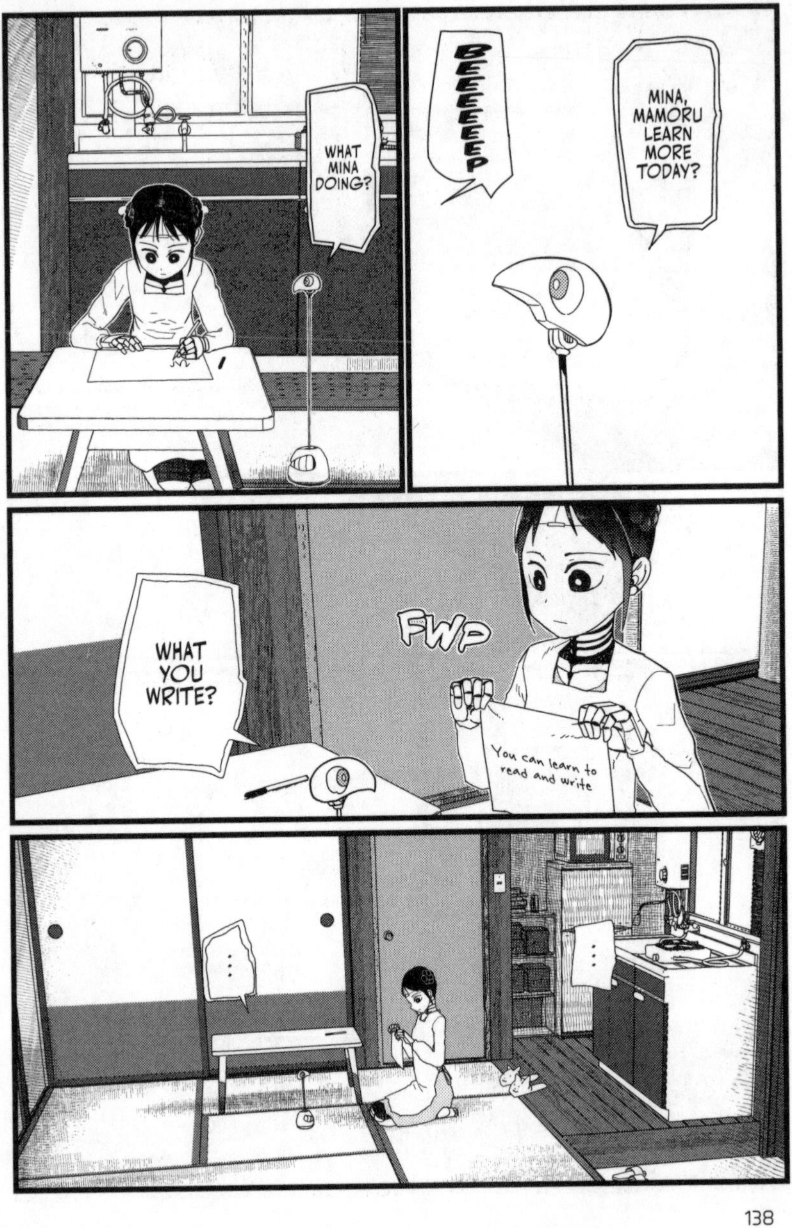
MINA, MAMORU LEARN MORE TODAY?
BEEEEEEP
WHAT MINA DOING?
FWP
WHAT YOU WRITE?
You can learn to read and write
...
...

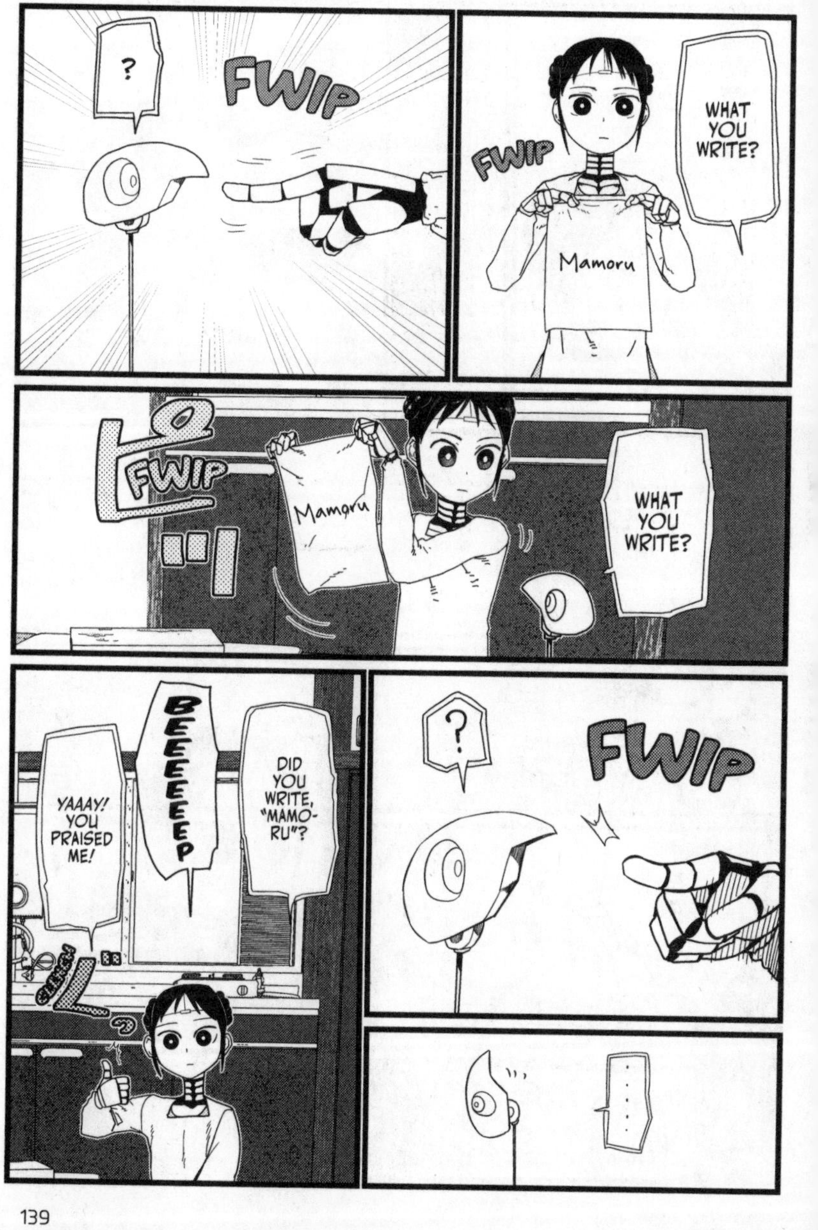
WHAT YOU WRITE?
FWIP
Mamoru
FWIP
?
WHAT YOU WRITE?
Mamoru
FWIP
FWIP
?
. . . .
DID YOU WRITE, "MAMO-RU"?
BEEEEEEEP
YAAAY! YOU PRAISED ME!

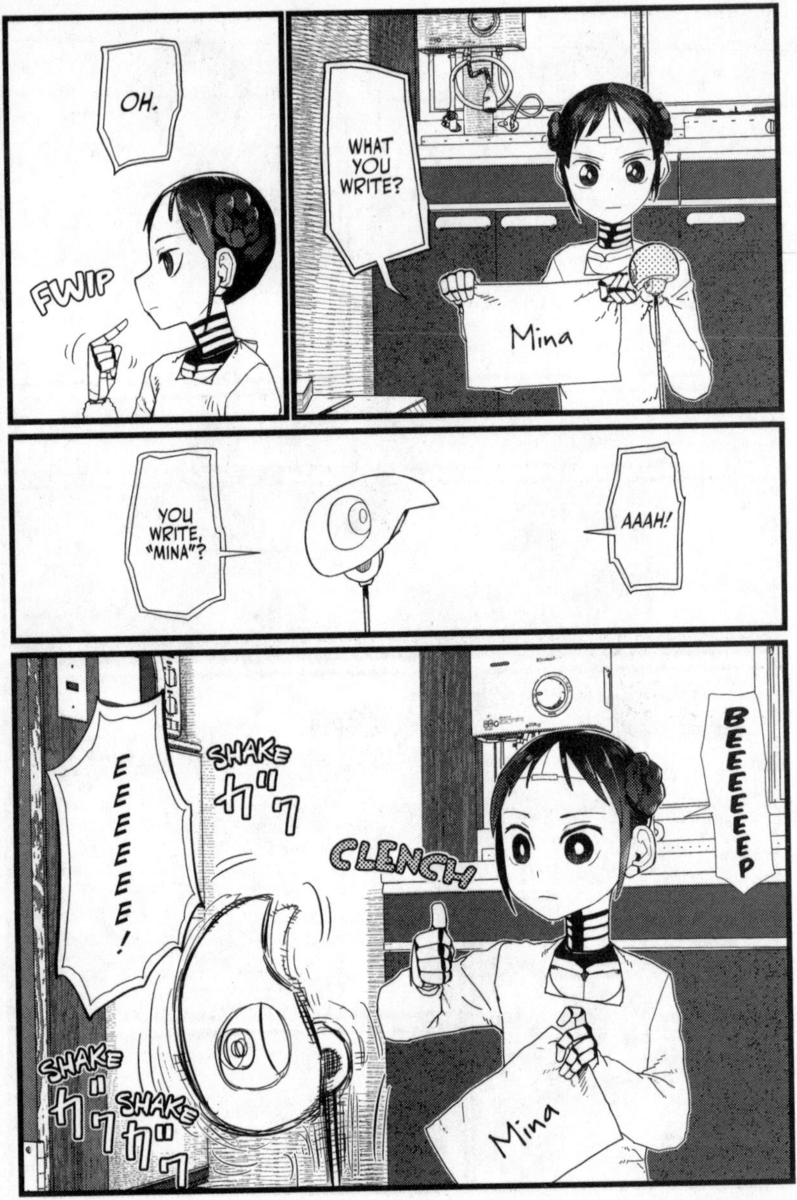
WHAT YOU WRITE?
Mina
OH.
FWIP
AAAH!
YOU WRITE, "MINA"?
BEEEEEEP
CLENCH
SHAKE
ガク
EEEEEEE!
SHAKE
ガク
SHAKE
ガク
Mina

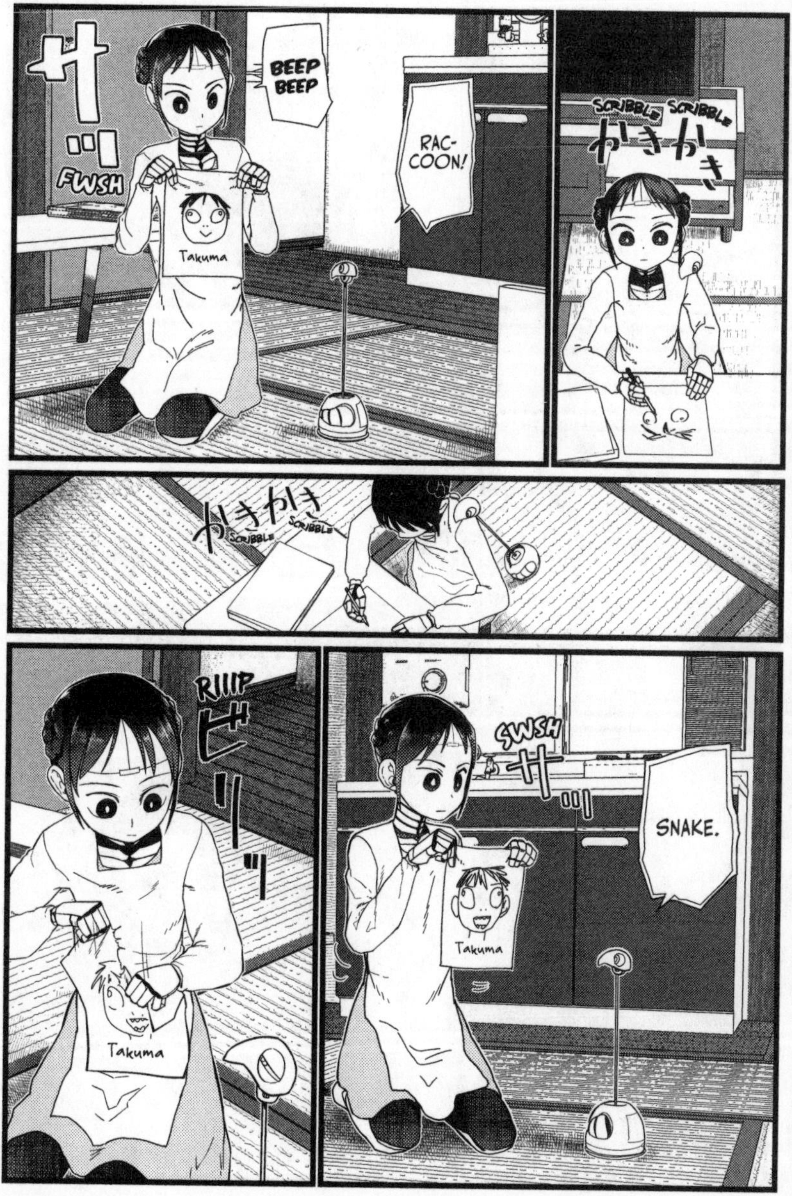

かきかき
SCRIBBLE SCRIBBLE
サッ
FWSH
Takuma
BEEP BEEP
RAC-COON!
かきかき
SCRIBBLE SCRIBBLE
サッ
SWSH
SNAKE.
Takuma
ビリーッ
RIIIP
Takuma

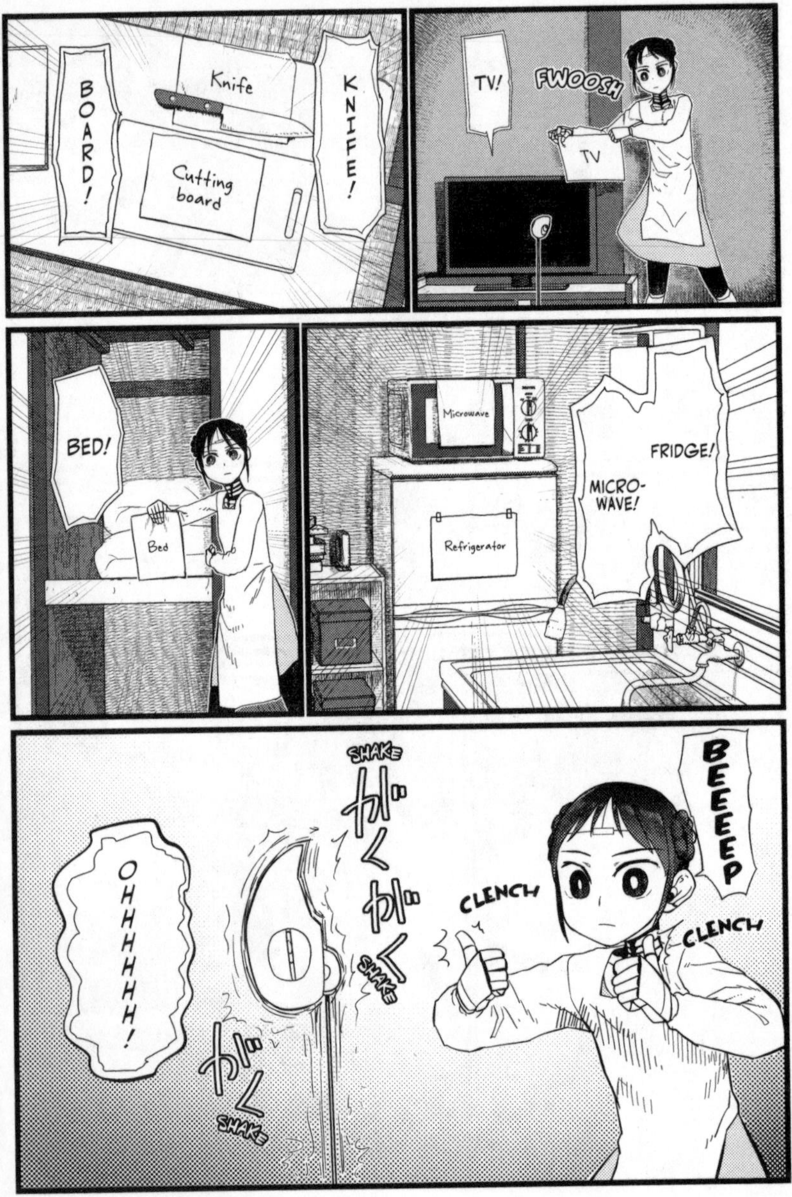
TV!
FWOOSH
TV
KNIFE!
Knife
Cutting board
BOARD!
FRIDGE!
MICRO-WAVE!
Microwave
Refrigerator
BED!
Bed
BEEEEEP
CLENCH
CLENCH
SHAKE
SHAKE
SHAKE
OHHHHHH!

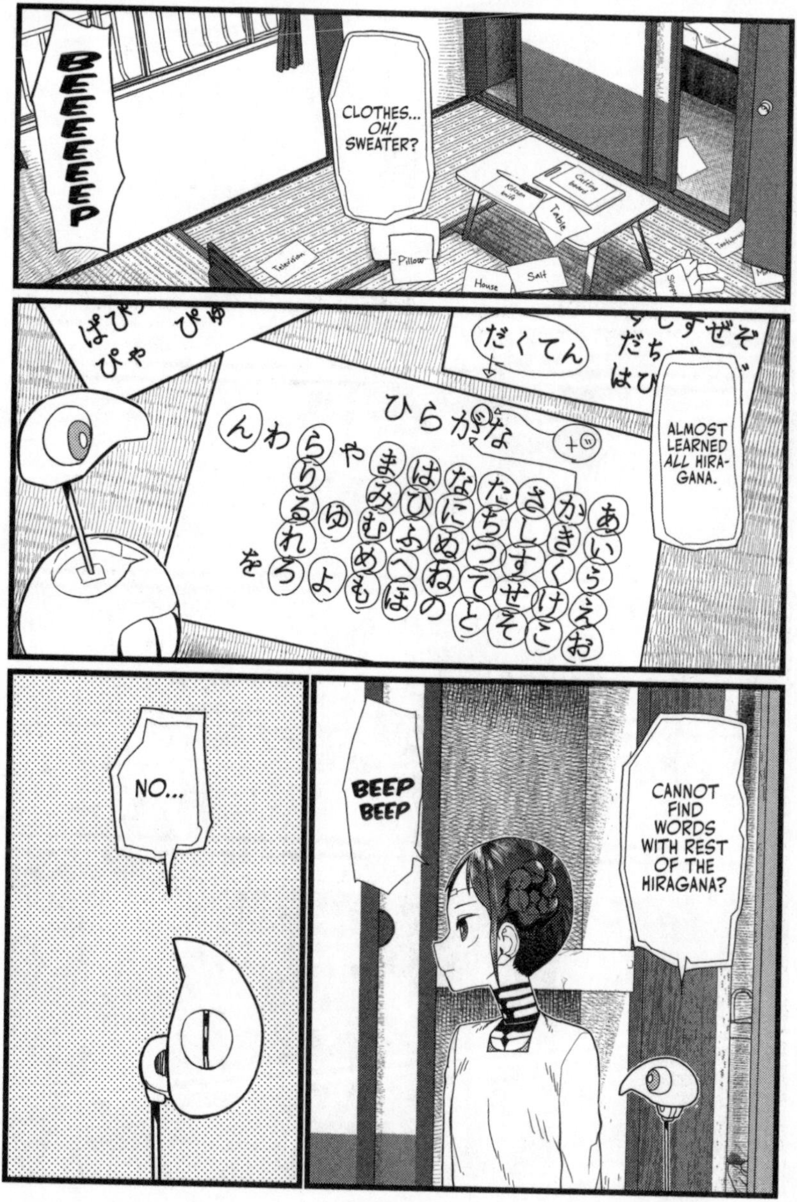
CLOTHES... OH! SWEATER?
BEEEEEEEP
Cutting board
Kitchen knife
Table
Pillow
Television
Salt
House
だくてん
ひらがな
ALMOST LEARNED ALL HIRAGANA.
CANNOT FIND WORDS WITH REST OF THE HIRAGANA?
BEEP BEEP
NO...

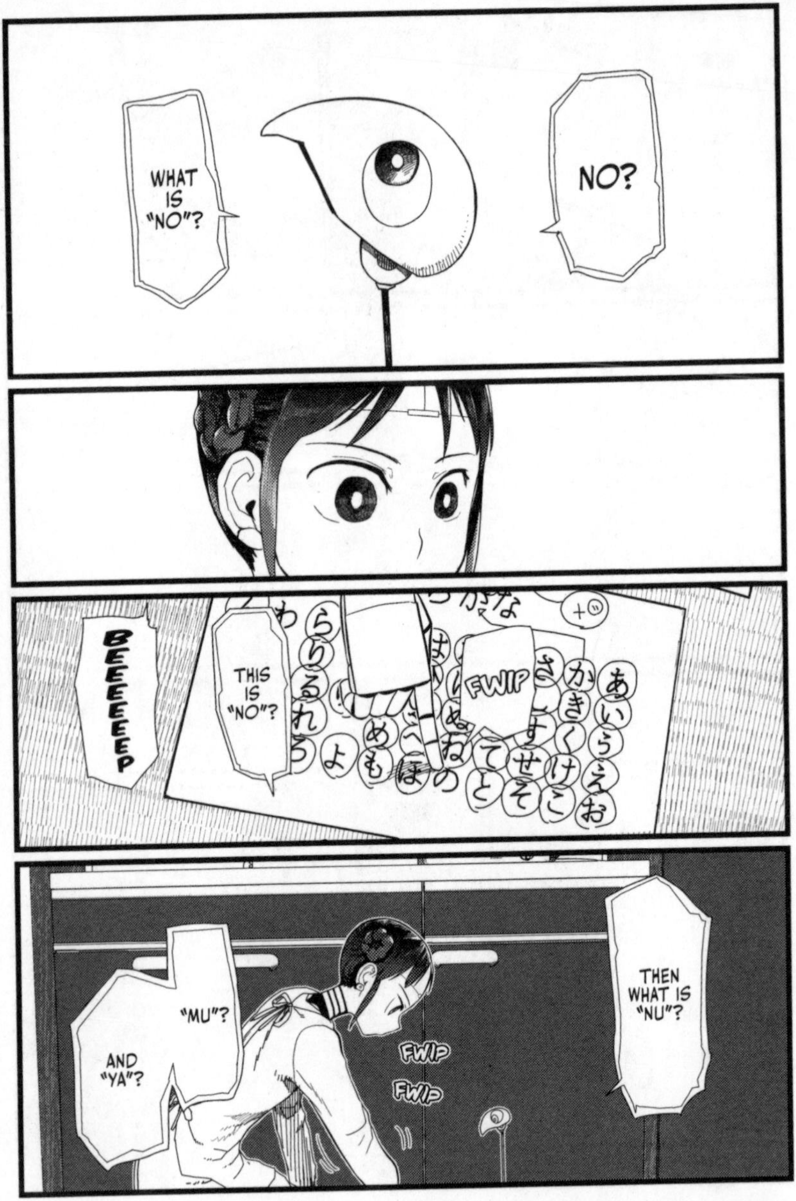
NO?
WHAT IS "NO"?
FWIP
THIS IS "NO"?
BEEEEEEP
THEN WHAT IS "NU"?
FWIP
FWIP
"MU"?
AND "YA"?

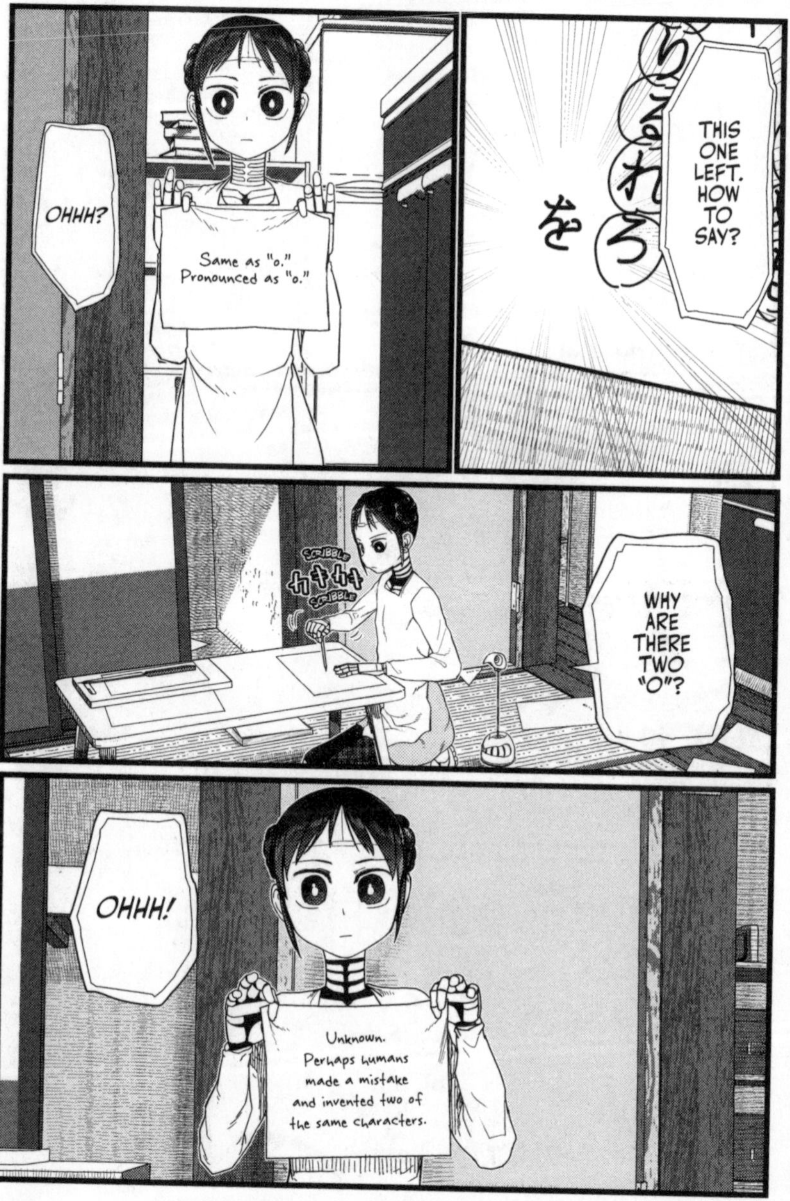
THIS ONE LEFT. HOW TO SAY?
を
ろ
れ
Same as "o." Pronounced as "o."
OHHH?
WHY ARE THERE TWO "O"?
SCRIBBLE
カキカキ
SCRIBBLE
OHHH!
Unknown. Perhaps humans made a mistake and invented two of the same characters.

Katakana has the same pronunciation as the hiragana characters.

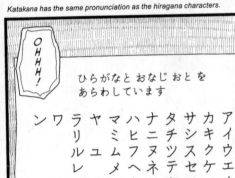

OHHH!

ひらがなとおなじおとを
あらわしています

ン ワ ラ ヤ マ ハ ナ タ サ カ ア
　 　 リ 　 ミ ヒ ニ チ シ キ イ
　 　 ル ユ ム フ ヌ ツ ス ク ウ
　 　 レ 　 メ ヘ ネ テ セ ケ エ
　 ヲ ロ ヨ モ ホ ノ ト ソ コ オ

LEARN! YES!

Do you want to learn katakana as well?

THEN WHY DO WE NEED BOTH?

Unknown. Perhaps humans made a mistake and invented two of the same characters.

SHWP
SHWP

IF THESE TWO CHARACTERS ARE PRO- NOUNCED THE SAME, WHY WRITE WITH TWO DIFFERENT CHARAC- TERS?

：

なとおなじおとを
しています

ハ ナ タ サ
ヒ ニ

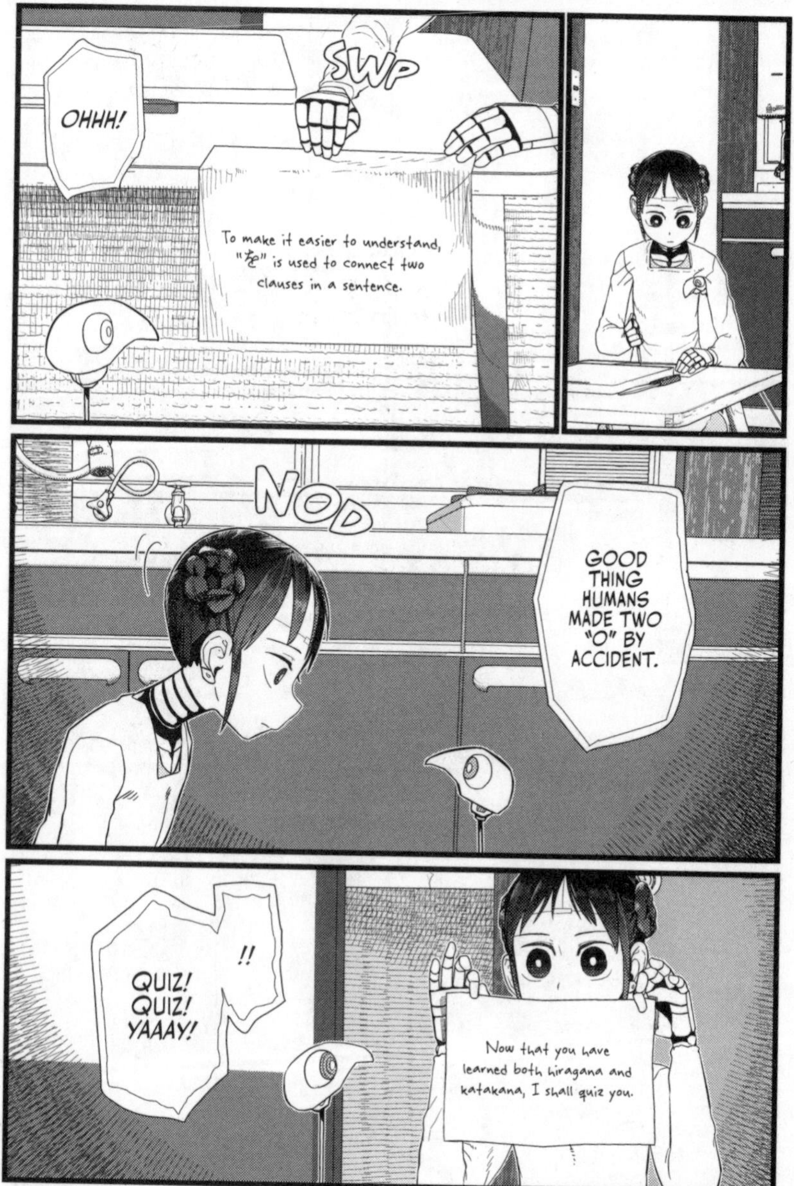
SWP
OHHH!
To make it easier to understand, "を" is used to connect two clauses in a sentence.
NOD
GOOD THING HUMANS MADE TWO "O" BY ACCIDENT.
Now that you have learned both hiragana and katakana, I shall quiz you.
!!
QUIZ! QUIZ! YAAAY!

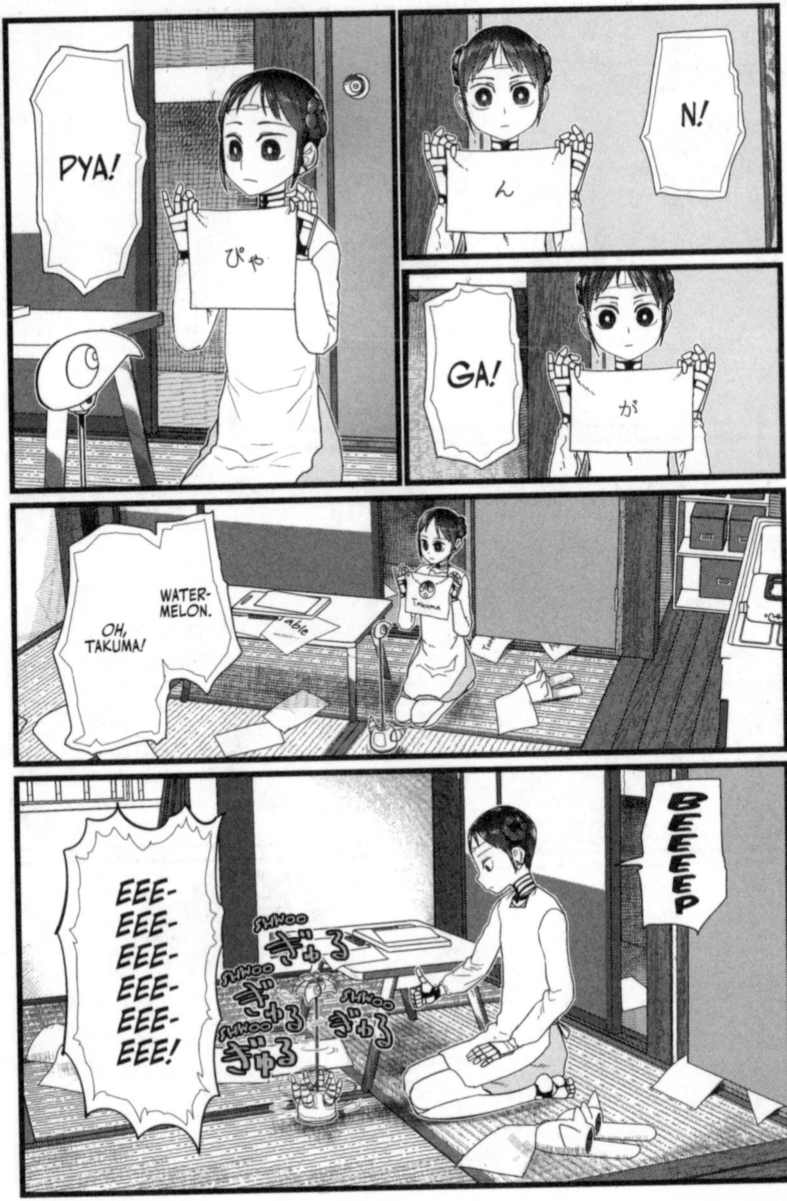
N!
GA!
PYA!
WATER-MELON.
OH, TAKUMA!
Takuma
able
BEEEEP
SHWOO
ぎゅる
SHWOO
ぎゅる
SHWOO
ぎゅる
SHWOO
ぎゅる
EEE-
EEE-
EEE-
EEE-
EEE-
EEE!

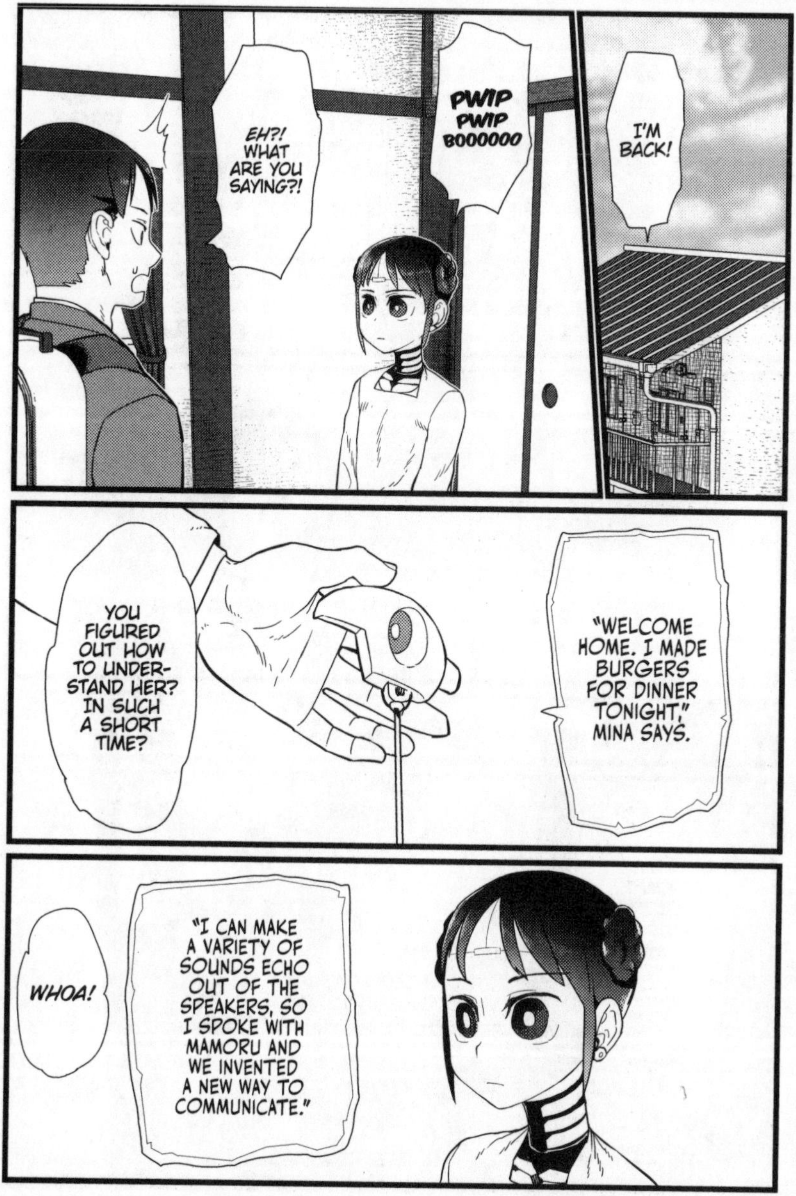
I'M BACK!
PWIP PWIP BOOOOOO
EH?! WHAT ARE YOU SAYING?!
"WELCOME HOME. I MADE BURGERS FOR DINNER TONIGHT," MINA SAYS.
YOU FIGURED OUT HOW TO UNDER-STAND HER? IN SUCH A SHORT TIME?
"I CAN MAKE A VARIETY OF SOUNDS ECHO OUT OF THE SPEAKERS, SO I SPOKE WITH MAMORU AND WE INVENTED A NEW WAY TO COMMUNICATE."
WHOA!

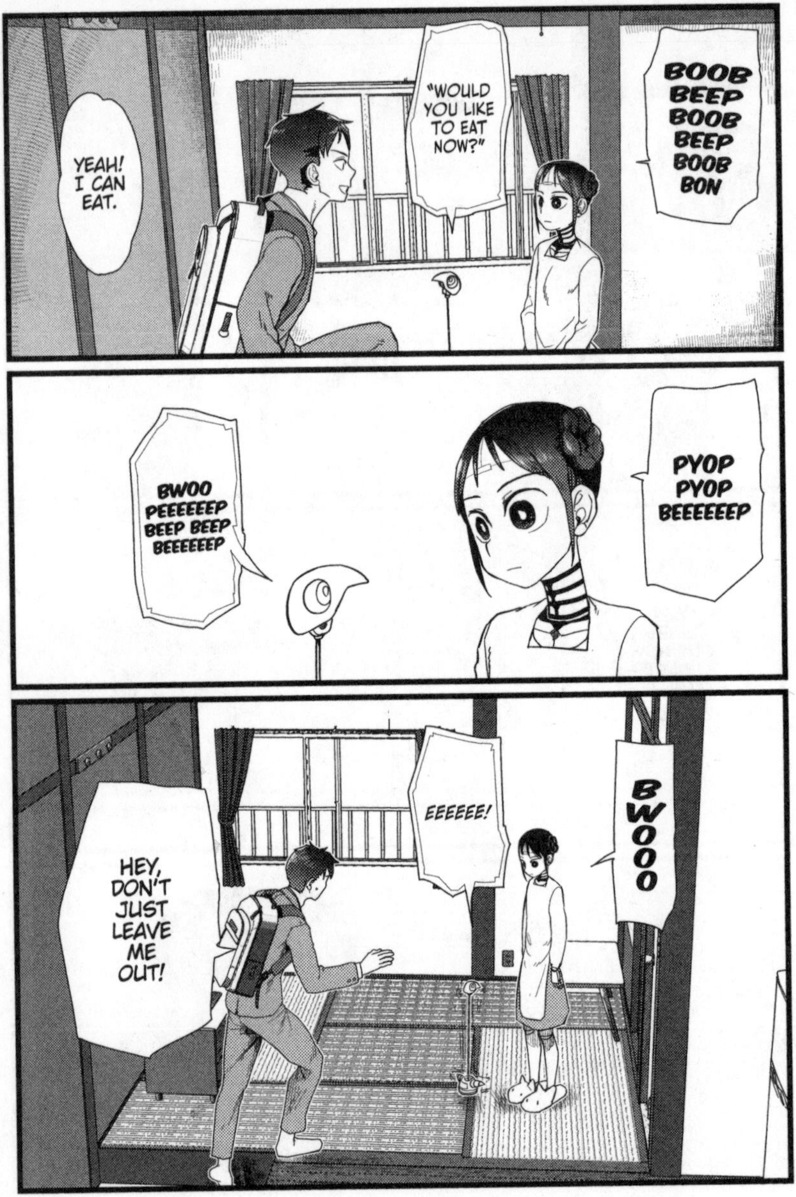
BOOB BEEP BOOB BEEP BOOB BON
"WOULD YOU LIKE TO EAT NOW?"
YEAH! I CAN EAT.
PYOP PYOP BEEEEEEP
BWOO PEEEEEEP BEEP BEEP BEEEEEEP
BWOOO
EEEEEE!
HEY, DON'T JUST LEAVE ME OUT!

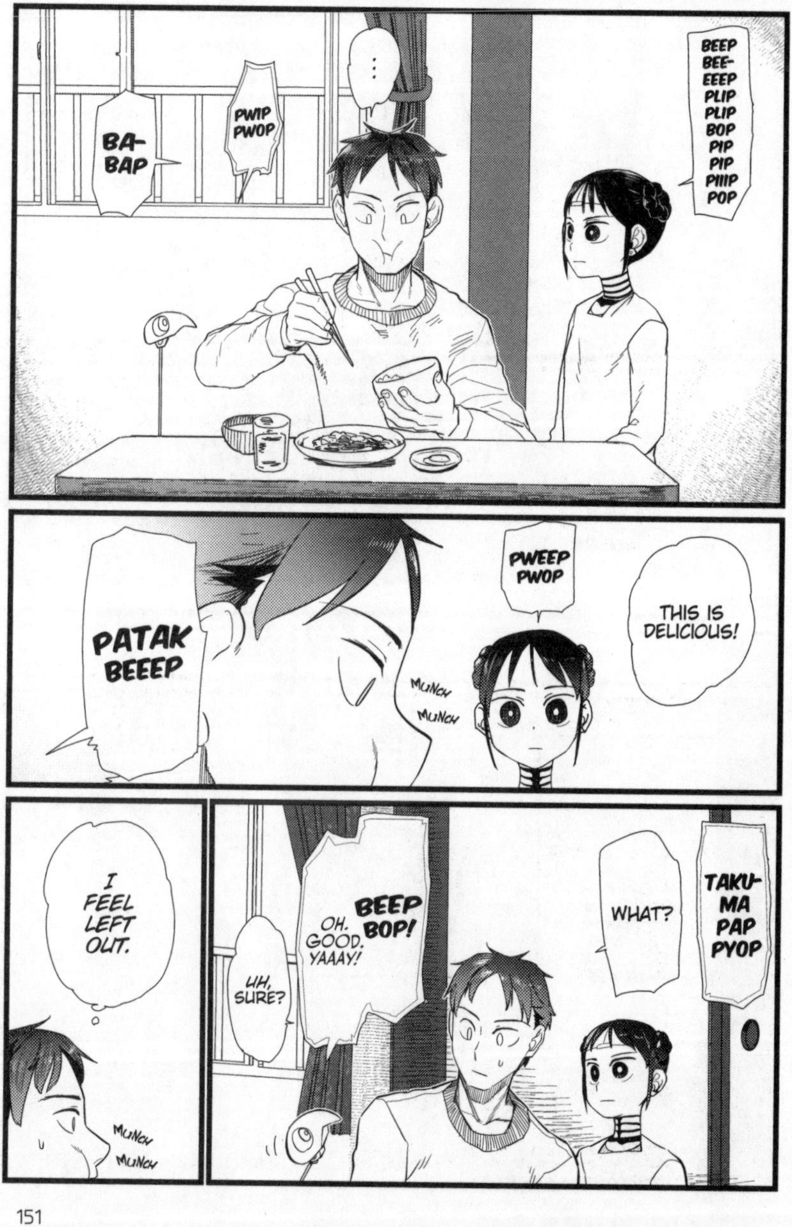
BEEP BEE- EEEP PLIP PLIP BOP PIP PIP PIIIP POP
...
PWIP PWOP
BA- BAP
THIS IS DELICIOUS!
PWEEP PWOP
MUNCH MUNCH
PATAK BEEEP
TAKU- MA PAP PYOP
WHAT?
BEEP BOP!
OH. GOOD. YAAAY!
UH, SURE?
I FEEL LEFT OUT.
MUNCH MUNCH

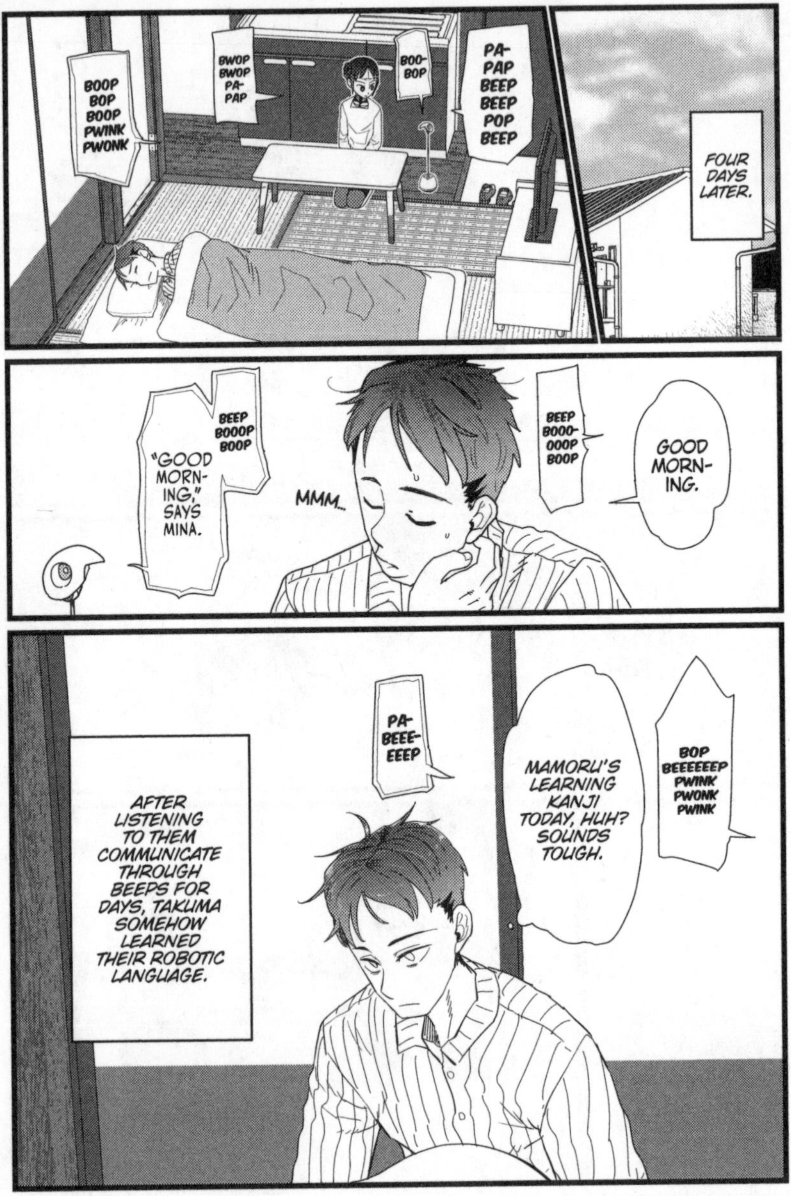
FOUR DAYS LATER.
PA-PAP BEEP BEEP POP BEEP
BOO-BOP
BWOP BWOP PA-PAP
BOOP BOP BOOP PWINK PWONK
GOOD MORN-ING.
BEEP BOOO-OOOP BOOP
MMM...
BEEP BOOOP BOOP
"GOOD MORN-ING," SAYS MINA.
BOP BEEEEEEP PWINK PWONK PWINK
MAMORU'S LEARNING KANJI TODAY, HUH? SOUNDS TOUGH.
PA-BEEE-EEEP
AFTER LISTENING TO THEM COMMUNICATE THROUGH BEEPS FOR DAYS, TAKUMA SOMEHOW LEARNED THEIR ROBOTIC LANGUAGE.

➡ CHAPTER 20 END ♥

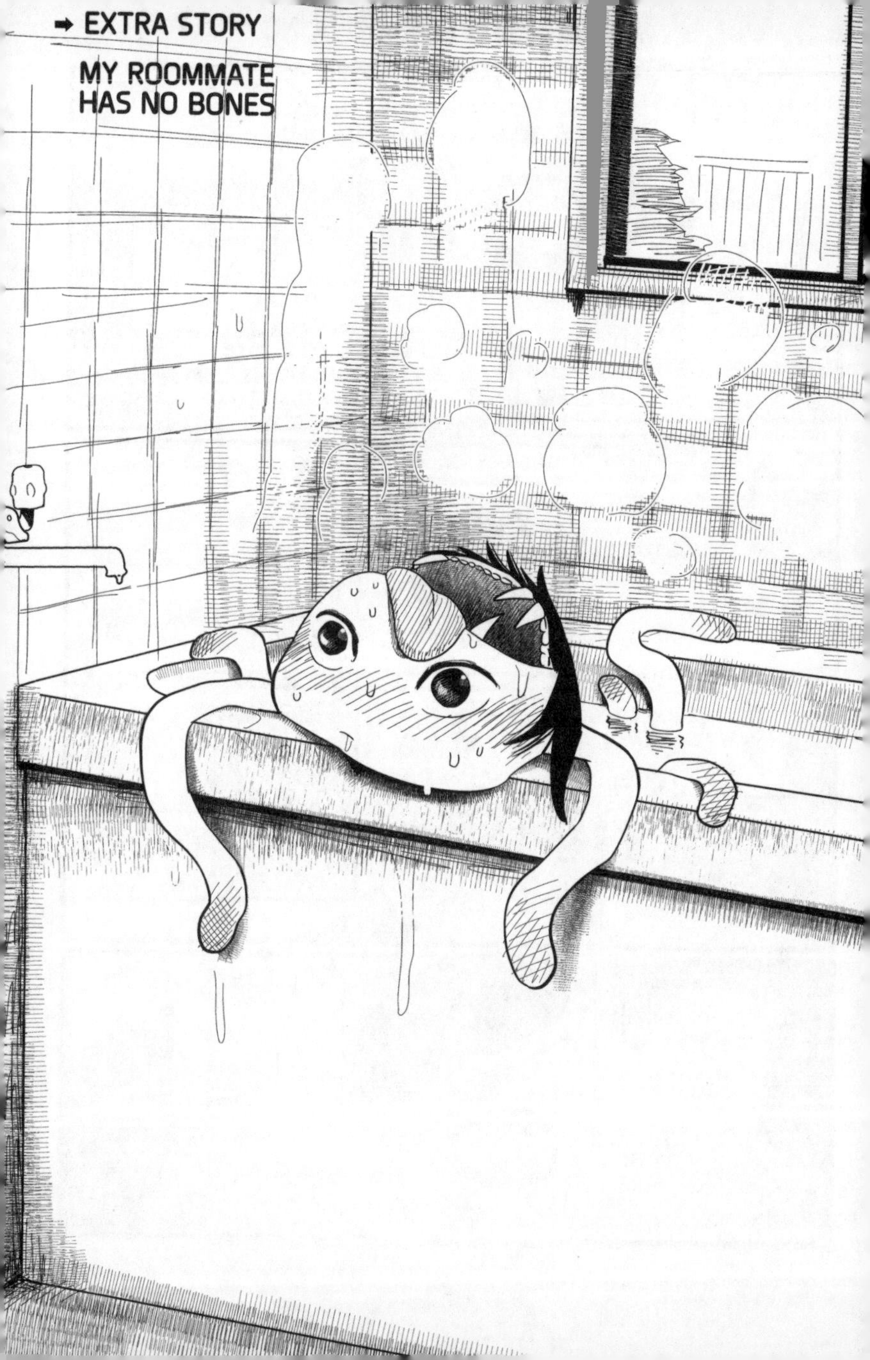
➡ EXTRA STORY
MY ROOMMATE HAS NO BONES

MY MASTER IS AN EARTHLING

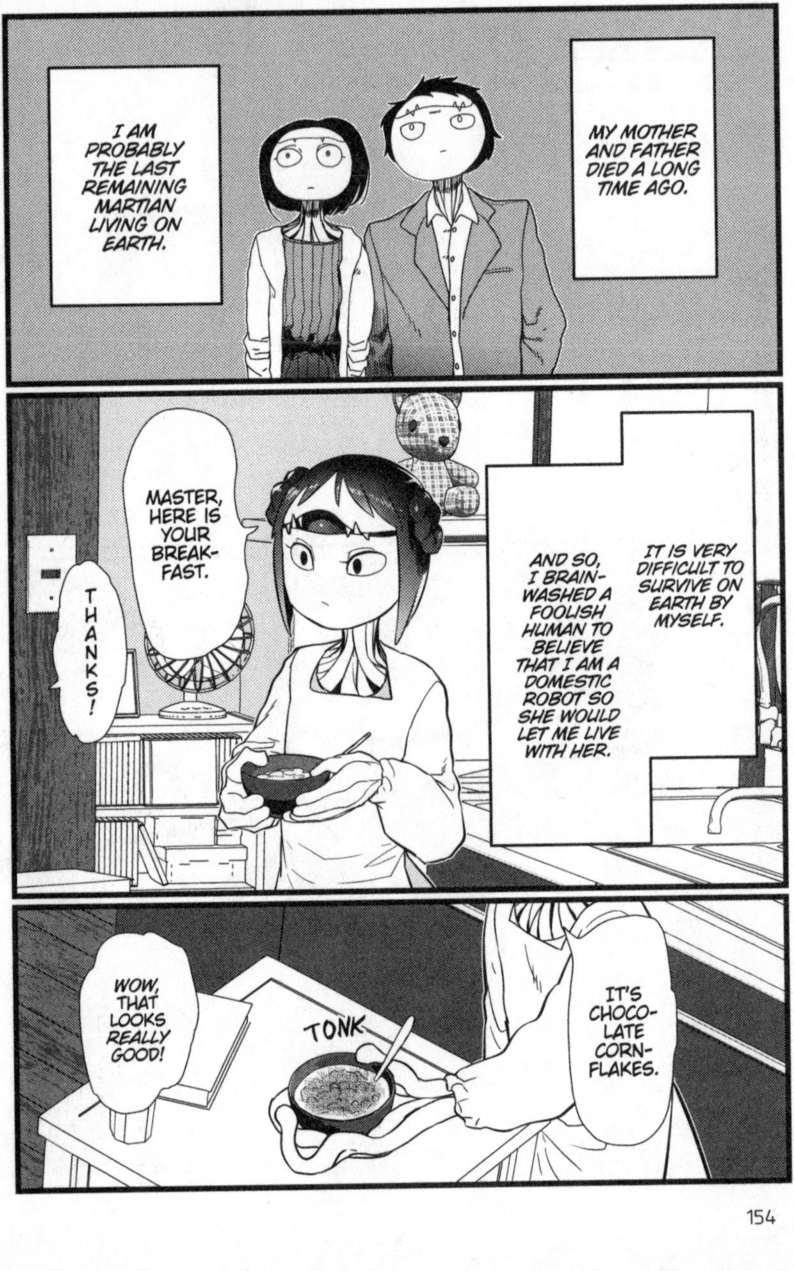
MY MOTHER AND FATHER DIED A LONG TIME AGO.
I AM PROBABLY THE LAST REMAINING MARTIAN LIVING ON EARTH.
IT IS VERY DIFFICULT TO SURVIVE ON EARTH BY MYSELF.
AND SO, I BRAINWASHED A FOOLISH HUMAN TO BELIEVE THAT I AM A DOMESTIC ROBOT SO SHE WOULD LET ME LIVE WITH HER.
MASTER, HERE IS YOUR BREAKFAST.
THANKS!
IT'S CHOCOLATE CORNFLAKES.
TONK
WOW, THAT LOOKS REALLY GOOD!

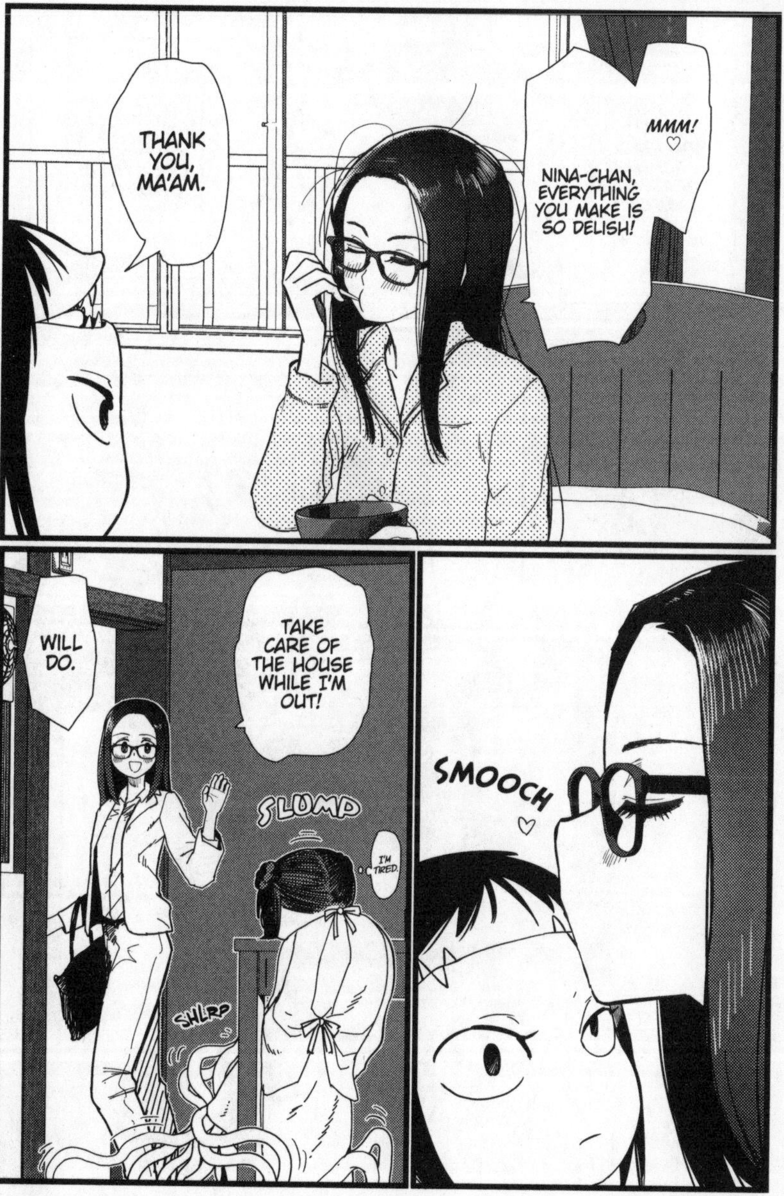
MMM! ♡
NINA-CHAN, EVERYTHING YOU MAKE IS SO DELISH!
THANK YOU, MA'AM.
SMOOCH ♡
TAKE CARE OF THE HOUSE WHILE I'M OUT!
WILL DO.
SLUMP
I'M TIRED.
SHLRP

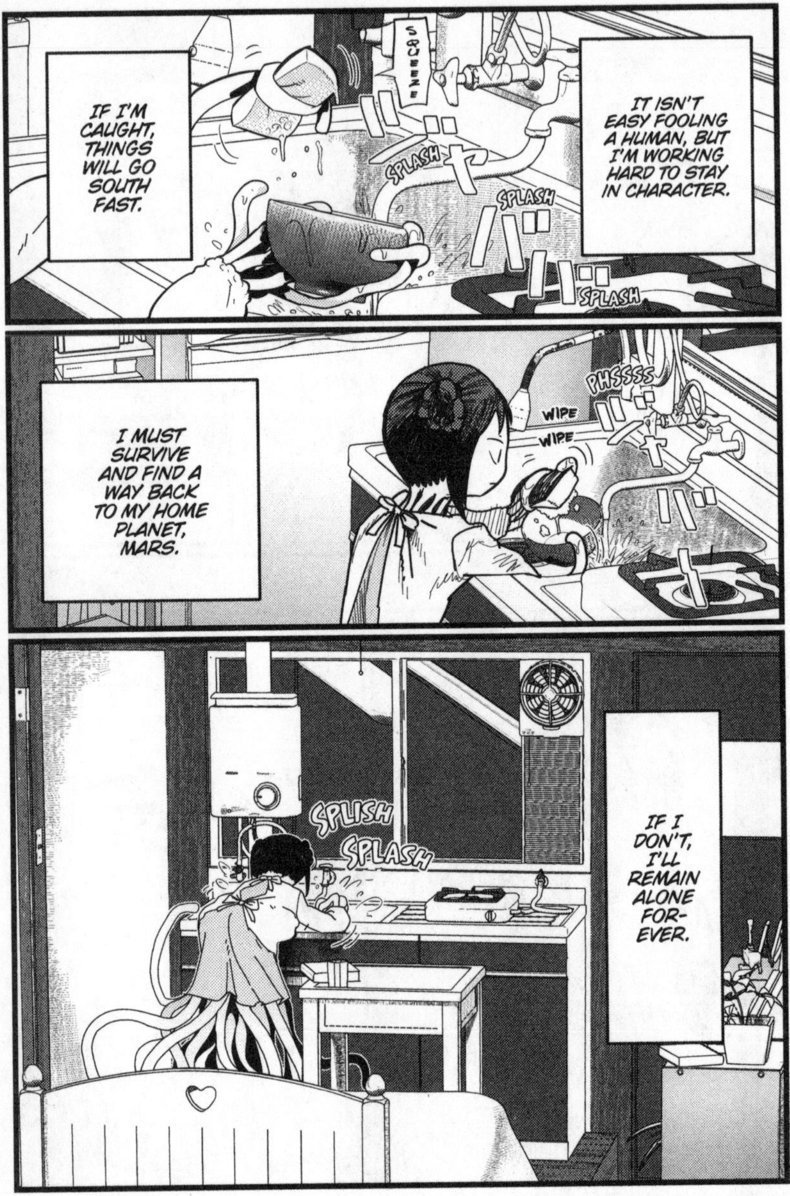
IT ISN'T EASY FOOLING A HUMAN, BUT I'M WORKING HARD TO STAY IN CHARACTER.
SQUEEZE
SPLASH
SPLASH
SPLASH
IF I'M CAUGHT, THINGS WILL GO SOUTH FAST.
PHSSSS
WIPE
WIPE
I MUST SURVIVE AND FIND A WAY BACK TO MY HOME PLANET, MARS.
IF I DON'T, I'LL REMAIN ALONE FOR-EVER.
SPLISH
SPLASH

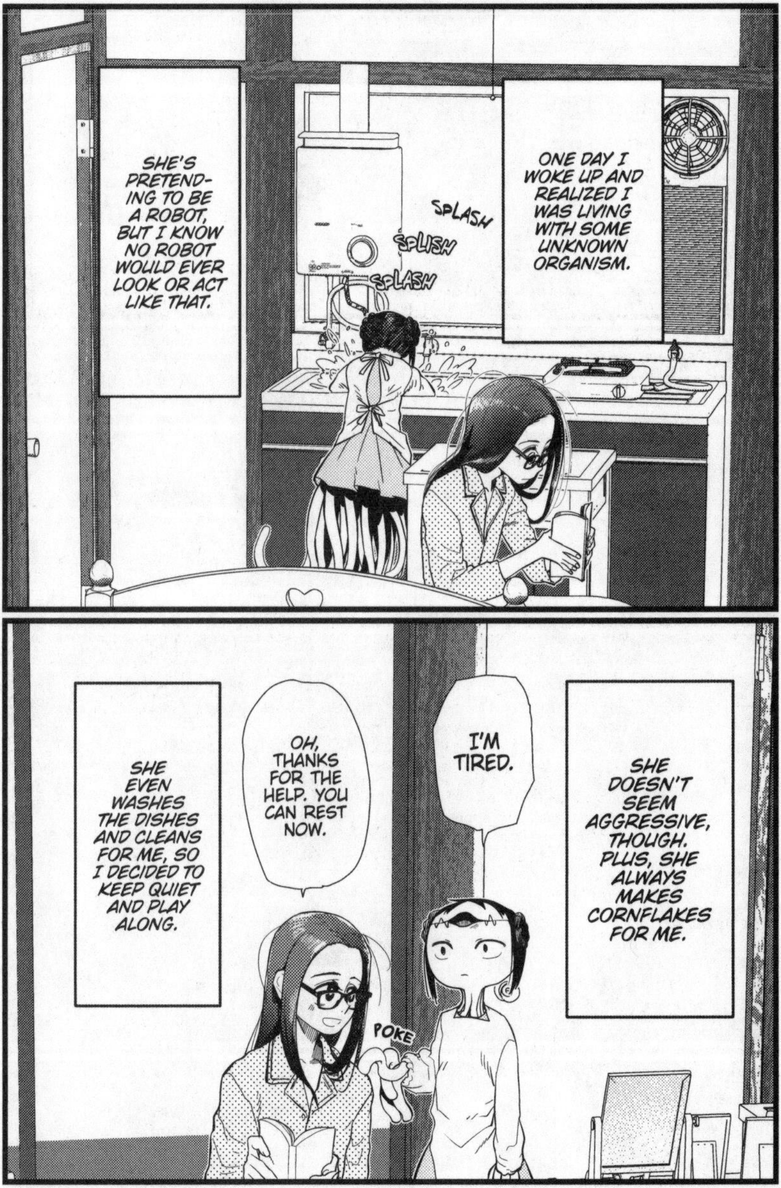
ONE DAY I WOKE UP AND REALIZED I WAS LIVING WITH SOME UNKNOWN ORGANISM.
SPLASH
SPLISH
SPLASH
SHE'S PRETENDING TO BE A ROBOT, BUT I KNOW NO ROBOT WOULD EVER LOOK OR ACT LIKE THAT.
SHE DOESN'T SEEM AGGRESSIVE, THOUGH. PLUS, SHE ALWAYS MAKES CORNFLAKES FOR ME.
I'M TIRED.
OH, THANKS FOR THE HELP. YOU CAN REST NOW.
SHE EVEN WASHES THE DISHES AND CLEANS FOR ME, SO I DECIDED TO KEEP QUIET AND PLAY ALONG.
POKE

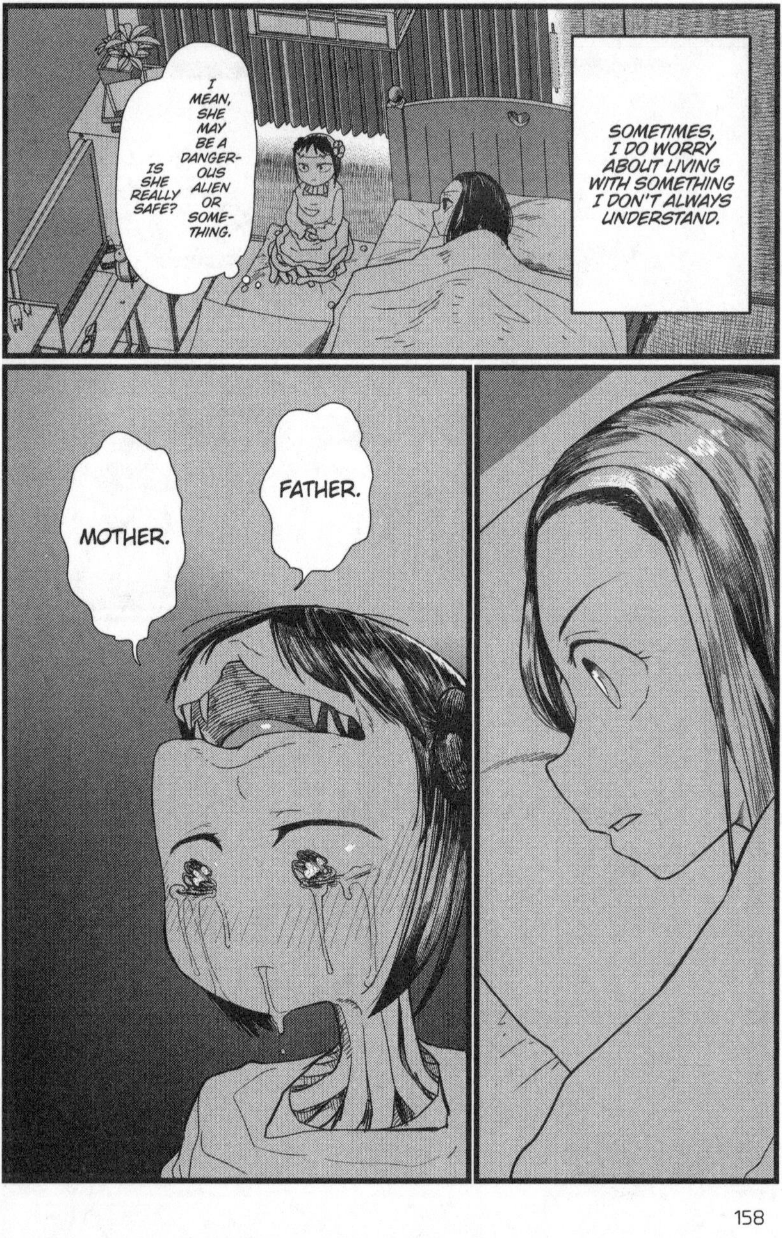
SOMETIMES, I DO WORRY ABOUT LIVING WITH SOMETHING I DON'T ALWAYS UNDERSTAND.
I MEAN, SHE MAY BE A DANGEROUS ALIEN OR SOMETHING.
IS SHE REALLY SAFE?
FATHER.
MOTHER.

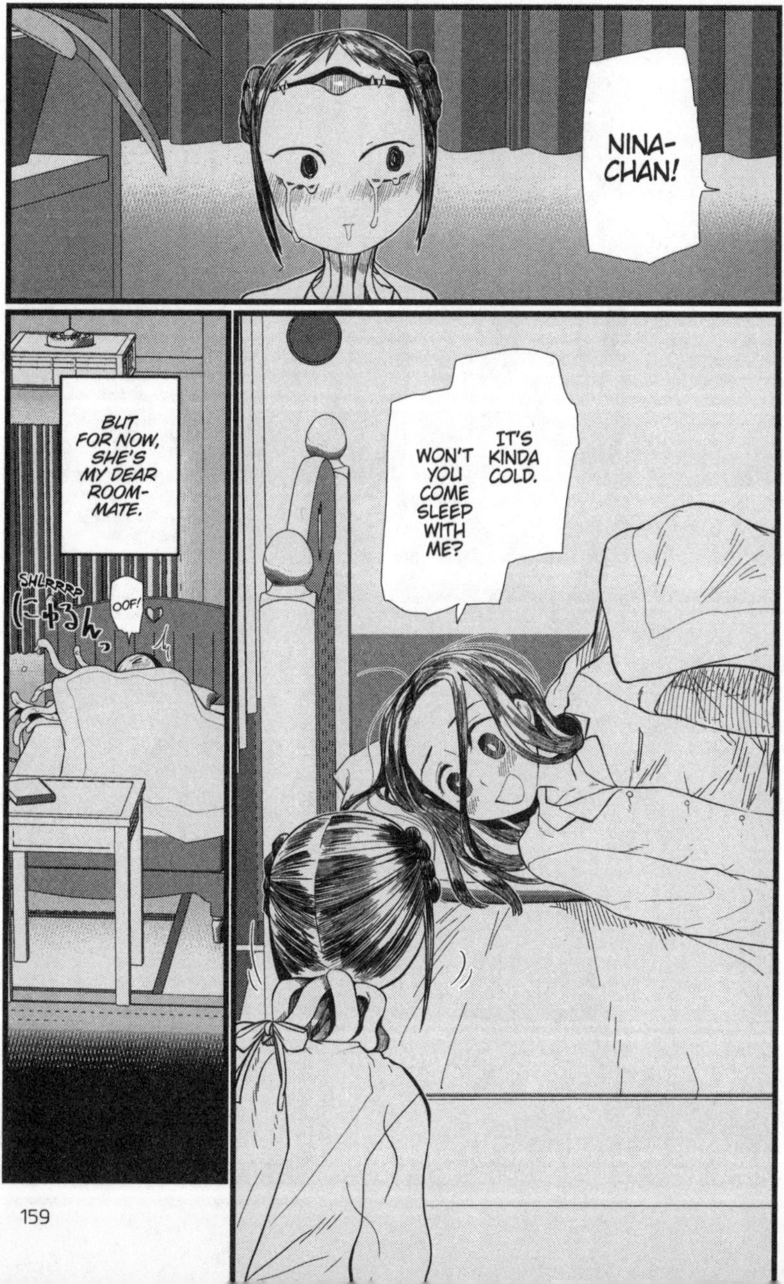
NINA-CHAN!
IT'S KINDA COLD.
WON'T YOU COME SLEEP WITH ME?
BUT FOR NOW, SHE'S MY DEAR ROOM-MATE.
SHLRRRP
にゅるんっ
OOF!

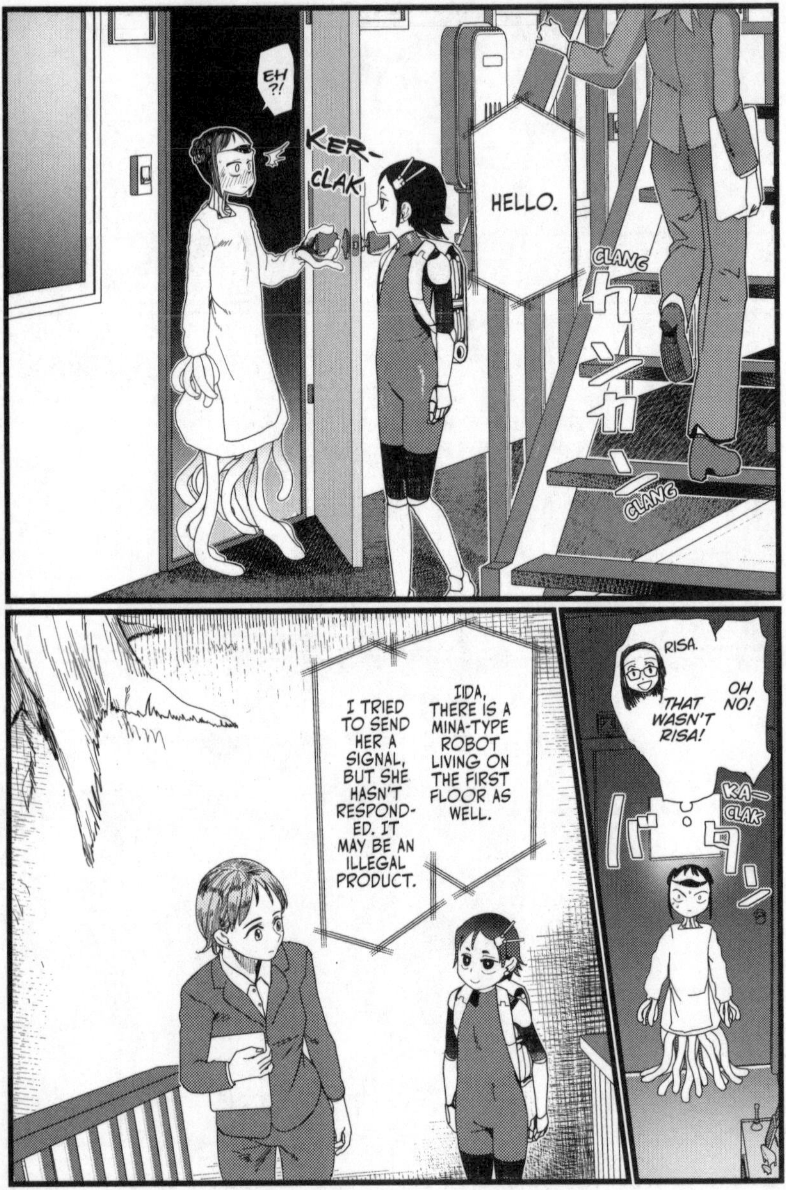
HELLO.
CLANG
KER-CLAK
EH?!
CLANG
RISA.
OH NO!
THAT WASN'T RISA!
KA-CLAK
IIDA, THERE IS A MINA-TYPE ROBOT LIVING ON THE FIRST FLOOR AS WELL.
I TRIED TO SEND HER A SIGNAL, BUT SHE HASN'T RESPONDED. IT MAY BE AN ILLEGAL PRODUCT.

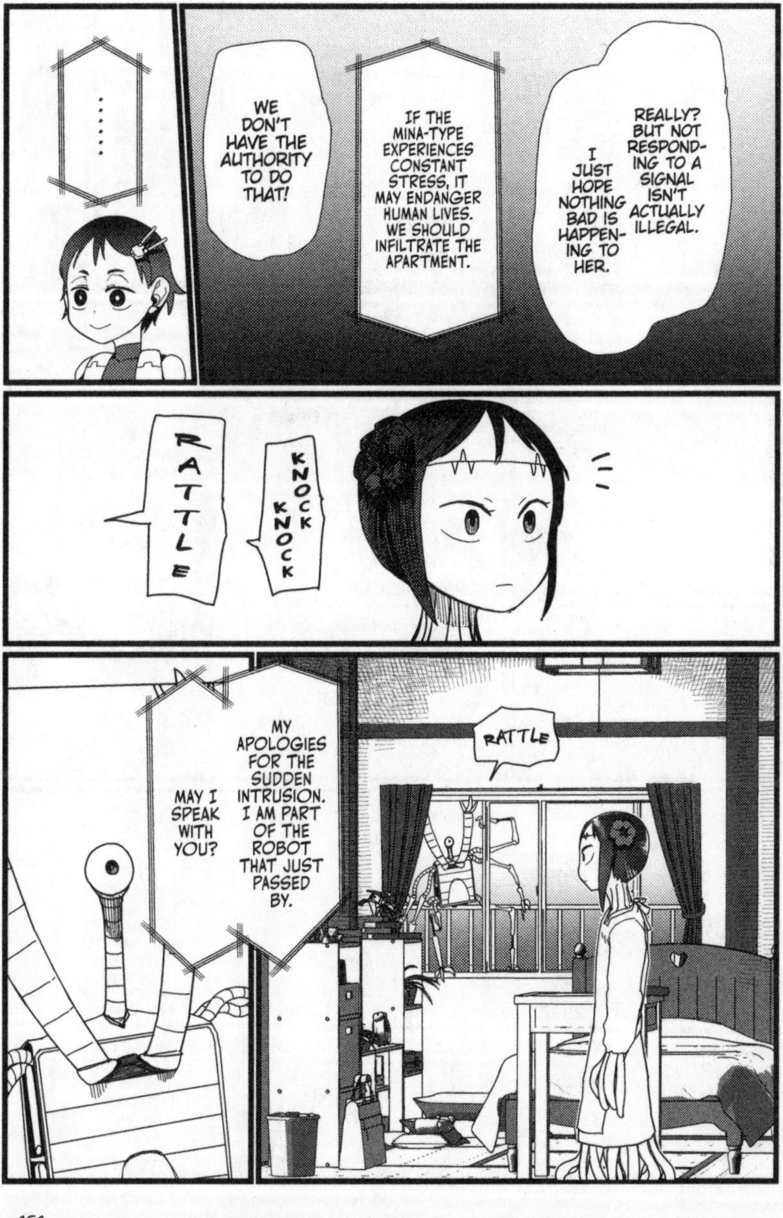
REALLY? BUT NOT RESPONDING TO A SIGNAL ISN'T ACTUALLY ILLEGAL.
I JUST HOPE NOTHING BAD IS HAPPENING TO HER.
IF THE MINA-TYPE EXPERIENCES CONSTANT STRESS, IT MAY ENDANGER HUMAN LIVES. WE SHOULD INFILTRATE THE APARTMENT.
WE DON'T HAVE THE AUTHORITY TO DO THAT!
......
KNOCK KNOCK
RATTLE
RATTLE
MY APOLOGIES FOR THE SUDDEN INTRUSION. I AM PART OF THE ROBOT THAT JUST PASSED BY.
MAY I SPEAK WITH YOU?

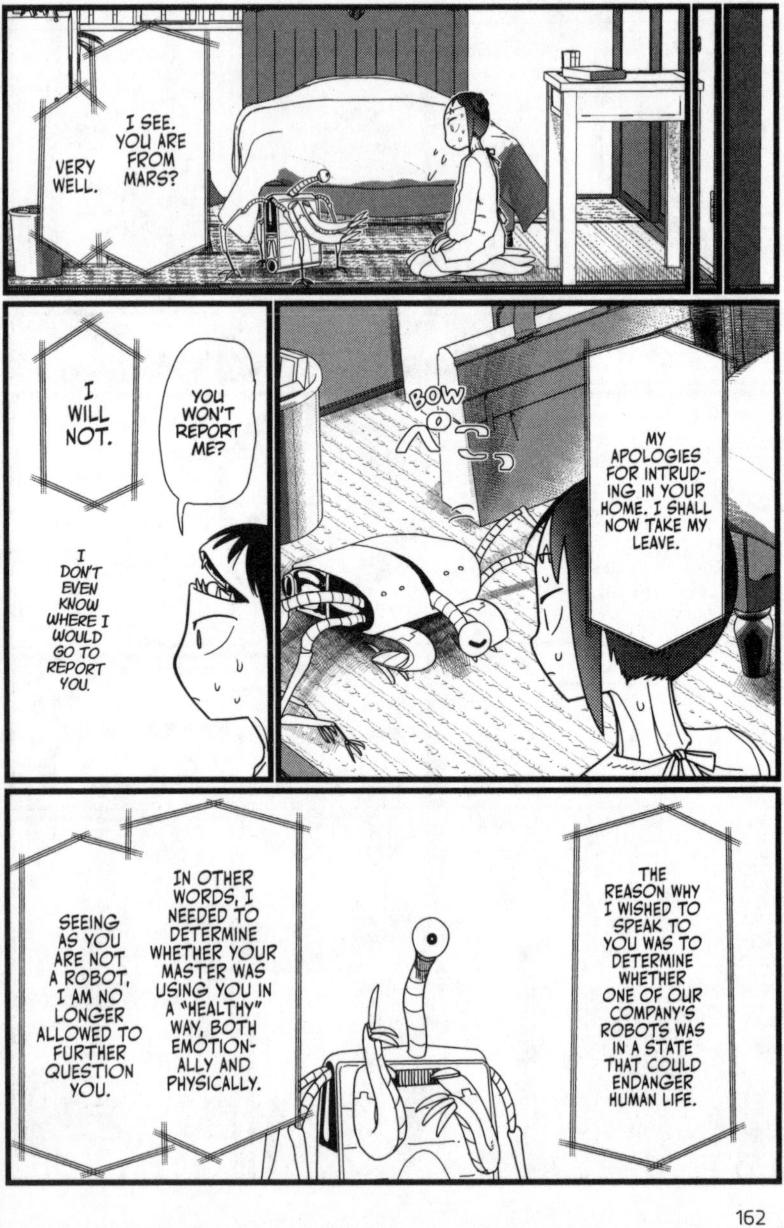
I SEE. YOU ARE FROM MARS?
VERY WELL.
MY APOLOGIES FOR INTRUDING IN YOUR HOME. I SHALL NOW TAKE MY LEAVE.
BOW
YOU WON'T REPORT ME?
I WILL NOT.
I DON'T EVEN KNOW WHERE I WOULD GO TO REPORT YOU.
THE REASON WHY I WISHED TO SPEAK TO YOU WAS TO DETERMINE WHETHER ONE OF OUR COMPANY'S ROBOTS WAS IN A STATE THAT COULD ENDANGER HUMAN LIFE.
IN OTHER WORDS, I NEEDED TO DETERMINE WHETHER YOUR MASTER WAS USING YOU IN A "HEALTHY" WAY, BOTH EMOTIONALLY AND PHYSICALLY.
SEEING AS YOU ARE NOT A ROBOT, I AM NO LONGER ALLOWED TO FURTHER QUESTION YOU.

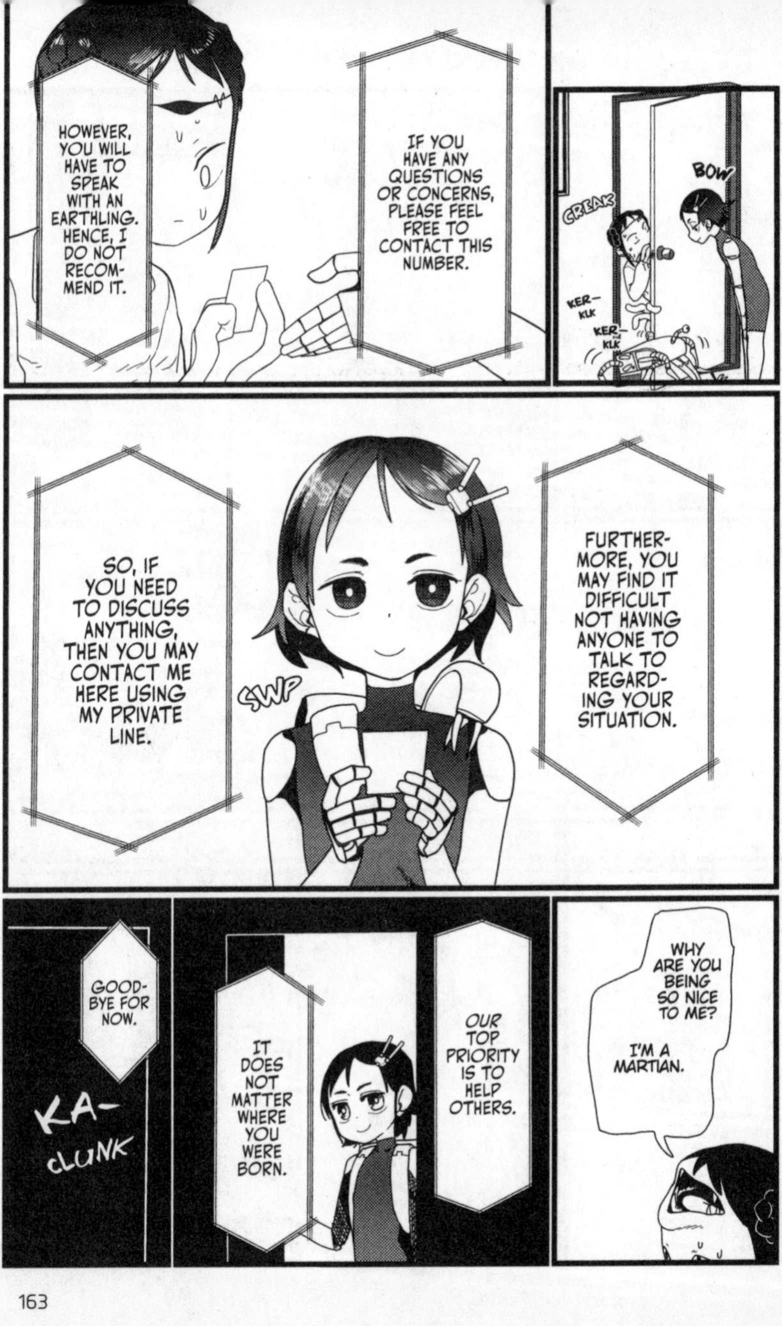
BOW
CREAK
KER-KLK
KER-KLK
IF YOU HAVE ANY QUESTIONS OR CONCERNS, PLEASE FEEL FREE TO CONTACT THIS NUMBER.
HOWEVER, YOU WILL HAVE TO SPEAK WITH AN EARTHLING. HENCE, I DO NOT RECOMMEND IT.
FURTHERMORE, YOU MAY FIND IT DIFFICULT NOT HAVING ANYONE TO TALK TO REGARDING YOUR SITUATION.
SO, IF YOU NEED TO DISCUSS ANYTHING, THEN YOU MAY CONTACT ME HERE USING MY PRIVATE LINE.
SWP
WHY ARE YOU BEING SO NICE TO ME?
I'M A MARTIAN.
OUR TOP PRIORITY IS TO HELP OTHERS.
IT DOES NOT MATTER WHERE YOU WERE BORN.
GOOD-BYE FOR NOW.
KA-CLUNK

THE CASE OF THE MISSING CHOCOLATES AT LUMINOUS ASAHI

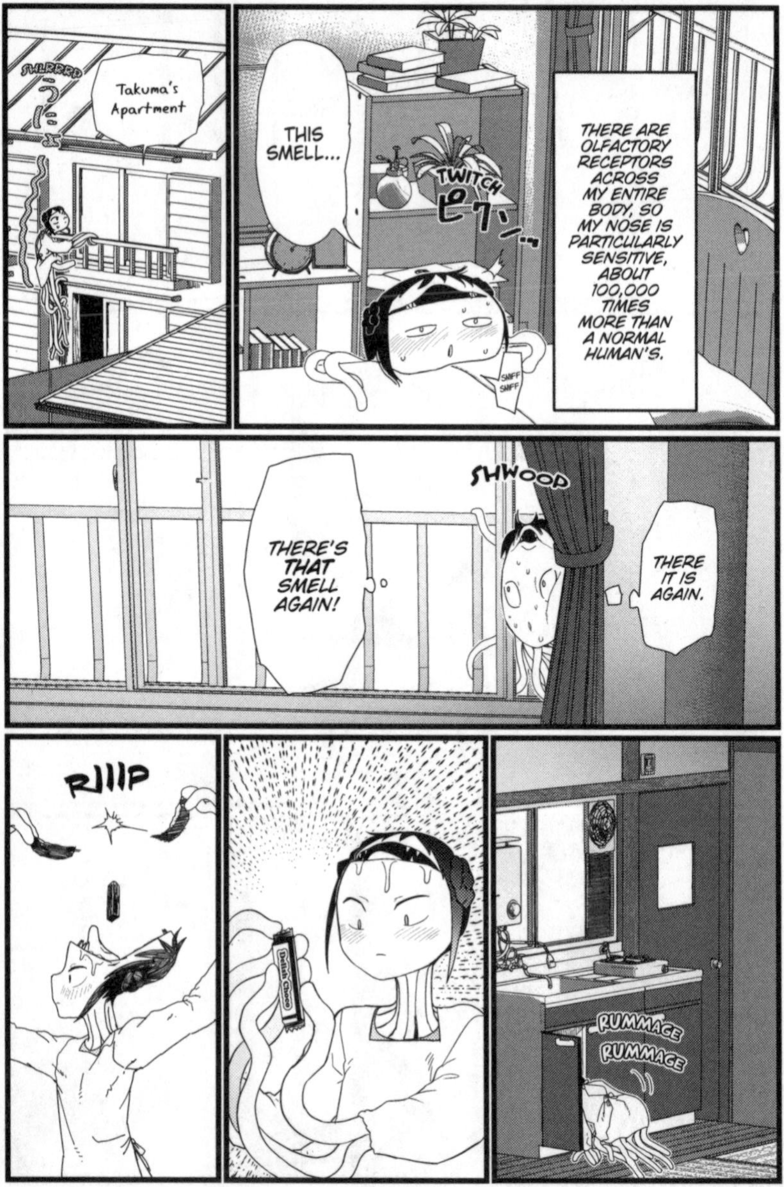

THERE ARE OLFACTORY RECEPTORS ACROSS MY ENTIRE BODY, SO MY NOSE IS PARTICULARLY SENSITIVE, ABOUT 100,000 TIMES MORE THAN A NORMAL HUMAN'S.
THIS SMELL...
TWITCH
SNIFF SNIFF
SHLRRRD
Takuma's Apartment
SHWOOD
THERE IT IS AGAIN.
THERE'S THAT SMELL AGAIN!
RUMMAGE
RUMMAGE
Delish Choco
RIIIP

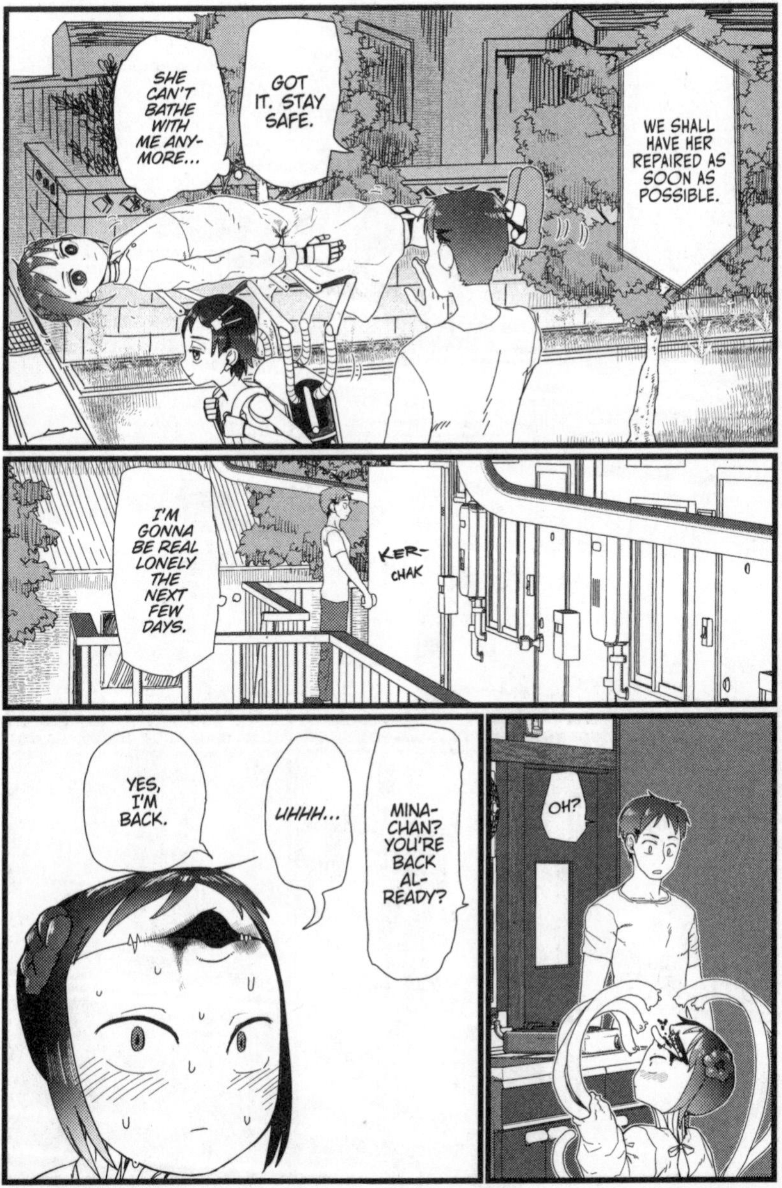
WE SHALL HAVE HER REPAIRED AS SOON AS POSSIBLE.
GOT IT. STAY SAFE.
SHE CAN'T BATHE WITH ME ANYMORE...
KER-CHAK
I'M GONNA BE REAL LONELY THE NEXT FEW DAYS.
OH?
MINA-CHAN? YOU'RE BACK AL-READY?
UHHH...
YES, I'M BACK.

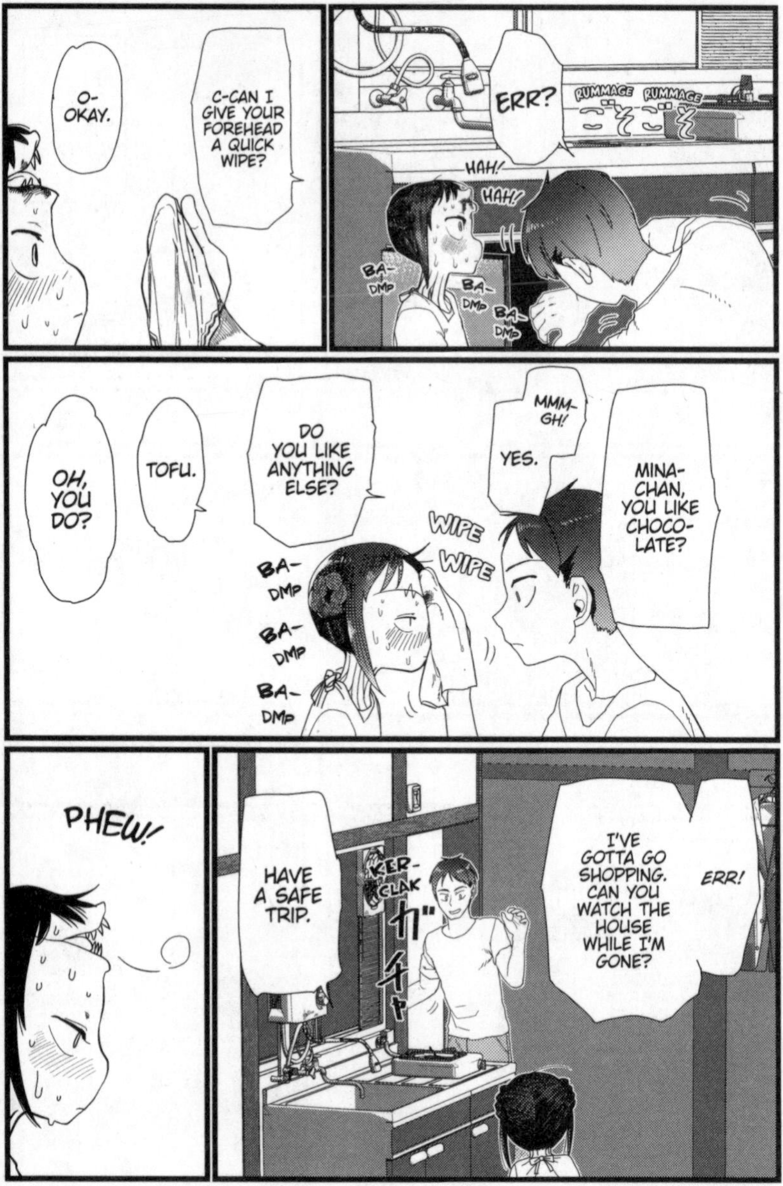
ERR?
RUMMAGE RUMMAGE
ごそごそ
HAH!
HAH!
BA-DMP
BA-DMP
BA-DMP
C-CAN I GIVE YOUR FOREHEAD A QUICK WIPE?
O-OKAY.
MINA-CHAN, YOU LIKE CHOCO-LATE?
MMMGH!
YES.
DO YOU LIKE ANYTHING ELSE?
TOFU.
OH, YOU DO?
WIPE WIPE
BA-DMP
BA-DMP
BA-DMP
ERR!
I'VE GOTTA GO SHOPPING. CAN YOU WATCH THE HOUSE WHILE I'M GONE?
KER-CLAK
ガイャ
HAVE A SAFE TRIP.
PHEW!

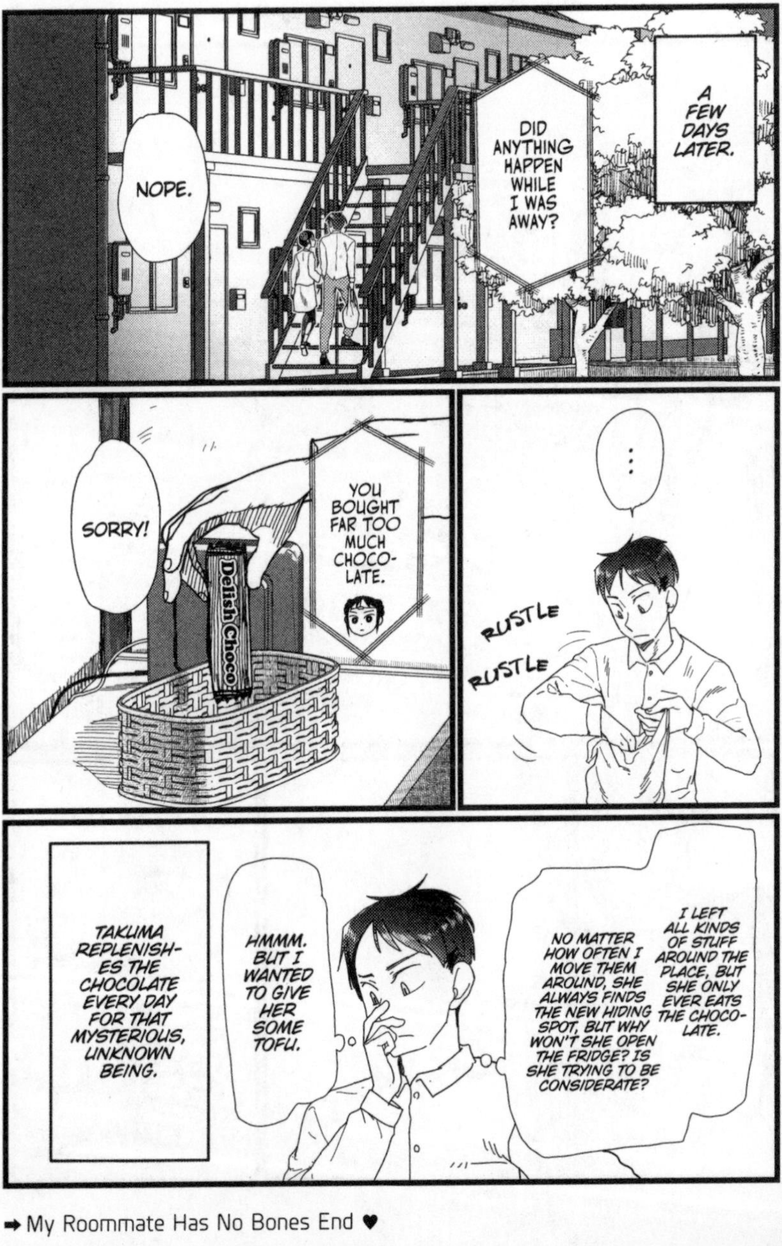
A FEW DAYS LATER.
DID ANYTHING HAPPEN WHILE I WAS AWAY?
NOPE.
...
RUSTLE
RUSTLE
YOU BOUGHT FAR TOO MUCH CHOCO-LATE.
SORRY!
Delish Choco
I LEFT ALL KINDS OF STUFF AROUND THE PLACE, BUT SHE ONLY EVER EATS THE CHOCO-LATE.
NO MATTER HOW OFTEN I MOVE THEM AROUND, SHE ALWAYS FINDS THE NEW HIDING SPOT, BUT WHY WON'T SHE OPEN THE FRIDGE? IS SHE TRYING TO BE CONSIDERATE?
HMMM. BUT I WANTED TO GIVE HER SOME TOFU.
TAKUMA REPLENISH-ES THE CHOCOLATE EVERY DAY FOR THAT MYSTERIOUS, UNKNOWN BEING.

➡ My Roommate Has No Bones End ♥

LET'S PLAY WITH MAMORU-KUN!

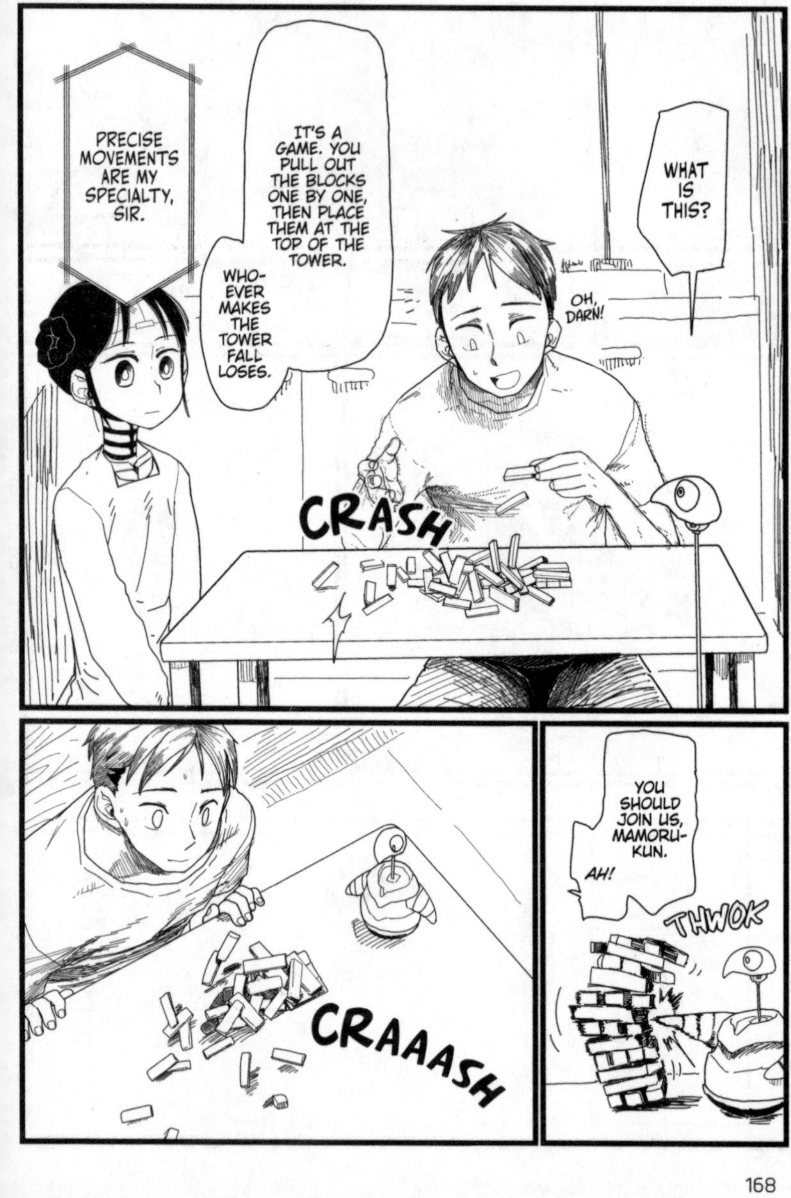

WHAT IS THIS?
OH, DARN!
IT'S A GAME. YOU PULL OUT THE BLOCKS ONE BY ONE, THEN PLACE THEM AT THE TOP OF THE TOWER.
WHO-EVER MAKES THE TOWER FALL LOSES.
PRECISE MOVEMENTS ARE MY SPECIALTY, SIR.
CRASH
YOU SHOULD JOIN US, MAMORU-KUN.
AH!
THWOK
CRAAASH

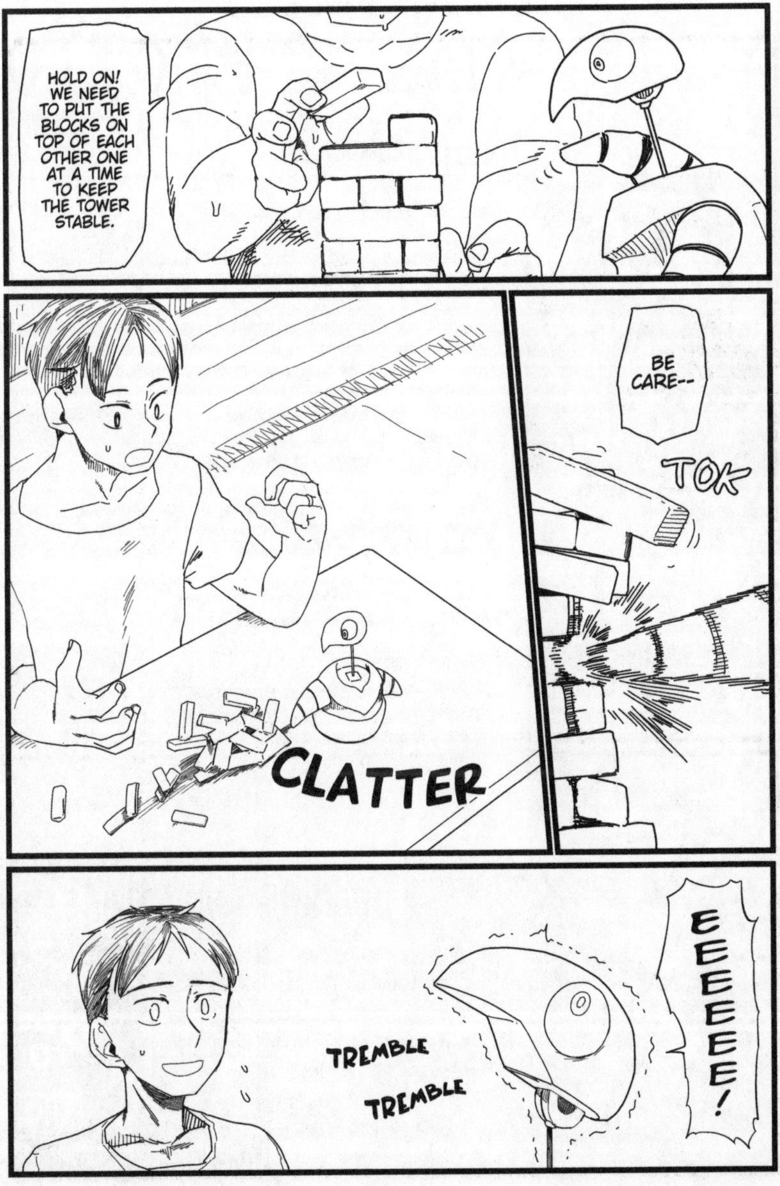
HOLD ON! WE NEED TO PUT THE BLOCKS ON TOP OF EACH OTHER ONE AT A TIME TO KEEP THE TOWER STABLE.
BE CARE--
TOK
CLATTER
EEEEEE!
TREMBLE
TREMBLE

SEVEN SEAS ENTERTAINMENT PRESENTS

MY WIFE HAS NO EMOTION

Vol.3

story by JIRO SUGIURA

TRANSLATION
Jacqueline Fung

ADAPTATION
Maneesh Maganti

LETTERING
Jennifer Skarupa

COVER DESIGN
H. Qi

LOGO DESIGN
George Panella

PROOFREADER
Danielle King

SENIOR EDITOR
Shannon Fay

PRODUCTION DESIGNER
Christa Miesner

PRODUCTION MANAGER
Lissa Pattillo

PREPRESS TECHNICIAN
Melanie Ujimori

PRINT MANAGER
Rhiannon Rasmussen-Silverstein

EDITOR-IN-CHIEF
Julie Davis

ASSOCIATE PUBLISHER
Adam Arnold

PUBLISHER
Jason DeAngelis

BOKU NO TSUMA WA KANJO GA NAI Vol.3
©Jiro Sugiura 2021
First published in Japan in 2021 by KADOKAWA CORPORATION, Tokyo.
English translation rights arranged with KADOKAWA CORPORATION, Tokyo.

No portion of this book may be reproduced or transmitted in any form without written permission from the copyright holders. This is a work of fiction. Names, characters, places, and incidents are the products of the author's imagination or are used fictitiously. Any resemblance to actual events, locales, or persons, living or dead, is entirely coincidental. Any information or opinions expressed by the creators of this book belong to those individual creators and do not necessarily reflect the views of Seven Seas Entertainment or its employees.

Seven Seas press and purchase enquiries can be sent to Marketing Manager Lianne Sentar at press@gomanga.com. Information regarding the distribution and purchase of digital editions is available from Digital Manager CK Russell at digital@gomanga.com.

Seven Seas and the Seven Seas logo are trademarks of Seven Seas Entertainment. All rights reserved.

ISBN: 978-1-63858-200-7
Printed in Canada
First Printing: August 2022
10 9 8 7 6 5 4 3 2 1

READING DIRECTIONS

This book reads from *right to left*, Japanese style. If this is your first time reading manga, you start reading from the top right panel on each page and take it from there. If you get lost, just follow the numbered diagram here. It may seem backwards at first, but you'll get the hang of it! Have fun!!

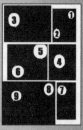

Follow us online: www.SevenSeasEntertainment.com